Managing Today's News Media

SAGE was founded in 1965 by Sara Miller McCune to support the dissemination of usable knowledge by publishing innovative and high-quality research and teaching content. Today, we publish more than 850 journals, including those of more than 300 learned societies, more than 800 new books per year, and a growing range of library products including archives, data, case studies, reports, and video. SAGE remains majority-owned by our founder, and after Sara's lifetime will become owned by a charitable trust that secures our continued independence.

Los Angeles | London | New Delhi | Singapore | Washington DC

Managing Today's News Media

Audience First

Samir Husni
University of Mississippi

Debora Halpern Wenger
University of Mississippi

Hank Price
*Northwestern University Media
Management Center*

Los Angeles | London | New Delhi
Singapore | Washington DC

Los Angeles | London | New Delhi
Singapore | Washington DC

For information:

CQ Press

An Imprint of SAGE Publications, Inc.

2455 Teller Road

Thousand Oaks, California 91320

E-mail: order@sagepub.com

SAGE Publications Ltd.

1 Oliver's Yard

55 City Road

London EC1Y 1SP

United Kingdom

SAGE Publications India Pvt. Ltd.

B 1/I 1 Mohan Cooperative Industrial Area

Mathura Road, New Delhi 110 044

India

SAGE Publications Asia-Pacific Pte. Ltd.

3 Church Street

#10-04 Samsung Hub

Singapore 049483

Printed in the United States of America

Library of Congress Cataloging-in-Publication Data

Husni, Samir.

Managing today's news media : audience first / Samir Husni, University of Mississippi ; Debora Halpern Wenger, University of Mississippi ; Hank Price, Northwestern University Media Management Center.

pages cm
Includes bibliographical references and index.

ISBN 978-1-4522-9257-1 (pbk. : alk. paper)

1. Broadcast journalism. 2. Television viewers. I. Wenger, Debora Halpern. II. Price, Hank. III. Title.

PN4784.B75H87 2016
070.1'9—dc23   2015024939

This book is printed on acid-free paper.

Acquisitions Editor: Matt Byrnie

Editorial Assistant: Janae Masnovi

Production Editor: Bennie Clark Allen

Copy Editor: Melinda Masson

Typesetter: C&M Digitals (P) Ltd.

Proofreader: Annie Lubinsky

Indexer: Karen Wiley

Cover Designer: Scott Van Atta

Marketing Manager: Ashlee Blunk

Certified Sourcing
www.sfiprogram.org
SFI-00453

15 16 17 18 19 10 9 8 7 6 5 4 3 2 1

DETAILED CONTENTS

C hange is the only constant. And while change in the media in general and the news media in particular has been occurring at a record speed, this book offers practical solutions on how to cope with and adapt to the evolving media landscape.

The philosophy and theories behind "Managing Today's News Media: Audience First" have a foundation in the works of two great Greek philosophers, Parmenides and Heraclitus.

Parmenides is the pre-Platonic Greek philosopher who theorized about permanence as reality; what is permanent, what lasts and what is stable is real. In other words, what you cannot destroy is what is real and true.

Heraclitus, on the other hand, was the theorist of change. He's the one famous for saying, "You cannot step in the same river twice," because the water keeps on flowing and changing. For him, constant change was the one reality. The only permanent thing in the universe, according to Heraclitus, is change.

So, how can we then create a systematic way of managing news organizations in a world of ever-changing audiences and news and information platforms? This book proposes a strategy; the "4 C's Strategy" is based on the premise that the focus of media managers today should be on the audience and not the platforms themselves. In Chapter 1 and throughout the text, we describe in great detail how customers, control, choice and change are all part of a strategy for successful media organizations.

WHERE WE ARE GOING

Between the three of us, we have been teaching and training media managers for decades. We've also worked as consultants or media managers ourselves for some of the top news organizations in the country.

This textbook will help prepare managers for jobs in today's media organizations, but we also cover the essential topics for any journalist who needs to understand the business of media. It is our belief that one of the great failures of journalism and mass communication education is that programs have neglected to expose students to the basic business principles that drive the success or failure of the organizations for which they work.

Throughout the book, we discuss how the audience-first approach to managing a news company changes the thinking about and execution of news-gathering and the news distribution process. We deal with subjects such as fostering innovation within an organization and the impact of the more interactive relationship news organizations now have with their audiences. Business models and new sources of revenue are discussed, along with an exploration of where multimedia journalism may be headed and how those who want to lead news media companies can prepare themselves for jobs and careers, now and in the future.

HOW WE GET THERE

We've structured the book in such a way that you can read individual chapters in whatever order seems most useful to you. Our goal is to provide a straightforward guide to what you need to know to work as a news manager today. All major forms of media are presented in their own individual chapters with an introductory chapter fully explaining the basis of our 4 C's Strategy.

In addition, in each chapter you will find real-world examples of business successes and failures, in-depth interviews and advice from industry leaders, and unique elements you won't find in other media management textbooks. We take on the topics of branding, business models and audience power as well.

Each chapter includes two innovative features: "Leadership Reports" and "Think and Do" exercises. The "Leadership Reports" involve interviews with CEOs, publishers, editors, producers, owners and media agency professionals in order to present a "reality check" on how the 4 C's Strategy can be put into practice.

And while it's one thing to read about how to do something, it's another to actually do it. The "Think and Do" sections provide exercises that will test what you've learned and your ability to execute the techniques discussed in each chapter.

For those in the classroom, this book is intended to be a tool of preparation for the world of news media. For the news manager, this book is intended to be a tool to enhance and enrich the work environment as many professionals seek solutions to the challenges facing the industry, rather than just updates on the latest technological changes.

This book is about the profession we love and how we manage the integration of media and technology in order to serve our customers better. It is not a theory book, although it is based on a theory. Our goal for "Managing Today's News Media: Audience First" is to present a practical handbook for every person interested in acquiring a better set of skills when it comes to managing media organizations.

There are many good books out there dealing with media, management of media, news media and other topics relevant to the subject. This one, however, simply put, is different. It is a hybrid if you will. "Managing Today's News Media: Audience First" is not an academic book and not a professional book; it is both.

That could not have happened, however, without the generous contributions from media organization leaders who took the time to talk with us, to teach us, and to share what they know about the ever-changing media landscape and how to manage and survive in such a world. Our goal is that you use this foundation to grow and prosper in your media world regardless of the platform.

We also want to thank family, friends, colleagues, students, reviewers, and editors who believed in the project and worked with us to make this a better book.

It's also important to thank you – our audience. We need your feedback on our first edition of this book so we can enhance and enrich subsequent editions of the text. Feel free to reach out and offer advice. Thank you.

We wish to gratefully thank the following reviewers:

Dan Caterinicchia, *Ohio State University School of Communication*

Steven Chappell, *Northwest Missouri State University*

Sumana Chattopadhyay, *Marquette University*

Cornelius "Neil" Foote Jr., *University of North Texas*

Derina Holtzhausen, *Oklahoma State University*

Mary Catherine Kennedy, *Mount St. Mary's University*

Samir "Mr. Magazine™" Husni   samir.husni@gmail.com

Deb Halpern Wenger   debora.wenger@gmail.com

Hank Price   hankprice@outlook.com

Audience First

"*The most important fight in journalism today isn't between short vs. long-form publications, or fast vs. thorough newsrooms, or even incumbents vs. start-ups. The most important fight is between realists and nostalgists.*"

—Clay Shirky
Author, "Here Comes Everybody"

BENEFITS

- In this chapter we examine how to put the audience first – before our own wants and desires – beyond what the trends tell us.
- We lay out the 4 C's Strategy – how customers, choice, control and change will impact you as a media manager.
- We reimagine the business of news media as a service for the audience and consider how that might change the relationship with the audience.

STATE OF THE AUDIENCE

For those in the news business, it truly is the best and worst of times. The news media is more fragmented than ever, even within the same channels, and consumers are bombarded by more information from those different channels on a constant basis.

Still, news consumption is every bit as robust as ever, perhaps more so, yet businesses devoted to the traditional delivery methods for news are foundering when it comes to maintaining and growing revenue. So, if the audience is there, why aren't the profits?

The one thing that's hurting the news industry more than anything else is that news managers often forget why they are in this business and know less than they should about who makes up both the existing and the potential audience. The tendency is to focus on the delivery platform – whether that's ink on paper or pixels on a screen – and to forget that business growth requires innovation, creation and audience connection. Too often, we also focus on where audience has been in the past rather than where they are now or where they're headed.

Until the most recent economic downturn, for decades news media have had the luxury of living in something of a bubble. The media told the audience what to read and hear and watch, and they did it – making money for media companies all the while. Though news organizations are still making money, they now have to work much harder to be necessary, sufficient and relevant to the audience. The key to success for media managers is to focus on understanding rather than resisting the customer's desire for choice and control.

Fight the Fear

Another significant obstacle facing traditional journalists is their own fear of the future. It's not unusual to hear media managers ask questions like "If newspapers go away, who will investigate government?" "If mainstream news media falters, who will cover the school board meetings or keep big business from riding roughshod over the consumer?" Those are legitimate concerns, but they're also the reason why we are entering a new era in which the role of journalists and journalism organizations is more critical than ever before. Whereas in the past journalists might have worked alone or on a small team, today's journalists have access to crowdsourcing, big data and a two-way conversation with the audience. Journalists will curate the sources available to create additional news coverage, including investigative reporting, so their role will change and evolve, not disappear. Curating – or selecting and highlighting the most important information on a topic – is a significant part of journalism's future; the only way that we can create the level of detail and volume of information we need to effectively serve the user is if we allow the user to be involved. News organizations need to provide a trusted source; the audience is looking to us to figure out what's real and what's not.

By making the consumer a partner, we increase resources and our ability to tell a more accurate story. But consumers are not willing to merely be a resource; they are demanding a seat in the editorial meeting, and those news organizations that figure out how to leverage and acknowledge audience contribution will succeed.

For example, one monthly newspaper in Germany called +3 (305,000 circ.) is heavily invested in audience involvement. The paper, with the tag line "Every opinion counts," asks the readers to comment or provide additional information and insight on the cover story of the next issue before it comes out. The paper uses social networks and emails to solicit comments on other upcoming stories, and combines and prints reader responses along with those of renowned experts and journalists. It's interactivity with the audience that produces great results. Iwan Ittermann, the newspaper editor, told us this approach makes the entire process "equitable" between readers and the paper. It is "before the fact," interactivity, not "after the fact."

As you'll see in Chapter 9, to do great journalism in the future, we must understand the opportunity that an engaged audience creates for us. In fact, the news media have no choice if we are to remain relevant and in business.

PHOTO 1-1 The future of journalism is bright for those who overcome their fear of change and embrace the consumer as an engaged partner.

THE BUSINESS OF JOURNALISM

At this point, in addition to advertising support, there are essentially three major business models for news media: the all-access model, in which an individual news organization's content is free or one price for all content on all available platforms; the "bait and switch" model, in which news companies offer limited free access and then charge for frequent use; and the a la carte approach, in which every form of delivery is priced separately, sometimes called the iTunes model.

Throughout the text, we explore the impact of these models on the news media organizations that have implemented them. We also make the case for both internal innovation and the creation of new journalism businesses or revenue streams. The news media cannot maintain and grow revenue if those involved fail to expand their thinking about the type of services they can provide to the audience.

News as a Service

At its core, news is a service. That doesn't mean it's nonprofit, but it does mean it has to consider more than profits. Journalism professor Jeff Jarvis argues that "journalism must shift from seeing itself primarily as a producer of content for masses to become more explicitly a service to individuals and communities. Content fills things; service accomplishes things."[1]

PHOTO 1-2 Just as the technology of journalism is changing, so is the business of journalism. Understanding new media models is essential to future success.

©iStockphoto.com/ scanrail

When considering new product development, it seems only sensible that you focus on those areas where you can serve an audience effectively.

Jarvis also contends that to provide a relevant and valued service means knowing those you serve, and that means building relationships with the audience. So, though analytics and ratings provide valuable data, there is more to a relationship than measurement.

Strategic thinking needs to include a new set of questions and answers. It is no longer location, location, location – as in simply where to find an audience – but rather relationship, relationship, relationship with that audience. We are in the relationship business. As a media manager, you must ask yourself, are you looking for a one-night stand, a love affair or a long-lasting partnership? What relationship are you trying to develop, and how is it different from all other media trying to reach your customer?

To help you think about what we're saying, let's dive into this analogy more closely. Consider what happened when Barack Obama was first elected president in 2008. People bought every newspaper they could get their hands on because of the significance of the event. Newspapers were completely sold out. For a lot of people, that was the first newspaper they had ever purchased, and quite possibly it would be the last. It was a once-in-a-lifetime event, and they grabbed that paper. The same can be said about the events of Sept. 11, 2001, or the Boston Marathon bombing. People who never watch television news were glued to their television sets for a day or two, but then they returned to their old viewing habits. That's a one-night stand, and it's no way to sustain a relationship with the audience.

PHOTO 1-3 According to a story in The New York Times, "The election of Barack Obama produced a clamor for newspapers that publishers said they had never seen. From The Cincinnati Enquirer to The Charlotte Observer to The Dallas Morning News, papers accustomed to years of declining sales pumped out extra copies by the thousands, and could not keep pace with demand."[2] Unfortunately for newspapers, that was just a "one night stand" as sales volume quickly returned to normal in subsequent days.

©iStockphoto.com/ EdStock

Then there's the love affair. People will sometimes become engaged with news and information because suddenly something has become important to them. Investors faced with a major economic downturn or a crash in the stock market become avid readers and viewers of the media. Similarly, brides-to-be buy stacks of magazines, which they pore over for months. But when the crisis or the wedding is over, the relationship with the media cools off and in some cases just ends.

Instead, what today's media managers are targeting is the long-lasting relationship. They are looking for customers – be they readers, listeners, viewers or users – who want to engage with their newspaper, television show, website or app every day. Just like people in a good marriage or partnership, these customers would feel incomplete without the relationship. Of course, that doesn't mean the relationship won't need to be revitalized every now and then, but it must be ongoing and mutually beneficial at its core.

Creating Relationships

So, how do you woo and keep customers? The advent of mobile and social media has changed both the news media's relationship with the audience and the metrics with which we judge success in our digital world. We've gone from tracking eyeballs, page views and stickiness to looking at engagement, passion, participation and interaction.

Yet, to many in the news business, the product is ink on paper or pixels on a screen, and those typically aren't the building blocks of a personal relationship.

In order to create a connection with the digital audience, media outlets have to examine that word "connection" more closely. The screen persona that they ask the audience to invite into their homes, cars or lives, in general, has to be more than just words, pictures and links. There has to be a true defining "connection" or "experience" for the consumer.

Imagine how that relationship might change if a media organization was asked to consider its products as human. With a magic wand it would strike the app, paper or video segment and imagine that its product could become human just that simply. Who would it be? If media could humanize and define itself as a living being, what sort of personality or characteristics would it have?

When media organizations can do that, they can better brand the product and produce a loyal and returning audience. Media outlets have to define the "person" that they have created before they can ever expect the audience to fall in love. If they demonstrate that they know who they are, as well as who they are informing, a valued relationship will ensue.

BRANDING THE NEWS

Because of the enhanced role branding is playing in journalism, there's a need for news and information companies to rethink the "wall" between editorial and marketing, and even sales. Branding discussions need to include every aspect of what a news media company does, as well as analysis of every interaction the company has with a "customer," whether that's a news consumer, an advertiser or a new potential business or content partner.

The most important thing for any organization is to fully understand its own brand and to understand the role the audience plays in defining it. One of the biggest challenges for journalism organizations is to figure out which of its efforts are critical to the brand and which are superfluous. That process should be followed by managers making tough decisions to jettison those initiatives that don't engage audiences with their brands. Through this effort, news outlets focus on improving their return on investment and, as such, improve the bottom line.

In Chapter 2, we explore in more detail how a brand is created, not only by the efforts of those within your organization but also, more importantly, by the audience itself.

The audience's view of your news operation will define your brand far more effectively than any campaign you can launch.

Packaging the Experience

A big part of branding is based on creating the right experience for the right customer. One audience segment may consume information on computers,

PHOTO 1-4 Brand helps a news organization focus on its core mission while also providing the consumer with a clear understanding of the product and its value.

another on mobile phones. Whatever package the product is wrapped in must be appropriate.

Fortunately, it's never been easier to become an "experience maker" in the news business. We have more access to audience data than ever before that help us understand what members of the audience are consuming in terms of news and information and how they prefer to consume it.

Yet, a significant obstacle to leveraging that information remains within many news organizations – the top-down, "we decide what news is" approach is as prevalent as it is outdated and dangerous to profitability. Web and print designer Joe Natoli calls himself a "User Experience Evangelist" and says news managers who rely only on their own experiences will have difficulty creating a positive content experience for others.

"It takes discipline, focus and practice to force yourself to step outside what you know to be true and to remember that the people who are consuming what you're creating are not you," Natoli tells us. "What matters is whether the person consuming it can understand what it is, that it relates to them, that it speaks to them in a language that they understand, in words and images that they understand and that have context to them in some way."

It's imperative for news managers to understand that the audience has never had more influence and control, so the news media have to work harder at maintaining relevance through targeted content and personalization.

NEW CHALLENGES

What some call the "Shirky Principle" will sound all too familiar to many in the news media. Clay Shirky is a writer, consultant and educator who focuses on the social and economic effects of Internet technologies. He says, "Institutions will try to preserve the problem to which they are the solution."[3]

News organizations have long been trying to hold on to a past in which barriers to entry kept those without a printing press or a TV license out of the news and information game. Many involved in "old media" may, in fact, have a warped self-perception. Traditionally, as an industry, an article in The New York Times has been perceived as having more intrinsic value than a blog post. Now, whether we like it or not, the audience may sometimes value a tweet more than a piece that took a reporter months to source and write.

This changing value system does not mean that customers disregard trusted sources; rather, they define who is to be trusted. News and information organizations have an opportunity to leverage the credibility they have built in the past as they develop ways to curate the audience conversation. In this way, media companies get an opportunity to reach new audiences and to tap into new content sources that were out of reach in the past.

However, reaching new audiences, especially younger audiences, may require a shift to both a user-centric approach and a broadening of the very definition of news. Writing in response to The New York Times' Innovation Report, media analyst Thomas Baekdal says the report is missing the point.

"They are so afraid of challenging the core product of journalism that all their suggestions are about all other things not directly related to their actual work, or changing how they work. Their 'innovation' is more like an added extra, like suggesting that their journalists become more active socially. That's not a bad suggestion, but it implies that social is just an extra task, while the core journalistic product can just stay unchanged," writes Baekdal.[4]

Bottom line: We need to do more than move current content to new platforms. News organizations must put everything on the table as they consider who they will serve and how they will provide that content, including an examination of what they believe news is and is not.

New Competitors

In fact, the redefinition of journalism appears to be taking place with and without traditional news organizations as non-media companies are now creating content of value to potential news audiences. Whether it's Coca-Cola creating a "brand journalism" website or Virgin Atlantic's native advertising on BuzzFeed, the audience is engaging with these stories and often accepting them right along with content produced by the Associated Press and NBC News.

So, how do news organizations compete? Audience trust and relationships are key. To facilitate the preservation and growth of both, we've developed this book based on the "4 C's Strategy."

PHOTO 1-5 "Audience First": Consuming news media comes in all shapes and forms. Different audiences utilize different platforms to satisfy their needs, wants and desires for the news.

Customer – News media companies must be platform-agnostic while keeping in mind that the audience may be platform-specific. Thus, each platform must be necessary, sufficient, and relevant.

Change – Change is the only constant in media today. Companies must be ready to continually adapt.

Choice – The audience has more options than ever, and news organizations must work harder to be the preferred choice.

Control – Sharing power and control with the audience is now a necessary part of running a successful news operation.

THE 4 C'S STRATEGY

The practice of putting audience first is based on a concept that begins and ends with the letter C. What we mean is that media companies must start by asking what customers want. We believe it's clear that they want choice and they want control. What makes delivering on the customers' desires more difficult is that news media companies are now operating in an ever-changing marketplace and a constantly evolving technological world. So, that leads us to the final C – change. Today's media companies have to be adept at adaptation, much more nimble than ever before.

Call Them Customers

Success in business is a matter of priority. Can you create such a great product that nothing could snatch it out of the hands of your customers? Not even a winning lottery ticket? OK, maybe that's pushing it, but you get the idea.

To create such a product, you have to know your audience, and you need to accept that the audience isn't made up of readers, viewers or users – it's composed of customers. For some, this may seem like heresy, but the top news managers we talked to while writing this book all believe in considering the audience first. Journalism is a business, albeit one that plays a particularly important role in supporting a free society.

You may have heard the expression "The customer is always right," but few businesses actually operate that way. In fact, it's not unusual for those in news organizations to show real disdain for their audiences. Yet, used in the best sense, the concept supports an ideal that a business should always make customer satisfaction a priority. In the news business, parallels can easily be drawn to terms like "trust" and "credibility," which are critical to the success of a news operation.

Yet, how can we expect to exceed anyone's expectations if we don't know who they are? When we define and target our audience, we can then meet and exceed their expectations.

Recognize Choice

There are two types of news available to our audience, regardless of platform – there is news as a commodity, and there is unique content that the audience can't get anywhere else. As you'll read in Chapter 4, The Wall Street Journal's leaders say their success has been based, in large part, on the paper's approach to providing exclusive content to its audience.

However, most news organizations operate in a competitive environment in which the audience has a significant number of choices for the same or similar content. In such situations, news is a commodity – coverage of a particular issue or event on any given platform or from any particular outlet will likely exhibit some differences, but there will be enough similarities to essentially make the product indistinguishable to the average audience member. Case in point: How often do you hear someone say, "I can't remember where I read it, but . . ."? The vast number of choices for commodity news makes your organization's branding critical to your success, along with your commitment to producing relevant and important content.

Cede Control

The power of audiences has never been greater. It is truly an on-demand world when it comes to news consumption, and news organizations have been forced to recognize that getting information to the audience in the way the audience wants it is key to maintaining relevance.

Of course, first you need to know enough about audience habits and desires to understand how that audience control should manifest itself in your organization. Years ago, for example, in the WFLA-TV newsroom in Tampa, Florida, a consultant recommended that the management team appoint an "audience champion." The idea was to have that person represent the audience in as many newsroom conversations as possible. Whether it was the angle of a particular story or a decision about where to strategically deploy resources in the future, the goal was to make audience desires more top of mind. Unfortunately, the concept was better in theory than in practice for several reasons – perhaps the most important is that this was before analytics made it possible to know so much more about the audience. In Chapter 7 and elsewhere, we'll hear how some media managers are putting audience analytics at the core of many management decisions.

In fact, devoting more time to researching and reporting on your existing audience and your potential audience is an important part of what makes a news manager successful.

PHOTO 1-6 Consumers now control both content and delivery systems. Journalists who accept and embrace these changes will be positioned to invent the future.

©iStockphoto.com/3Dmask

Embrace Change

Earlier technological advancements used to outlive humans. Now it's not unusual to find yourself wondering what the heck you're going to do with that expensive piece of hardware you bought just three years ago. It's OK to grumble, but that can't keep you from adapting to the ongoing change of the technological revolution. Most of the news media leaders we showcase throughout the book are confident that media technology will continue to evolve in the foreseeable future, and all plan to push their organizations to keep up.

Part of that commitment to change means educating yourself about what's happening outside your core industry – keeping on top of social and technology trends that have the potential to impact the media business. Knowing what technologies the members of your audience are using and how they're using them is essential. In Chapter 11, we share how some experts who are focused on the big picture suggest that you future-proof a news organization.

LEADERSHIP REPORTS

One of the most powerful components of new media is its ability to engage expertise and viewpoints on any topic on a much larger scale than in the past. The authors have capitalized on this capability through a series of interviews with some of the best minds in the news management business. Each chapter will focus on a particular medium and will feature two to three interviews with those who are innovating and leading the way into the future of the news and information business.

For each medium-specific chapter, the authors will rely on these industry experts to describe what they've done to succeed and how they've done it. We will provide a summation and recommendation for readers who wish to replicate best practices or avoid missteps.

THEORY IN PRACTICE

Most news media managers have risen through the ranks of their organizations, and few have had the opportunity to explore foundational management theories. In each chapter, we will explore one aspect of theory that may help you better understand how to navigate the challenges you will face as a manager. However, we want to be straight with you – this is not a text on management theory. Instead, we focus on giving you "fresh from the front lines" experiences and advice from veteran news managers.

THINK AND DO

Each chapter will conclude with an opportunity to put what you've just read about into practice with exercises grounded in real-world scenarios. Here are some things to consider as you finish reading this chapter:

- First, be sure you understand the importance of audience relationships and the 4 C's Strategy. How might the evolution of this relationship affect and continue to affect those in news leadership positions? Consider both positive and negative aspects of this new paradigm.
- Select a news media entity or a news product and try to explain how the 4 C's – customer, change, control and choice – are currently at play. For example, if you take Time magazine, NBC's "Today" show and Bleacher Report, how are they approaching their audiences? Who is the customer, and how do you know? How much change has taken place recently? Who is in control of the product or the medium, and what's your evidence? What other choices does the audience have now, and how should that influence the organization or product?

EXECUTIVE SUMMARY

So, why write a book about putting audience first? For two important reasons: First, somewhere along the way, too many news organizations seem to have lost respect for their audiences. Audiences have often been perceived as "the great unwashed" – less informed, less educated and less important than the journalists who gather and deliver the news. Without a mutual respect between audiences and those who serve them, journalism organizations can never regain the trust and credibility, or the profitability, they used to enjoy.

Which brings us to our second point – news organizations are also too critically important to the preservation of an informed and democratic society to let outdated thinking destroy them. Today's media managers must meet the needs of an ever-changing audience, and that means they must fully understand the audience and its members' expectations. Rather than focusing too narrowly on the platform for delivery and the form of the message, media managers must understand that content is king only when the audience provides the coronation.

Journalism's future is changing as fast as the technology used to bring it to the audience. Therefore journalists and those who manage news organizations must learn to be flexible and adaptable, as well as informed and innovative. Too much is riding on them to do otherwise.

NOTES

1. Jeff Jarvis, "A Degree in Social Journalism," BuzzMachine, April 26, 2014, retrieved from http://buzzmachine.com/2014/04/26/degree-social-journalism/ on Feb. 16, 2015.
2. Richard Perez-Pena, "Newspapers a Hot Commodity After Obama Win," The New York Times, Nov. 5, 2008, retrieved from http://www.nytimes.com/2008/11/06/business/media/06paper.html?_r=0 on Nov. 13, 2014.
3. "The Shirky Principle," The Technium, April 2, 2010, retrieved from http://kk.org/thetechnium/2010/04/the-shirky-prin/ on Feb. 16, 2015.
4. Thomas Baekdal, "What If Quality Journalism Isn't?" Baekdal Plus, June 12, 2014, retrieved from http://www.baekdal.com/insights/what-if-quality-journalism-isnt/10C3F189EE6048BBB4D5CB448CE6F069DAC6C08B6F9E7F72EF24FC33EAC1F946 on Feb. 16, 2015.

Be the Brand

"Brand matters, and it matters more than ever, but what does that brand stand for? If it's 'we're special' or 'we're unique,' it's not going to work. The audience is in charge and they will determine your brand based on performance, not promotion. Promotion is a Media 1.0 concept; the 'Law of Attraction' is what works in today's marketplace. Attraction is the defining dynamic of influence in our increasingly postmodern culture, and it is 180 degrees from what mainstream media companies currently practice."

—Terry Heaton
Media Consultant, Author of PoMo Blog

BENEFITS

- In this chapter we explore the commoditization of media, the resulting transfer of power from mainstream media to the consumer and the role brand now plays in news consumer decisions.
- We explore the opportunity to create new, nontraditional journalism brands.
- We examine cable news as a media branding example.

THE IMPORTANCE OF BRAND

Major media companies are in transition as they move from platform-based businesses to brand-based businesses. This transition is changing the relationship between journalists and consumers in a two-way world where users now have a voice in the news process. Faced with continuously emerging competitors, news managers must adapt to the playing field while not losing sight of ethics and standards.

How Did It Get This Way?

Enabled by the printing press, newspapers first appeared in Europe in the mid-17th century. Beginning with broadsheets, newspapers quickly evolved to a state that would look familiar to a reader today. Because they were virtually the only form of mass media, newspapers proliferated throughout the world.[1] By 1828, around 120 newspapers were being published in New York state alone, 20 of those in New York City. By the mid-20th century, when electronic journalism first appeared, newspapers were the dominant source of daily news and information throughout the world. In the United States, most cities of any size had multiple newspapers.[2]

With the nationwide emergence of television during the 1950s, newspapers began to feel competition from local stations – not so much as alternative journalism sources, but as activities that took up time formerly devoted to newspaper reading. This was especially true for afternoon newspapers that found themselves competing with prime-time network programming as some former readers became viewers.

By the 1960s, newspapers had begun to consolidate. Because television competition was primarily in prime time, morning papers began to emerge as the dominant newspapers in their markets.

Television, meanwhile, began to develop its own forms of journalism with news being one of the program elements. Because the U.S. government limited the number of available television licenses, and because of the limited amount of network programming available at that time, most communities found themselves with a maximum of three commercial television stations (CBS, NBC and ABC affiliates) offering local and network newscasts.

By 1980, a status quo had developed in local communities across the United States with one daily morning newspaper per market and three major local television stations. The emergence of a single daily paper made newspapers robust journalistically and as an advertising vehicle. The emergence of one paper per market meant those papers controlled daily access to the homes of their subscribers, making them an essential advertising option for local merchants who wanted to use the print medium. A limited number of television licenses and networks allowed television stations to narrow their field of competition as well. Like newspapers, television stations derived their profits primarily from advertising.

Television had also settled into a structured culture. Television stations did not attempt to compete with the robust journalistic product being produced by newspapers, but they did possess two unique attributes: video and immediacy. By 1980, the model for television newscasts had hardened into a formula of half-hour increments featuring "anchors" sitting behind desks introducing video-heavy stories. The half-hour newscasts were subdivided into news, weather and sports segments.

Traditional Models Still Predominate

The year 1980 is significant because the newspaper and television business models that were in place at that time still exist today. The culture of that era – limited platforms and exclusive user bases – has made it difficult for journalist organizations, once secure in the knowledge of a stable status quo, to compete in a world of unlimited choices and exploding new platforms.

Yet, even as the media status quo of those days was being solidified, its base was starting to erode. Home Box Office and "superstation" WTBS both had used community antenna television (CATV) to launch national services during the 1970s. CNN was launched in 1981, quickly followed by a wide range of specialized entertainment cable channels. By 1990, television news ratings were clearly dropping.[3]

As the 21st century dawned, Internet, cable, satellite and wireless services were giving consumers unlimited new choices. Though the future was upon them, daily newspapers and local television stations continued to dominate local advertising dollars, creating little incentive to adjust their cultures or even take new journalism competitors seriously.

By 2012, major newspapers had lost so much readership that many were no longer economically robust. Some failed; others curtailed services; all searched for a new business model using digital platforms.[4] Television stations, with diversified entertainment programming in addition to local news, fared better. Still, local news viewership was in steep decline. Both newspapers and television newscasts also suffered from an aging viewer base.[5]

In a platform-dominated world, limited choice meant news availability was also limited. In today's world of exploding technology and unlimited platforms, news is no longer exclusive. It has become a commodity.

PHOTO 2-1 When the same news is available on multiple platforms, it becomes a commodity and loses its unique brand value.

©iStockphoto.com/scyther5

The 4 C's Strategy: Choice

In the good old days, options were limited. You wanted a decaffeinated soda; there was 7UP. A box of tissue; there was Kleenex. A bowl of cereal; there were Kellogg's Corn Flakes. Nowadays, the customer has more choices than time to make a selection. We're living a brand delusion. There are still some big, powerful brands out there; the only difference is customers now have a choice. The question today is, what will make your brand uppermost in the customer's mind?

Many of the CEOs, publishers and producers we've interviewed have indicated that if your brand is not No. 1 or 2, you're better off exiting the market. So part of that strategy of choice is to ensure that your brand is a first or, at the worst, a second preference for the consumer. Today it is imperative that your brand stand out if you hope to be on your customer's playlist.

The commoditization of news has implications not just to business models, but also to journalism. A journalist writing for a captive audience is under far less pressure than one who is subject to consumer choice.

Audience choice creates some fundamental questions: How should news organizations react? How must journalism business models change to be viable in a future dominated by choice? What is the role of ethics? Do users have a role to play in journalism? Must news always be a commodity, or does some journalism have unique value? How does a journalistic organization define itself in a way that makes it valuable to a consumer? How do the answers to all of these questions relate to the concept of a news media brand?

The Rise of Brand

Brand is perhaps best described as the unique features and benefits consumers believe a product offers. A strong brand motivates consumers to act on those benefits. For instance, when thinking of Wal-Mart, consumers might think "low price." When thinking of Mercedes-Benz, consumers might think "luxury and high status." Both of these brands motivate the consumer.

Media brands function the same way. When thinking of The Wall Street Journal, a consumer might think "unique and important financial news." When thinking of Turner Classic Movies, the consumer might think "great old films." In some cases the names of media organizations also proclaim the brand. History, Better Homes and Gardens, and FlightStats are examples.

Brand perceptions are built over time. They are the result of every contact – positive and negative – between the consumer and the product or service. Strong brands are always based on unique value over time.

Susan Gunelius, an author of numerous books on branding, says, "At its core, a brand is a promise to consumers. The brand promise incorporates more than just those tangible products and services. It also includes the feelings that consumers get when they use your products and services." Gunelius goes further, saying, "Brands are built by consumers, not companies. Ultimately it's the way consumers perceive a brand that defines it."[6]

In talking about brand, John Lavine, founder of Northwestern University's Media Management Center, says, "It's not necessarily what the newspaper (media company) thinks or wants its brand to be. It is how the consumer or reader perceives the newspaper (media company), the images and feelings and meanings that are conjured up in people's minds when they think about or look at the paper."[7]

One of Lavine's colleagues at Northwestern, professor Bobby Calder, goes on to explain, "Branding is the activity that goes on inside the newspaper first, to come up with an idea that has great meaning for readers. You have to find out what, in their minds, is a great idea – something that is so linked to their lives and needs that it would make them use the newspaper more. These ideas must be informed by consumers and they have to make sense to consumers. The newspaper then has to 'be' that idea – to translate the idea into content of the paper and related services."[8]

Gunelius, Lavine and Calder all emphasize the role of consumers – or audience – in brand creation. Marv Danielski, president and general manager of KSDK-TV in St. Louis, says that when it comes to television, "The audience has always been in charge of what they watch and when they watch it," but with the changes brought by digital technology, "it's all about one-to-one relationships. You really have to start thinking of the audience as being connected to the station for brand characteristics that go beyond the fact 'Hey, we're on television.' Good broadcasters, good cable people, good Web folks understand 'My audience comes first because I am now in the service business.'"

As we indicated earlier, brand is also the result of every touch point, good or bad, with the consumer. This means a brand can also be negative, creating a barrier between the media organization and the audience. Fred Young, former senior vice president of news for Hearst Television, says brand defines an organization in a positive way "but only until you screw up. A big, bad mistake can take your brand down the toilet." Young says, "Look how the 'Today' show brand took a hit with the Ann Curry episode. Look at the '60 Minutes' hit with Lara Logan. Your brand is the most important thing you have, but once it becomes tarnished, you are in trouble."

Putting these ideas together, we learn that "brand" distinguishes an organization based on unique consumer benefits. At its best, brand is the fulfillment of a promise to consumers. But brand is more than a promise. It is the very character of an organization – both positive and negative – based on every point of interaction between the consumer and the media organization.

Because brand is a departure from traditional platform-based thinking, it is especially difficult for established media companies to transition their relationship with consumers from platform power to brand power.

Leadership Report – Douglas Clemensen

PHOTO 2-2

Courtesy of Doug Clemensen

Founding Partner, Clemensen & Rovitto LLC

Branding expert Doug Clemensen is a founding partner of Clemensen & Rovitto LLC, an international news consulting and market research firm. Clients have included ABC News, CBS News, Fox News Channel and major groups in the United States, Europe and Canada. Clemensen has a unique perspective because his career has spanned decades – from the 1980s through today, making him intimately familiar with the change in relationship between audience and media.

You've spent decades researching news audiences and advising major media companies. How has the relationship between audiences and media providers changed over the years?

The relationship has moved in two, nearly opposite directions, and it has moved simultaneously. On the one hand, the connection between the audience and most news providers has loosened. This is particularly the case with "traditional" news sources like the national broadcast networks, which once controlled their competitive landscape either because of scarcity or because of regulatory advantage. We now know that what the networks assumed to be active consumer preference was, in fact, little more than habit, created by artificially limited choices. The minute the choices multiplied, the habit crumbled. On the other hand, the connection between the audience and some news providers has intensified. News sources that offer unique value, have clear brand identities, or provide a distinct point of view generate as much, and sometimes more, consumer loyalty than ever. Fox News Channel is an obvious example. In the United Kingdom, BBC News is an equally obvious (though utterly different) example.

We keep hearing that news has become a commodity and that the future of news is about brands. Is news actually a commodity? If so, what does that mean for the future of news organizations?

It is necessary to distinguish between news itself and the organizations that provide it. News itself is sometimes a commodity and sometimes not, and it always oscillates between the two states. That is what makes the news business so dynamic and challenging. Consider the Edward Snowden story. It was broken by three news organizations, led by The Guardian. In its early stages, the story was anything but a "commodity," because the supply of information was limited and, to some extent, still is. But that won't last. It never does, because the moment such a story breaks, a thousand news organizations chase it. Such stories become commoditized very fast. The commoditizing of news sources is a different matter and almost entirely the result of the inertia of news organizations themselves.

Consider two examples: daily newspapers and the daily local news programs that appear on television. Both, through their own inertia, have allowed themselves to become commoditized.

For the better part of a century, daily newspapers pursued largely identical news agendas, which they presented and communicated in largely identical ways. The points of differentiation – broadsheet versus tabloid, typographic choices, the use of color – were insubstantial. The result, of course, is that the newspaper business is on its last legs.

Similarly, the typical local news program has changed little in the last half-century: four people sitting behind a desk, presenting news, weather and sports in that order. The points of differentiation – personalities, graphics, the occasional special "feature" – are trivial. The result is that local news shares are declining and the demographic makeup of the news audience is aging.

How does a news organization reinvent itself as a brand? How do you figure out which elements are critical and which are superfluous?

Inventing a brand is much easier than reinventing one, because the need for reinvention usually arises when a brand is in trouble. The most important step in successful branding, from which everything else flows, is to define a core mission and then eliminate everything that is superfluous or contradictory to that mission. That is much easier said than done, and few organizations are capable of doing it completely.

Are some news organizations already brands? Can you give an example?

There are a few, but not many. I've already mentioned several examples: Fox News Channel, MSNBC, BBC News. There are others: The Wall Street Journal, The Economist, Le Monde in France. In the digital space, where clarity, focus and brand differentiation are easier, there are even more: The Huffington Post, Slate, Politico, on and on.

Note the examples I haven't mentioned: ABC News, CBS News, NBC News, CNN. These are examples of news organizations that once were brands but no longer are. They dramatize the difference between an era when being a familiar "household name" was sufficient and the present era when branding success requires more focus.

"Tribes" and "psychographics" are both popular terms when talking about consumers. How do you look at particular groups of consumers? How do you target them?

The jargon of audience and consumer measurement often gets in the way of clarity and focus, and these terms – I plead guilty, since I've used such jargon often enough myself – are no exception.

The problem with such jargon is that it substitutes abstractions for reality. In reality, there are no "millennials" or "Gen Xers." Those are terminological fictions. In defining groups or the potential "targets" of a brand, it is more useful to understand unsatisfied needs and interests than to cook up artificial psychographic categories.

The same thing is true of simple demographics. There are, to be sure, not insignificant differences between younger and older consumers, between rich and poor, between those with more formal education and those with less. But some of the most common demographic categories used by marketers – "women 25 to 54" comes to mind – are utterly useless. They have no predictive value. They say nothing whatsoever about behavior. To succeed, targeting of any kind has to begin and end with behavior – and with the products or services that might change behavior.

(Continued)

(Continued)

The goals should be:
First, identify what the real market opportunities are.
Then, understand the target.

In producing a consumer-driven, branded product, how do you answer the old question of balancing "what they want versus what they need"?

The dichotomy between "want" and "need" is false, because it presupposes a conflict that doesn't exist. Journalism serves two masters and always has. In the "marketplace" of information and ideas, news organizations must inescapably deal with things that are both important and interesting.

It would be foolish to pretend that, along the way, no points of uncertainty or tension arise. Not every important thing is interesting, and not every interesting thing is necessarily important. But that has always been the case, and there is no calculus for striking a precise balance between the two. It is the job of journalism to provide both and, as often as possible, to combine the two. The false dichotomy between "want" and "need" also presupposes that the two poles of the spectrum are clearly understood. The truth is otherwise. Consumers often can't articulate what they "want." They often realize what they want only after they've seen it, read it or bought it.

Conversely, those who think they know what consumers "need" are often speaking from on high, without regard for or any understanding of the actual needs of those they serve. Successful brands listen to people and try to anticipate what they "want" or "need" before they actually realize it for themselves. Did anyone know they "wanted" or "needed" an iPad before the iPad was created?

Is there still a wall between journalism and advertising? If so, has the wall moved? How should it be protected?

I hope so, if by "advertising" you mean advertising for products and services other than the promotion of news itself. Journalism competes in a commercial world, but it is fundamentally different from the other products and services that compete in that world. Its success and survival depend, quite literally, upon a wall of separation. The wall has most certainly moved or, to put it more precisely, has become more porous. I wouldn't for a moment pretend to know how this can be slowed or reversed. But news organizations that figure it out are more likely to succeed both journalistically and commercially. There is abundant evidence that consumers have become fundamentally skeptical of major institutions of all kinds: government, business, the news media. News organizations that can convincingly buck this trend can also become great brands. It may seem counterintuitive to say it, but resistance to commercial encroachment is the best business strategy for the news business.

The Brand Experience

Jim Joseph, president of Cohn & Wolfe North America, is an expert on brand theory and its application to start-up businesses. The author of several books, Joseph defines brand as "the kind of experience you deliver to your customers with each and every interaction. The more compelling the experience, the faster you will build brand loyalty. In fact, the experience you build becomes your brand in your customer's mind."

Although Joseph agrees with Clemensen's ultimate interest in understanding unsatisfied needs, he believes there is value to naming psychographic clusters, provided common interests are sufficiently narrowed. "A tribe," he explains. "A group of people who have very similar attitudes and behaviors. You can talk to them in the same way, and they will relate it back to you. It's not mass. It's not everybody. It's clusters."

But what happens to traditional media companies that still see themselves as appealing to traditional broad audiences? Joseph says, "They made their bets on media, and it paid off for them, but now it's so much more fragmented. This sets up opportunities for new companies to come onto the scene that appeal to the 'tribes,' these clusters of consumers that we understand emotionally. It is an entrepreneur's opportunity."

Perhaps nowhere are consumers more clustered than in their choice of cable news channels.

Branding Example: Cable News

When Turner Broadcasting launched CNN in 1981 as the first cable news network, a decision was made to purposefully downplay personalities. CNN's brand was simply news available 24 hours a day. "CNN started life as a de facto monopoly," says Doug Clemensen.

That monopoly evaporated in 1996 with the launch of two competitors, Fox News Channel and MSNBC.

The brainchild of former NBC executive and political consultant Roger Ailes, Fox News Channel immediately began to distinguish itself from CNN by offering personality-driven programs, a greater use of graphics, lighting and upscale sets, anchors who dressed and looked more glamorous, and the slogan "We Report, You Decide." Almost immediately, critics of Fox News Channel accused it of being politically conservative, a charge Ailes denied. What is not in dispute is that Fox's audience became heavily conservative.

The third cable news network to emerge, MSNBC, also launched in 1996. Originally a joint venture between NBC and Microsoft, MSNBC attempted to brand itself as a younger, tech-heavy choice for news and information.

As distribution of Fox News Channel grew, the network slowly overtook CNN in viewership, surpassing it in 2002. In 2012, Fox News celebrated ten years as the No. 1 news network in cable television.[9]

Distribution for MSNBC also grew, but viewership lagged significantly behind both Fox and CNN. By 2006, MSNBC had grown in audience but continued to finish "a distant third to its cable news rivals in the ratings."[10] NBC News President Steve Capus decided to create a more distinctive brand for MSNBC, telling The Washington Post, "It's time to push . . . and grow the channel in a way it hasn't to date."[11]

Capus hired new management, and MSNBC began to deliberately move to the political left. Program hosts, especially in prime time, became more liberal.

PHOTO 2-3 CNN's original brand was simply 24-hour news. The advent of Fox News, with a conservative brand, split the CNN audience. The audience was further split when MSNBC created a liberal brand. Today CNN is suffering because it does not have a clear target audience, nor does it have a compelling brand. Thus the CNN logo is no longer compelling. The Fox logo, conversely, stands for a clear brand. MSNBC, seeking to also have a clear brand, has been much less successful in appealing to its target audience. The MSNBC logo also suffers from confusion with the NBC network.

©iStockphoto.com/Stratol

In 2010, MSNBC unveiled a new marketing plan "embracing its politically progressive identity with the new tagline 'Lean Forward.'"[12]

At the close of 2013, Fox News Channel was still the No. 1 cable news network, MSNBC was No. 2 and CNN was No. 3.[13] Fox News and MSNBC both had specific brands that attracted fiercely loyal audiences. CNN's weak brand identity caused the network to have far fewer loyalists.

In a 2012 interview with Politico, "several staffers throughout the organization described CNN as a troubled network suffering from an absence of editorial leadership. 'There is no editorial guidance, no editorial culture,' said one staffer. . . . 'How often do you see something that's fresh and distinctive?'"[14]

Doug Clemensen considers brand failure the cause of CNN's low ratings. "When its monopoly evaporated, it lost its way, and it's still fumbling. Now consider the rather different case of MSNBC, which started life as a loose and incoherent alliance between Microsoft and NBC News. When that went nowhere, someone made the bold decision to counterposition Fox News Channel by providing a blatantly liberal point of view. MSNBC is a long way from toppling Fox, but it is in much better shape today than it was five years ago."

At the end of 2013, CNN chief Jeff Zucker said he plans "massive change at CNN," and that CNN "need(s) more shows and less newscasts." He proposed news coverage "that is just not being so obvious." Instead, he wants more of "an attitude and a take."[15]

Ekaterina Walter, who writes on marketing for Forbes and other business publications, is not shy in her assessment. "Does CNN seriously think they still have control of their brand? This is the reason CNN lost their way. If I don't know who I am and where I stand, how will the viewer know?"

Will these changes create a more viable brand for CNN? Time will tell. Clemensen says, "One possibility is for them to become explicitly apolitical because their competitors are explicitly political. If I were marketing CNN today, the most obvious option to consider is to attack them (Fox and MSNBC) for their bias."

Jim Joseph agrees: "Maybe CNN's brand should be objectivity, a news source that doesn't filter it."

Walter says, "I would take a stand. The reason any channel is successful is because you are appealing to a particular audience, but you are also taking a stand. When you have a very clear purpose for your function, it shapes everything you do."

Brand Distinctions

In looking at cable news, we learn brands must be targeted, offer specific user benefits, have a strategy to build user relationships and be understood throughout the media organization. But those things alone are not enough. The brand must have unique and distinctive benefits that the targeted consumer sees as important and valuable.

Leadership Report – Marv Danielski

PHOTO 2-4

Courtesy of Marv Danielski

President and General Manager, KSDK-TV, St. Louis

Marv Danielski, president and general manager of KSDK-TV in St. Louis, is a former senior vice president of Frank N. Magid Associates where he led a team of expert brand and marketing consultants to develop and oversee brand integration strategies for media companies. He has also served as a brand expert on the corporate staffs of both Hearst Television and Gannett Television.

How do you create a brand?

There have to be unique characteristics and distinctions, but most importantly, it's got to be valuable to the consumer. How relevant is that brand to the community you serve? One of the things I fundamentally believe makes a big difference is your values. Your values in journalism.

(Continued)

(Continued)

Your values in how you serve the community. Your values in how you connect yourself to real people that you serve. That's a big change for a lot of folks.

Every great brand – I don't care if it's Procter & Gamble, I don't care if it's Nike – understands there has to be a relationship between what my services are, what products I provide and what that value is to the consumer.

How does that fit with brand versus commodity?

Information has become commoditized, but brands don't have to become commoditized if they do the right thing with that information – if they provide the right experience at all those touch points. The difference between being a commodity and being a brand is that the brand actually means something to the consumer – it means something to the audience – and that the audience feels good about their choices using that brand on a daily basis.

You really have to stand out for valuable distinctions. [For news], investigation can be a distinction; a more humorous style can be a distinction. At some point you must have some kind of sustainable competitive advantage. And you must present that distinction in a way people will say, "That's worth my time. That's worth my effort to watch them, to use their website, to download their mobile app."

What if those distinctions are taken? Are there other ways to build a brand?

Take Fox [television stations], for instance. The Fox brand can be convenience. They are on in many different [time slots]. If they are solid and they are at different times than the other stations, then convenience becomes a brand. Fox stations across the country have successfully done the convenience play. Geography can be a great play. Caring can be a great play.

So, convenience can be a brand?

We are surrounded by convenience brands: Jimmy John's, 7-Eleven, PDQ, Amazon – which is one of the greatest convenience brands of all time. Those kinds of brands exist in people's lives; why not in media too?

What part does marketing play in building a media brand?

Go Daddy is a brand, and they have used marketing to create a whole kind of sensibility. You can say the same thing about Google. You can say the same thing about Yahoo. They provide search, but anybody can provide search. In this day and age of different kinds of services, when the products are all pretty good and they are competitive, the brand and the marketing supersede the product. You choose these brands because of the marketing.

By marketing, I mean not only advertising but being ubiquitous. Being on all of those critical touch points, being on the cell phone, finding that kind of shelf space. Search is just search, but Google has done all the marketing things right to make them really stand out.

The product or service has to fulfill at a level that meets expectations. People will choose a brand because there is a sense of tonality to it that makes you feel good that you've chosen that brand. The value of the marketing, when looking at the value of the brand, is actually much higher than people think. The value of the brand needs to be created, and the value of the brand needs to be reinforced.

You've been known to use the word "connectivity." What does that mean?

Every touch point is critical. When I go to a website and can't find what I'm looking for, I'm disconnected. The word "connectivity" comes back to "Do I feel part of that brand?" With social media, connectivity becomes even more important. Connectivity takes place in a lot of ways: emotional, informational.

Connectivity based on emergency is one of the most important connections local television stations have with their communities. When something like Sandy Hook takes place, people are choosing their brand at that place and time. Do I trust you to serve me in my time of need?

During the Boston Marathon bombing, I thought Facebook was the strongest brand I found because they were aggregating great content from all kinds of sources. There was a real sense of social immediacy. It was fascinating. Facebook then started to offer up options: "Here's what you can do right now." All of a sudden, it took on a whole new mentality. Then it went into the healing mode. Social media created a new media sensibility for a group of people who didn't rely on traditional media, but they aggregated traditional media in a way that made the understanding of the event even quicker and more possible.

THE RISE OF TARGETED MEDIA BRANDS

As we have seen, large platform-based media companies are faced with the challenge of transitioning to a brand culture while still trying to protect their traditional advertising bases. But what about small start-up media companies? Does audience fragmentation create the opportunity to create new journalism organizations?

Jim Joseph believes branding is the key to journalism entrepreneurism. "Understanding who you are as a brand and as a person and understanding your audience and how they live their lives is essential. A lot of people talk about one-on-one relationships, and I think that's true, but I think it's clusters of one-on-one."

A brand must not only be targeted, but it must be consistent, meaning the brand will have a negative side, says Joseph. "Inconsistency is what troubles people. Inconsistency is what causes people to not understand your brand. Brands can be polarizing. They can have negative elements. It's OK if they don't buy into you."

Apple and Microsoft are both examples of consistent brands that have negative sides. Apple loyalists feel Microsoft products are less intuitive, harder to use and biased against the Apple culture. Microsoft loyalists see Apple products as limited to consumers and not appropriate for corporate integration. These negatives actually reinforce the strengths of each brand.

Ekaterina Walter, a branding innovator, agrees with Joseph. "This is a radical change in mentality. What is my niche, and who can I satisfy? How can I make this content important to users long term?"

Leadership Report – Ekaterina Walter

PHOTO 2-5

Courtesy of Ekaterina Walter

Chief Marketing Officer, Branderati

Ekaterina Walter has led strategic and marketing innovation for Intel and Accenture. She is author of The Wall Street Journal best-seller "Think Like Zuck," and co-founder and chief marketing officer of Branderati. Walter writes on branding and marketing for Forbes, Fast Company, The Huffington Post and Entrepreneur.

What new opportunities do you see for journalists?

In the social era, people don't buy products anymore. They choose brands.

With the democratization of information, it is hard to keep things exclusive. So the shift is to the quality of the information. How do I provide value in a different way?

Building communities of people so you can reach them in a specific way is an opportunity – to go from being just a purveyor of news to actually providing value. You need to ask, "Who will want my news and information product?"

How do you have a two-way conversation with these communities?

We don't buy products, we invest in the brand, so we want to feel we are part of the conversation, part of the decision-making process. This is especially true with millennials. Millennials consume more information than everybody else, and they are more natural in a two-way conversation. Millennials are naturals for an information brand that reaches them by phone. Studies show they love their phone better than sex.

We are in an age when there is a lot of noise out there. The digital noise is increasing. From the beginning of time until 2003, all of the information produced during that time is now cranking out every 48 hours. The problem is, how do you stand out? The answer is the continuing value of what you provide because you can't get a viral hit every single time. You need people to sample and come back for what you are offering.

The reality is people will consume your content value, but you must also provide great customer service. You must think of them as social communities who are on Facebook, Instagram, et cetera, et cetera. You are cranking out content every day that satisfies your social communities.

How do you mobilize those social communities?

Advocates. In a two-way conversation, people can push back, which leads to creating advocates who will come back and use your services no matter what happens. In this age of advocacy, the number of viewers you have is not as important as the number of actual advocates.

As advocate consumers become journalists, there is a volunteer army of journalists, and some of them write better than the people who get paid to do it. With the amount of information that exists, why wouldn't you want to get it for free?

Is there competition from nonjournalism companies?

Businesses are becoming publishers and direct competitors to news organizations. Intel's website IQ.intel.com, for instance, aggregates news about technology. They provide aggregation, social response and service response in real time. Cisco and Pepsi do the same thing. Not only are they aggregating the best on a particular passion point or topic; they are actually creating content. They have people in roles like editor and chief content officer. They see themselves as building media brands.

Theory in Practice – Branding Theory

The theory of brand loyalty explains the relationship of customers' psychology with the brand of a company. According to this theory, the positive behavior of a customer toward a brand has three different aspects: emotional attachment, brand evaluation, and behavioral aspect.

When Walter says, "We want to feel we are part of the conversation, part of the decision-making process," she is talking about both an emotional attachment and a brand evaluation that result in loyalty. Extreme loyalty produces advocates for the brand.

The value-based brand theory explains that brands require satisfying user needs over the long term. Success is dependent on the brand's ability to continuously provide unique, consistent value.

Both Fox News loyalists and MSNBC loyalists believe they receive specific value (political agreement) that is reinforced daily and long term. The consistent message and continuing relationship of each network to its core users creates fierce, emotional loyalty.

At its core, brand "represents a symbolic construct created within the minds of people that consists of all the information, expectations and personality associated with a company, product or service. It can symbolize confidence, passion, belonging, or a set of unique values. A brand is an experience," says Walter.

FOCUS ON THE FUTURE

We live in an age of electronic innovation. Media disruption early in the 21st century came from the development of new distribution platforms (Web, wireless) and product innovations such as tablets and smartphones. The future is about a much more unified world in which the consumer is less dependent on specific platforms and devices. Instead, media users will expect a constant stream of information and two-way communication, much of it pre-filtered to their interests, all of it seamless.

In a world of constant information, Doug Clemensen says, "There is, in my view, little future for 'generic' news sources. To survive, news organizations will have to offer something specific and unique, whether that means content or a point of view."

PHOTO 2-6 A strong brand distinguishes a media company's unique value to the consumer, allowing multiple connection points across platforms.

©iStockphoto.com/ IvelinRadkov

The future is also two-way, which means a brand must be both conversational and relevant. Marv Danielski believes relevancy is the key: "To be relevant you must provide relevant information. What is it that I can provide that is really important to people? If you are going to ask people to join the conversation, you've got to give something to the conversation. And that conversation is built on relevant, important, interesting information. There has to be linkage from platform to platform. You must think of yourself as driving multiple wheels simultaneously. Make sure the audience relationship is thought about all the time."

The reward for creating a specific, relevant brand goes beyond consumer usage. It builds advocates for your brand. Ekaterina Walter goes so far as to say, "If you don't build a fanatical following of advocates – people who understand who you are and actually advocate on your behalf, who you mobilize and connect with in a meaningful way – you are not going to be successful."

This world of seamless communication is the enemy of platform-centric media, but the friend of brand-based media. Brand frees media from the restraints of a particular platform, but brings with it direct accountability to consumers who demand specific benefits, a two-way conversation and the kind of value that causes them to become advocates of the brand.

The good news is that journalism is not about technology. It is about information, communication and relationships. Media brands that prove their value to consumers will remain valuable no matter where technology takes us.

EXECUTIVE SUMMARY

New technology has created two massive social changes: choice and connectivity. Choice means consumers now have an unlimited number of ways to spend their time, giving them power over which media companies succeed and which fail. Connectivity means consumers now have a voice in media, creating a two-way conversation.

This rise in consumer control has put platform-dependent media companies at risk. No longer able to sustain their businesses using old media platforms alone, companies must now play by the consumer's rules. That means competing on the basis of brand value.

While a threat to many traditional media companies, the rise of brand also creates opportunities for new media entrants, bringing diversity and even more choice to the consumer. Because journalism is fundamentally about information, not technology, the future is bright for companies willing to compete on the basis of brand value.

THINK AND DO

You are the new general manager of television Channel A. A is a moderately successful station with a website named RegionalNews.com. The station also has a mobile app named Mobile News Now.

The Background

While somewhat successful, Channel A's ratings and revenue lag far behind two competitors: Channel B and Channel C. Both B and C have websites and mobile apps with larger numbers of users than A.

Channel B is known as "the breaking news station." The emphasis on breaking news carries over to Channel B's Web and mobile sites. Channel B is usually the highest-rated station, but during big news events, Channel B's television news, website and mobile site all experience even larger audiences. Channel B does such a good job of covering breaking news that it would be very difficult for any other station to match Channel B's effort.

Channel C is known as "the investigative station." Channel C regularly produces unique investigative stories that air on its television station, has video excerpts on its mobile site and gives even greater detail on its website. Channel C's ratings and mobile/Web usage are normally second to Channel B, but Channel C's ratings and mobile/Web usage often spike during major investigative stories, causing Channel C to temporarily pass Channel B.

Channel A's past strategy has been to try and offer the best of both Channel B and Channel C. During breaking news situations, A always tries to compete with B. A also has an investigative unit that produces stories designed to compete with C. In addition, A has a strong emphasis on weather and owns the market's only Doppler radar system. The station also has a consumer affairs unit, a health expert, a science reporter and a community affairs department. Though Channel A's television newscasts, mobile site and website all offer a wider variety of news than the other stations, A lags in third place across all platforms.

Research shows that Channel B and Channel C are very strong stations. Channel B "owns" the breaking news image. Channel C "owns" investigations. Viewers see Channel A as second place in both breaking news and investigations. A has a reasonably strong reputation for weather coverage and does a fairly good job in consumer affairs reporting, health advice and education reports. Viewers also value A's many community events. Unfortunately, these efforts have not been enough to lift Channel A out of third place.

The Goal

You must find a way to make Channel A the No. 1 station on television, mobile and the Web. Channel A's owner is willing to invest in your plan, and you will be given a reasonable amount of time to be successful, but you must become No. 1 on all platforms.

Write a statement describing Channel A's new brand. Explain why you believe the brand will be important to viewers/users and why it will eventually put A in first place on all platforms. Explain what resources you will add to A and which current efforts you will give up. Give the brand a name.

Things to Consider

- Do Channel B and Channel C currently have brands? If so, what are they? Are those brands consistent over all platforms?
- Does Channel A have a brand? If so, what is it?
- Weather coverage, consumer reporting, health, education and community events all bring users to Channel A. Are you prepared to abandon any of these efforts in order to build a new brand? If so, which ones?
- In choosing a new brand for Channel A, how will that brand be extended to RegionalNews.com and the Mobile News Now app?
- How will the new brand affect coverage of regular news events?
- Once in place, how will you market Channel A's brand?

NOTES

1. "Newspapers Getting Started: The Development of the Modern Newspaper," Center for History and New Media, George Mason University, 2005, retrieved from http://chnm.gmu.edu/worldhistorysources/unpacking/newsmod.html on Jan. 20, 2014.
2. "The Early History of Newspaper Publishing in New York State," New York State Library, May 14, 2009, retrieved from http://www.nysl.nysed.gov/nysnp/history.htm on Jan. 20, 2014.
3. Mark R. Gould, "History of TV News – Part 1," American Library Association, 2012, retrieved from http://www.atyourlibrary.org/culture/history-tv-news-part-1 on Jan. 18, 2014.

4. Rick Edmonds, Emily Guskin, Amy Mitchell, and Mark Jurkowitz, "Newspapers: Stabilizing but Still Threatened," The State of the News Media 2013, retrieved from http://stateofthemedia.org/2013/newspapers-stabilizing-but-still-threatened/ on Jan. 18, 2014.

5. Barbara Boland, "Study: Network News Viewers at All-Time Low; Half Under Age 30 Never Watch News," CBS News, Jan. 10, 2014, retrieved from http://www.cnsnews.com/news/article/barbara-boland/study-network-news-viewers-all-time-low-half-under-age-30-never-watch on Jan. 18, 2014.

6. Susan Gunelius, "What Is a Brand? Part 1 – 5 Factors That Define a Brand," AYTM, 2015, retrieved from http://aytm.com/blog/research-junction/branding-factors/ on Jan. 18, 2014.

7. "A No Nonsense-Look at Newspaper Brand," Readership Institute, Northwestern University, 2012, retrieved from http://www.readership.org/brand/brandlook.asp on Jan. 18, 2014.

8. Ibid.

9. "Fox News Channel Marks Decade as the Number One Cable News Network," Press Release, January 2012, retrieved from http://press.foxnews.com/2012/01/fox-news-channel-marks-decade-as-the-number-one-cable-news-network/ on January 18, 2014.

10. Lisa de Moraes, "Rick Kaplan Out at No. 3 MSNBC," The TV Column, The Washington Post, June 8, 2006, retrieved from http://www.washingtonpost.com/wp-dyn/content/article/2006/06/07/AR2006060702355.html on Jan. 18, 2014.

11. "Rick Kaplan Exits: It's Time to 'Grow the Channel in a Way It Hasn't to Date,'" MSNBC, June 8, 2006, retrieved from http://www.mediabistro.com/tvnewser/rick-kaplan-exits-its-time-to-grow-the-channel-in-a-way-it-hasnt-to-date_b9996 on Jan. 18, 2014.

12. "MSNBC to 'Lean Forward' in Two-Year Brand Campaign," MSNBC News, Oct. 5, 2010, retrieved from http://www.nbcnews.com/id/39507182/ on Jan. 18, 2014.

13. Rick Kissell, Fox News Remains Ratings Champ as 2013 Comes to Close: "It and Rivals CNN, MSNBC Down From Last Year," Variety, Dec. 16, 2013, retrieved from http://variety.com/2013/tv/news/fox-news-remains-ratings-dynamo-as-2013-comes-to-close-1200964903/# on Jan. 18, 2014.

14. Dylan Byers, "In Crisis, CNN Aims to Rethink the Brand," Politico, June 26, 2012, retrieved from http://www.politico.com/blogs/media/2012/06/in-crisis-cnn-aims-to-rethink-itself-127385.html on Jan. 18, 2014.

15. Mike Allen and Alex Weprin, "Zucker Plans Massive Change at CNN," Capital, Dec. 3, 2013, retrieved from http://www.capitalnewyork.com/article/media/2013/12/8536789/zucker-plans-massive-change-cnn on Jan. 18, 2014.

chapter 3

Audience Power

"The new and permanent controlling role of the audience is not going to change. I don't think we are going back."

—Scott Libin
Internet Broadcasting

BENEFITS

- The rise of consumer power has moved control of media decisions from companies and institutions to information consumers who are empowered by choice and by their ability to communicate directly with each other.
- Information consumers are demanding "a place at the table" not only to choose content, but to produce it themselves.
- To be effective, journalists must find new ways to understand audiences and serve their needs as part of a two-way conversation.

STATE OF THE MEDIUM

Media companies have not always recognized the fundamental role consumers play in the journalism process. A newspaper has value only if people choose to read it. A television news program will fail without sufficient viewers. A website is only viable if people access it.

Even when recognized, the role of consumers in mass media has traditionally been minimized. Mass media audiences by definition are made up of large numbers of people, often with widely conflicting views and interests. Without a clear audience or target to serve, professional journalists have based content decisions primarily on their own perspectives and experiences. The lack of user input created a top-down mentality, further minimizing the consumer's role in the journalism process. Most mainstream journalism organizations continue to be structured and function in a top-down manner. As we will see, even though media is undergoing radical change, for the moment traditional media companies remain profitable and therefore powerful.[1]

The 4 C's Strategy: Control

This is by far the biggest change that's taken place in the modern media landscape – control has basically shifted away from the media companies to the users and customers of those media companies. Today's customers are asking not only for choice, but also for control of their written and visual content. And in fact, they are demanding and practicing control. They feel empowered by online and social media where they can voice opinions immediately. The increased number of news and information outlets also gives consumers more control, allowing them to find what they need for themselves.

That shift in control affects the strategy of your media organization. Whether it's revenue or content decisions, your future is controlled by the hands of those customers. It becomes very important to know your customer and your audience in order to serve them and your own business interests well.

PHOTO 3-1 Traditional mass media presents a one-way message to a large group of people. The audience is diverse, but the message is not. Today's targeted media can create individual two-way conversations.

©iStockphoto.com/ Robert Churchill

Technology Impact

Mass media as we know it was a phenomenon of the 20th century, a time when innovative technologies such as radio and television were invented and widespread, but today's consumer-driven technologies such as Internet and wireless were largely unknown. Federal licensing of broadcast stations restricted the number of radio and television stations available. Newspapers, pressured by the rise of television, consolidated in most markets with stronger papers buying weaker ones. The result in most communities was a single metro newspaper wielding enormous editorial and advertising power.

The rise of new technology such as cable television and the Internet radically changed the equation by giving consumers new and wide-ranging media choices. Personal two-way media devices such as smartphones and tablets gave consumers the ability to connect directly with each other. These two social phenomena, choice and connectivity, changed the mass media equation, moving power from media companies to media consumers.

Just as there is an inverse role between profitability and risk taking, there is also an inverse relationship between the size of audience and consumer input. The larger a media organization's audience, the less responsive that company's products are to the interests of individual consumers. The smaller and more targeted the audience, the more important user input becomes.

Rachel Davis Mersey, associate professor of journalism at Medill, argues that today "there are no more mass audiences. That's something organizations have to accept from the beginning. The organizations we see being particularly successful at reaching mass audiences are doing it because they aggregate a number of targeted audiences. Think about something as ubiquitous as Facebook. Facebook has a large mass audience because it serves a number of different smaller audiences' varieties of needs. High schoolers are on there for a very different reason than you and I. Ultimately Facebook's success in the marketplace is being able to aggregate all those targets into one product."[2]

Business Model Breakdown

If Mersey is right, then the business model of "old" media, selling mass audience access to large advertisers, is particularly challenged. Steve Gray, former managing publisher of The Christian Science Monitor, agrees, saying old media business models are breaking down.

"What's really happening is that the lopsided old 'mass media' information system – a few providers sending limited amounts of information to huge audiences – is now being engulfed and dwarfed by an information system that is truly 'mass' on both ends – sending and receiving." Gray argues that the "mass media era" was a 150-year bubble that began with high-speed printing and ended with the advent of the Internet.[3]

Mersey's and Gray's views are forward looking, the logical results of a media world where consumer choice, connectivity and power continue to grow. The world we actually live in is more complex because traditional mass media such as newspapers and television still remain powerful forces within the marketplace. These competing forces put media companies in the difficult position of serving an audience through business models that are in transition.

Ironically, traditional mass media such as television and newspapers, even with shrinking audiences, continue to command a large share of advertising dollars, meaning local newspapers and television stations are still profitable. In the case of television, even with continuing loss of audience, new sources of revenue such as retransmission consent rules, which force cable companies to negotiate with broadcasters before carrying their programming, and digital sub-channels, which allow television stations to broadcast more programming with one signal, are helping profits remain stable. However, this need to serve new targeted audiences on emerging platforms while still maintaining established media businesses creates both economic and cultural stress.[4] To remain profitable, companies must continue to invest the majority of their resources in producing content for traditional platforms. The value of that content is then extended by repurposing much of it on Web and mobile news sites. But extension of existing content is not enough to satisfy news consumers. Empowered audiences also demand new kinds of content on new platforms, much of it two-way, most of it not yet profitable.

Scott Libin, vice president for news and content at Internet Broadcasting, a leading news site hosting company, says websites are very dependent on traditional newsgathering for content: "There are some terrific television station websites out there, but I think they are terrific because of their association with the television station. They are heavily subsidized, and the content tends to come primarily from the television stations."

Brand Extension Challenge

Libin believes extending existing content to Web and mobile sites is in fact critical to advancing a company's brand. As users interact with familiar brands on new platforms, he says, the power of the brand is extended: "Once they have bought into your credibility and your value as a brand, I think then they will open their minds to 'Well, if this trusted source of mine thinks this is worth exposing me to, then maybe I will give it a shot.' If we don't do that, we will be not a brand, but sort of a vending machine."

To avoid "becoming a vending machine," brands must stand for something. That means a two-way conversation has to be an equal partnership, but not one in which journalism companies cede their responsibility to provide truth. Journalistic integrity is essential to maintaining any news organization's brand. It is also a baseline demand from news consumers.

These competing pressures: the practice of journalism, resource allocation, constant advances in technology and brand protection – all challenged by the rise of consumer power – make finding balance in the transition from traditional media to future enterprise challenging.

Jacques Natz, senior vice president with SmithGeiger, a news research and consulting firm, says companies must find ways to achieve balance while always advancing the two-way conversation: "It's a careful dance. You have to be intuitive and smart and build an engaged community. You can find out if your efforts are having impact by doing research. 'Am I making more people loyal to my various brands on all these platforms?' I think ultimately if you do a great job, that halo effect can help you build preference."

Understanding and Engaging Audience

Natz also points out that different platforms often appeal to different kinds of users: "Younger users, who are used to using social and digital to consume news, are far less loyal, so you have to attract them by being sparkling on those platforms for them to understand there's also a benefit to becoming regular TV viewers. I think that's where we are with a generation of people who are heavy Instagram users, heavy Facebook users, heavy Twitter users. We have to impress them on those platforms, then the product has to respond accordingly by doing the same thing."

Natz says new platforms have also created new expectations, especially among younger viewers: "They are very 'now' oriented. Anything that happened three hours ago is too old. The bar is really high. They expect context and the very latest in terms of what is happening."

Libin believes building relationships with younger users is also the key to success on traditional platforms: "I think that social media have given us the first truly interactive opportunity to manage that relationship when people are away from television. And I think we have to earn that relationship. They have to engage voluntarily. But if you are delivering to them content that is of enough value, I think you earn the right to send them a little promotion at a key moment – and I think this is where we have our best chance of getting people back from the digital realm to the broadcast."

Adding to the complexity, consumers also decide which technologies will be accepted and which rejected. Those decisions are based not on which devices are most advanced, but rather on which are most popular with an individual's cohort group. Thus Apple loyalists will likely buy the latest iPhone even when an Android product may be technically superior.

The current media world is thus in flux, with audiences clearly taking control; yet traditional media still commanding the majority of advertising dollars. The division of platform preference by age also complicates the equation.

Understanding the future means understanding the empowered role of audience, differences in generations and the importance of two-way conversation. Add to this the economic and cultural pressure to serve old and new platforms at the same time.

Leadership Report – Scott Libin

PHOTO 3-2

Courtesy of Scott Libin

Vice President for News and Content, Internet Broadcasting

Scott Libin is a specialist in digital journalism at Internet Broadcasting, a major provider of local news Web and mobile sites. He has three decades of experience as a journalist, news director, consultant, coach and educator. He has served as news director of both WCCO-TV and KSTP-TV in Minneapolis/St. Paul and is a former resident faculty member with the Poynter Institute in St. Petersburg.

You were at one time a traditional news director, but are now on the cutting edge of digital journalism. How have things changed?

It has been a really interesting ride. I graduated from college in 1981. I was taught journalism by mostly cranky, crusty newspaper guys who told me and my fellow aspiring journalists that news was what the editor said it was. And if we were fortunate enough to ever become editors, news would be whatever we said it was. It was not the business of readers or listeners or viewers to express their opinions. If they didn't like it, they could go elsewhere. The truth is, consumers of news didn't really have that many options. It was a lopsided relationship.

(Continued)

(Continued)

Good work occurred, meaningful journalism was committed and I think people were pretty well informed. Yet, there wasn't the kind of respect for audience that has developed since then. The pendulum swung. We went from that arrogance to a point of desperation. "Just tell us what you want. Never mind if it's really news or not; just tell us what you want, and we will provide it." That was the extreme.

If media has gone from one extreme to another, then the question has to be asked. Do editors and news directors really understand audience? Are they trying to understand it, or are they just saying, "Tell me what you want, and we will try to do it"?

The pendulum has swung back a little. Consumers of news expect more from media. They want to be heard and to be considered. I also think they expect some editorial judgment to be exercised beyond simply overnight ratings or the latest Google Analytics or comScore or whatever metrics might be available. Simply pandering does devalue the brand. It has to stand for something.

Audiences expect journalists to stay ahead of them and offer things journalists believe are important, but not to the exclusion of the audience's own feedback, which has become immediate and uninterrupted. We get more feedback than we ever imagined, and it can become a little overwhelming. I think that cuts both ways.

The ability to communicate with people is no longer exclusive. Anybody can do it. It's not just that you can reach all those people. You must have a message they choose as more valuable than the thousands of others that bombard them all day long.

About 60 television stations depend on your company for their websites. How do you interface this new media to old media? How dependent is the website on the television station?

One of the things we tell our clients is use your digital presence – your desktop, mobile site and social media presence – to promise people what they can get from you during the day. So if we're going to have this great new stadium site look at 11 o'clock this morning, tell me before I leave the house what time I can find that on your site, and I'll go there and check it out if I'm interested in it. We need to be skilled at promising continuing information through the day to an audience that is largely headed out and away from television. But most are never without a screen of some sort in front of them. So, we need to say, "Here's what you can count on from us. You don't have to go to a TV." That keeps you in contact with your customers and them in contact with your brand.

TECHNOLOGY ADVANCEMENT

Looking forward, we must remember that today's technology represents only a moment in time. Just as consumer adoption of earlier technology led to development of the smartphone, new opportunities for consumer choice are constantly being introduced, displacing older technologies.

Jacques Natz cites traditional websites as one example. "I think the concept of a website is starting to age because you've got all these other platforms that are bombarding you live with the latest whereas by the time I get to a website, that's information someone wrote two hours, four hours, six hours ago."

The answer, according to Natz, is to look not at technology, but at consumer interests. "Everybody's got to be thinking live," he explains. "Websites should be live; they should be evolving to that because mobile is live, mobile is immediate. I dial up the news I want, however much news I want. And so I think, just like newspapers and television stations are having to respond, websites are now having to respond and become live because that's my – the consumer's – expectation of news. News is not what happened recently. It's what is happening right now."

A 2014 Deloitte report recognized that in today's consumer-driven world, adoption of technology will constantly alter the playing field: "Consumers are gaining more power than firms because they are quicker to adopt disruptive technologies . . . not only do consumers have more options – and more convenient access to them – but increased communication among consumers gives rise to more power."

Pat McDonough, senior vice president for Nielsen, says consumers clearly understand the power they now wield: "I think they do, and I think the younger they are, the more they take that power for granted. You watch a 5-year-old. They don't understand the concept that their show is not on now. Their show should be on every minute of every day wherever they are. That's their expectation because that's what they are used to."

FIGURE 3-1 The vast number of media choices means consumers have not only gained power, they now expect information delivered when, where, and how they want it.

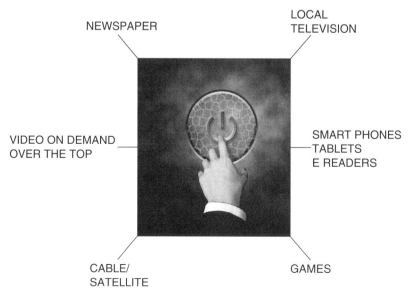

NEWSPAPER

LOCAL TELEVISION

VIDEO ON DEMAND OVER THE TOP

SMART PHONES TABLETS E READERS

CABLE/ SATELLITE

GAMES

©iStockphoto.com/ABDESIGN

Theory in Practice – Social Construction of Technology

All media is enabled by technology. From Gutenberg's invention of the printing press in 1448 to today's constant digital advances, disruptive technology has enabled every advance in communications.[5] Of course, not all advances are equal. A technology only becomes disruptive when consumers choose to adopt it. The iPad became a disruptor, but 3-D television did not. Why? The difference was consumer adoption.

The social construction of technology (SCOT) theory[6] argues that technology by itself has no power to determine human action. Instead, human action shapes technology. Today's vast array of tablets and operating systems were developed because human interaction with the iPad and iPhone led to Google's creation of the Android operating system, which ultimately led to wearable and embedded devices. The human need for greater storage of digital media led to cloud technology, which led to devices that rely primarily on cloud storage such as the Kindle Fire.

In shaping our understanding of audience power, we must remember that advances in technology by themselves do not drive the conversation or, for that matter, the future.

Technology becomes viable only when users adopt it. Technology enables the two-way conversation, but does not create it. The drivers are sociological needs that are inherent within the consumer.

This relationship between technology and the consumer can be confusing because it is not linear. Innovation expert Mike Docherty theorizes that breakthrough innovation comes when consumer needs and technology intersect. "To me," he says, "it's all about finding and exploiting the intersections between unmet needs, enabling solutions (e.g., technology) and marketplace opportunities."[7]

Both the SCOT theory and Docherty's intersection theory are displayed in the consumer's relationship with smartphones.

Smartphones began with the introduction of two disruptive technologies: texting on cell phones and introduction of the BlackBerry email device for business. Both intersected new technology with consumer need. The enthusiastic acceptance of texting by consumers and the overwhelming demand for BlackBerry devices by business users led to the development of the iOS (Apple) and Android (Google) smartphone operating systems. Interestingly, both Motorola, a leader in the development of texting, and BlackBerry, the developer of wireless email, were eventually marginalized by Apple and Google.[8]

Taking these theories to the next logical step, one can say that social media began with an intersection of new technology and user interest (texting and the BlackBerry device). Consumer adoption of those technologies then led to the development of operating systems, which created smartphones and tablets, which in turn enabled social media as we know it today.

EMPOWERMENT OF SOCIAL MEDIA

The motivation of social media is as old as two neighbors talking over a backyard fence. For hundreds of years, that conversation required the physical presence of both people in the same place at the same time. The advent of the telephone in the late 19th century meant conversations no longer required a physical face-to-face presence. A century later, cell phones brought portability and texting. The introduction of smartphones in the 21st century added pictures, videos and access to social media sites such as Facebook and Twitter. The group also expanded from just two neighbors to sometimes the entire neighborhood, even a worldwide neighborhood.

Social media often involves large groups, but it is fundamentally a one-to-one communication. The result is that a single person's opinion can suddenly become important, reaching across a town, a country or the world. This empowerment gives individual news consumers the ability to not just judge content, but produce it. Top-down media organizations, used to dictating content as a one-way conversation, now must deal with user pushback from vocal consumers demanding to be a part of the conversation. If the media organization does not respond, consumers are willing to withhold their two most valuable assets: their time and their money.

Prior to today's age of connectivity, audience power was thought of as the audience's ability to influence media by reacting to it. That definition is now too limiting. Today's audiences are able to influence media in real time, sometimes affecting content even as it is being created. Consumers are also quick to produce content themselves, sometimes bypassing traditional media completely.[9]

PHOTO 3-3 Even though social media involves large networks, it is fundamentally a one-to-one communication, not unlike two neighbors talking over a fence. This means a single person's opinion can suddenly become important.

©iStockphoto.com/DusanVulic

What is the role of the journalist in a world where the consumer is an active part of a two-way conversation, producer of content and even judge? The answer is to go back to human need. Few consumers have the desire to receive only unfiltered information. Most want a "trusted source" to provide relevant news and information and to help them understand the world around them. The fact consumers demand a two-way conversation, and even produce content themselves, does not diminish their need and desire for a reliable provider of news and information. One can argue the role of "trusted source" becomes even more important.[10]

The route to becoming that source for consumers starts with understanding the consumers' needs and interests. One way to begin that process is through research.

Leadership Report – Jacques Natz

PHOTO 3-4

Courtesy of Jacques Natz

Senior Vice President/Senior Consultant, SmithGeiger

Jacques Natz is a former director of digital media content for Hearst Television and a leader of several major market news organizations. As part of SmithGeiger's consulting services, Natz helps companies adapt to a new landscape of empowered, connected consumers. Winner of Peabody, duPont-Columbia and other journalism awards, Natz has pioneered social media efforts for many of his clients.

You are on the front lines of trying to understand a connected audience. What are you seeing regarding user control and production of news content? Is that real?

It's definitely real. You now have news consumers who are news providers. Everyone now sees themselves as having a seat at the table. If you now post a mug shot of a missing person, or someone on the run, on Facebook and ask your community to share it to keep people safe, they take that very seriously. And you'll find that that's generally the most engaging point in your day in social media. So, you start to see where community and news consumers now feel like they are an integral part of the process and are sources every day for the news. Therefore, they expect you to be listening more to them in addition to trying to get stuff from them.

Are your media clients accepting that this is the new way, that the user now has a place at the table?

To varying degrees. I think we are all trying to figure out the balance in a dynamic fashion because of the work flow that has to go into doing the traditional and very necessary feet-on-the-ground journalism and augmenting that with people who can consistently engage community and training people who are used to doing feet-on-the-ground journalism and also have expertise in this new area. There's a big learning curve.

There's also the constant questioning of "Is this tactic effective?" Or "Am I simply wasting time creating this Instagram video that I'm going to put on Facebook that gives people an understanding about a story that I've got coming up at 11 o'clock? Am I doing it in a way that's not traditional marketing that will endear them and cause them to become more loyal?"

How do you get the maximum amount of engagement? How do you know if you are getting the maximum amount of consumption of your core product, which is still important?

By redefining the digital and on-air product, are you now able to attract younger viewers to television news who otherwise would not go there?

I think that's the only way we are going to get them there. The younger viewer is from a generation of consumers who never even saw their parents sit down and watch television. Their parents were busy in dual-income households, and people have been using two and three screens to consume media for a number of years, so they didn't see the habits the baby boomers saw, which is "My parents did it this way, so I do it this way." They are starting their own habits and formulating the way they consume news and what their patterns are going to be.

If their parents didn't watch television news, they certainly didn't read the paper. Where does this leave the daily newspaper? Is there any hope for newspapers in a digital world?

Some newspapers have gotten smarter. They are doing video. But, newspapers suffer from a core problem of not being able to deliver fast enough in an environment where immediacy is starting to become the primary need. Some newspapers became successful on the Web before broadcasters did. The problem is that now it is all about mobile. Some media organizations get more than 50 percent, more than 60 percent of their impressions on mobile because of that need for immediacy. It has redefined news, and those lengthier pieces that newspapers did – I think there is a smaller appetite for that. I think there is still an appetite – that good columnist, that good sports columnist that you would not otherwise have – but I think that's why newspapers are struggling. Some have done it well, but most, I think, are still trying to figure it out in a mobile environment.

AUDIENCE MEASUREMENT AND RESEARCH

The traditional way to measure audiences is by platform. Newspaper and magazine circulation, for example, is measured by the Alliance for Audited Media, formerly known as the Audit Bureau of Circulations. The AAM is a nonprofit newspaper-centric organization whose role is to provide unbiased information for not only print circulation, but print extensions such as Web, mobile and email.

Full measurement of Internet audience is still in its infancy with most Web and mobile use not yet measured. ComScore is a leading Internet technology company that attempts to measure Internet use in local markets. ComScore is accredited by the Media Rating Council, an industry-funded national accrediting organization.

Unfortunately there is no single standard for measuring media audiences. Of the companies partially measuring audience, the largest and best known is Nielsen.

Founded by Arthur C. Nielsen in 1923, Nielsen is best known for television ratings, but the firm also measures a wide range of other behavior from consumer purchases to radio listening.

Often criticized by television stations for using outmoded technologies with perceived inaccuracies, it is nonetheless critical for media managers to understand Nielsen for two reasons: First, Nielsen produces the only universally accepted measurement tool for allocation of the annual $50 billion U.S. television advertising pool. Second, spurred by start-up companies such as comScore and Rentrak, Nielsen is working hard to not only update its television measurement systems, but expand its portfolio of tools to eventually measure all media usage.[11]

Nielsen's primary measurement tool is based on consumer panels made up of users representing particular demographic groups. Nielsen claims to have 250,000 panelists across 25 countries that use in-home scanners to record purchases. The company then attempts to match these data to media usage. Its primary goal is to create data that will be useful to advertisers.

Because of the size and scope of its research, Nielsen is a good source to help us understand the growing power of media consumers.

PHOTO 3-5 As the nature, complexity and choice of media have grown, so has the difficulty in measuring consumer use and engagement. Though often criticized, Nielsen is the largest and most influential audience measurement company.

©iStockphoto.com/scanrail

Randy Duchaine/ Alamy

Leadership Report – Pat McDonough

PHOTO 3-6

Courtesy of Pat McDonough

Senior Vice President, Insights and Analysis, Nielsen

Pat McDonough is a key developer of Nielsen's broadcast, cable, online and mobile measuring systems. During her 30 years with the company, she has played a role in every major advancement in the audience measurement process. McDonough is a thought leader in the U.S. media landscape and has shared her expertise with media executives in Europe and Canada.

Tell me how audience measurement has changed over the years.

It used to be very, very simple in that we were measuring television content across TVs and now we are measuring video content on television, which is still the primary means that we get our video, but we're also getting it online on computers, we're getting it on mobile phones, we're getting it on tablets, we're getting it out of our households. It really has just exploded in terms of the choice that the consumer has.

How has that changed the consumer's use of media?

The consumer has adapted, and they realize they can watch what they want, where they want to watch it. Twenty years ago, if you wanted to watch "The Cosby Show," you mostly watched it at home in your house on Thursday night. You can get "The Cosby Show," or anything since, on one of your devices today wherever you are. We are watching television and video as we commute. We're watching it in places where we didn't watch it before.

What do you think the key is to attracting younger viewers?

I think we have to go where they are. We used to get breaking news on the radio, or you watched it on TV. Now you are getting it continuously all day, online, on your phone; you're getting it tweeted. Good news content that is (well) produced and available is still compelling, but most of us have gotten the news before the evening news telecast.

Nielsen measures all kinds of things besides television. How do you see the future of measuring audience?

I see the future as a combination of traditional panels, where you are metering devices in a household, just as today we have television sets, computers, tablets and smartphones measured, supplemented by electronically coded content that we will be tracking on a broader census base. It will evolve where you are using the panel to give you the richness of information and interaction, combined with more of a census-based measure of how many people saw that video.

Do you think at some point you will be able to measure how people are using all of their time in a day?

We're pretty close to that now. We're not completely there. With the addition of the Nielsen audio assets, we've added radio. If you look at our most recent cross-platform

(Continued)

(Continued)

report, we are up to 11 hours of content that we are measuring every day on the consumer. That includes panels for electronic measurement, mobile phones and tablets, as well as traditional TV, which is still the largest share of media consumption, and adding radio as well.

Are you getting into qualitative information as well as quantitative – the reasons people make media decisions?

We are. We're actually doing that with video. We're looking at "menus" households are on during any given time in the day, "menu" meaning are you on Netflix, video on demand, your DVR list; are you watching live television? We're looking at the interaction in households between that and the household numbers. At the same time, we're able to anonymously tie consumption data to video. In other words, I can say that viewers of "American Idol" bought these brands using credit card information. These are the advertising vehicles that overdeliver in a program like "Idol."

It sounds like you can theoretically measure any metric.

I wouldn't say everything, but we are getting closer and closer. We have home scan data that give you grocery store purchases. We have credit card information that tells us things like what kinds of people are heavy restaurant customers. You really are getting to the point you can say, "Here's how an advertising campaign delivers, and here's a subsequent list of people who saw that campaign and went shopping."

If I were an entrepreneur starting a new video information business, are you saying I could come to you and get product usage information tied to people's video usage – the kind of information that would help me create my new business?

Yes. The challenge is understanding why something takes off. That is the awareness challenge for new content, but I think the need for significant news content is not going away, and that will still drive advertising dollars. I don't think that's changing at all.

I think content providers have to follow the consumers. What we've seen is new devices, such as smartphones, develop new uses, but then consumption is really driven by content providers making more content available. And once that content is available, the device then becomes mainstream. We are almost there with smartphones today. We are not there with tablets, but we will be.

So, we produce content and make it available, then the consumer chooses? Whatever consumers choose, we do more of?

Absolutely, because good content is still really the driver.

In a multiplatform world, audience measurement is also complicated by a brand's ability to reach beyond its core platform, both by choice and as the result of content aggregators.

Magazines, for example, point out that AAM primarily verifies print circulation, which is only one part of a magazine's total brand experience. To address this need for fuller measurement, the Association of Magazine Media has created what it calls Magazine Media 360°, a system of "measuring audiences across multiple platforms and formats." According to MPA President and CEO Mary Berner, "It's an attempt to present a comprehensive picture of consumer demand for magazine brands. And in such, it captures print and digital editions; it captures websites, including desktop, laptop, mobile and video."

The Magazine Media 360° system relies on gaining data from third-party suppliers such as Nielsen and comScore.[12]

Media companies are therefore faced with two related challenges. In order to effectively monetize their product, media brands must find new ways to measure total audience usage. Perhaps even more importantly, they must also understand audience in ways that allow them to advance brand relationships.

PSYCHOGRAPHICS, TRIBES, AND OTHER QUALITATIVE MEASUREMENTS

Demographic segmentation is one of the most common approaches to subdividing markets and is the primary product Nielsen provides. With this strategy, the larger market is divided into groups based on several defined traits. Age, gender, race, marital status and income are among the most commonly used segmentation traits. For instance, an advertiser might wish to reach a group of women aged 25 to 54, or high-income earners.

While demographic segmentation is a useful tool, it is also limited because it gives only a one-dimensional view. Women 25 years of age are very different from women 54 years of age. A high-income banker is different from a high-income athlete.

Psychographics, sometimes referred to as lifestyle segmentation, looks at consumers based on common interests and actions. Women runners who eat healthy foods would be a psychographic segment as would high-income boating enthusiasts. Psychographics study common denominators based on the way consumers think and act. Thus a psychographic group could include people of different ages, sex, income and other identifying traits.

Tribal segmentation adds to the psychographic equation the emotions and motivations of consumers. In theory, content producers who can satisfy consumers on both emotional and rational levels have a better chance of creating a strong relationship.[13]

Scott Libin believes market segmentation is important, but should not be the only measurement a journalist uses: "We talk in the technology space about ways to get our heads around personalization and contextualization. Not just who you are, but where you are and what you are doing so we can serve those needs better. We might be able to narrow it down to people who share certain interests and certain concerns. I think that's a worthy pursuit. We want to make news relevant, but I worry about what is lost. We want to offer people things that challenge them a little, give perspective and provoke them to think in different ways. But it's a delicate balance. People don't want to be schooled. That's not what they come to us for."

In media segmentation, demographics, psychographics and tribes can all play important roles. The more a content producer knows about media consumers, the more content can be tailored to fit the user's needs and interests. The important thing is to understand the audience in a way that makes content relevant to the user.

Terry Mackin, a media entrepreneur, says, "I still like the concept of community. Very tribe-like. It's a college community, it's a housewife with infants, it's a young professional, it's a Hispanic household. I look at the communities and ask how large, how sustainable, what's the direction of that trend? Then look horizontally. Then you put in the bets and the risks."

THE AUDIENCE "PERSONA"

Market segmentation tools such as psychographics allow content producers to see common audience wants and needs as a big picture. But wants and needs by themselves are not a target. Rachel Davis Mersey believes the next step is to create a "representation of the goals and behavior of a hypothesized group of users" called a persona.

Persona builds on demographic, psychographic and tribe segmentation to build a fictional user who can serve as a target for media content. A persona is hypothetical because it represents a group of consumers that do not really exist. It is an amalgamation and therefore an archetype, or model, of the ideal consumer.

Done right, personas help content producers understand audience motivations, interests and likely reaction. Mersey says persona is important because "people will only learn about things they are motivated to learn about. That is to say, people will accept what they need to know from an organization that delivers what they want to know. Think of your favorite newspaper or magazine. You are more willing to read about topics that may not be of particular interest to you because they are in a source that understands who you are and serves your needs."

BEHAVIORAL SEQUENCE MODELING

Still another way of looking at media consumers is through behavioral sequence modeling, a process of looking at how decisions are made and the roles people play in the decision-making process.

Marketing expert Larry Percy believes, "When we communicate with advertising or other marketing communications it is important to remember that we are talking to individuals, but as individuals in a role." By understanding the roles consumers play, as well as the various stages of decision making, Percy believes behavioral sequence modeling can create understanding of the complex nature of an audience and thus also an understanding of the opportunity to advance a brand relationship.[14]

Though behavioral sequence modeling is often thought of as an advertising tool, the process also has value in learning how consumers make media decisions. Understanding the stages of consumer brand choice can identify points in the process during which decisions can be affected in a positive way.[15]

Behavioral sequence modeling is a far more complex subject than can be addressed here, but it is important because it illustrates there are many ways to look at audience behavior. The process of building a media brand requires today's managers and journalists to always be open to new ways of understanding audiences.

PHOTO 3-7 Persona is a fictional person representing a group of consumers. Persona helps target a media message by personalizing the characteristics of consumers who share common interests. What type of persona would you say this woman represents based on the image provided?

©iStockphoto.com/ Dean Mitchell

FOCUS ON THE FUTURE

"Figuring out" the future requires understanding the changing role and power of audience and having the will to act. Because of their vast resources and experience, traditional media companies should be in the best position to lead this charge. Unfortunately this is often not the case. The inverse relationship between profitability and risk can cause traditional companies to be reactive in the marketplace, allowing others to develop new ideas, then adopting the ones that show success.

Equally important as investment is the need for companies to overcome cultural hurdles. One path to cultural change is to think no longer of "old vs. new" media, but rather of what platform is appropriate for a given audience and message.

Natz believes companies must also think beyond platforms, focusing their energy on user engagement. "That engagement commitment is equally as important as the commitment to find the truth and do good journalism," he says. "You have to realize that those two concepts, engagement and good journalism, are now tethered because essentially every reporter, every journalist, has a live unit attached to them. I think we've gotten to the point where the concept of engagement and live, progressive reporting is critical."

The roles of curator and conversation leader that lead to engagement are based in part on a deep understanding of target users' wants, needs and interests.

As we have seen, Nielsen and other companies continue to make progress measuring consumer use of media, and to some degree they are seeking qualitative insight into consumers. However, the primary goal is to help businesses advertise effectively, not to measure consumers' content needs and interests. The data are helpful, but remain primarily a quantitative measurement system. As McDonough says, "The challenge is understanding why."

If we are to fully understand today's empowered consumer, we must also create tools that give deeper insight into consumers.

EXECUTIVE SUMMARY

Today's media consumer is empowered in two ways: by choice and by connectivity. Choice allows the consumer to decide how to spend time and money. Connectivity allows the consumer to be part of a two-way conversation. Empowered consumers now demand news and information on their schedule, chosen device and forum. They also want a say in the journalism process and even the ability to produce content themselves. Ultimately consumers act as judge, choosing to invest or withhold their time and money.

The consumer's natural tendency to organize by group also plays out in media. Social media sites such as Facebook, LinkedIn and Pinterest are driven by consumer-produced media, further increasing the consumer's power. We'll talk much more about the impact of this phenomenon in Chapter 9.

Adapting to a consumer-driven landscape is especially difficult for traditional companies organized in a "top-down" manner. "Top-down" means news and information products are created by the companies, then presented to consumers for their use in a one-way conversation. No longer content with this system, consumers are forcing the conversation to become two-way and even "bottom-up." Media companies that do not adapt to this reality are faced with a decaying business model.

Traditional media companies are particularly challenged to deal with empowered users because company culture, organization and structure were all created for a one-way conversation. Furthermore, most media revenue still comes from traditional television and print products, meaning companies must continue to produce traditional product while also adapting to activist consumers who demand personalized media available where, when and how they choose.

In order to build a relationship with empowered consumers, organizations must create a level of trust that begins with understanding consumer needs and interests. Becoming a consumer's "trusted source" means more than just providing targeted news and information. It also means providing important news and information consumers are not seeking, but are willing to accept because their "trusted source" deems it important.

Whatever role media takes in the future, be it the evolution of traditional brands or entrepreneurial in nature, audience power will be the key determiner of success.

THINK AND DO

You are the editor of a major newspaper's home and garden section. Because of the decline in newspaper circulation, your section has been substantially reduced and, instead of running every day, is now available only on Thursdays.

Since your section was reduced, a number of readers have written letters to the editor complaining about the change. Most of the letters complain about the loss of Today's Area Recipe, a feature that has been in the paper many years and was formerly published daily.

Because of the complaints, the paper's publisher has asked you to come up with a solution. You're the leader of a company task force that has developed a number of options. They include:

1. Publishing Today's Area Recipe every day in another section of the paper.
2. Publishing Today's Area Recipe on the newspaper's main website every day.
3. Creating a new app or stand-alone Web business called Today's Area Recipe.
4. Ignoring the letters and continuing to publish Today's Area Recipe in the Thursday section.

The publisher has agreed to support whichever position you choose, but first wants your task force to describe the process you will go through to make the right choice. What are the strengths and weaknesses of each option? What resources do you need to aid your decision? How will audience power affect your decision?

Things to Consider

- Reader complaints indicate there is a desire for Today's Area Recipe to be published every day, but how important are these complaints? Do most readers feel that way? How do you find out?
- What cultural and economic issues come into play if Today's Area Recipe moves to another section?
- What are the advantages of using the Web instead of the paper? Are there downsides?
- How will an app-based stand-alone business be organized? Will it be part of the newspaper or a separate company?
- What is the downside of ignoring the complaints?

NOTES

1. Todd Spangler, "Media and Entertainment Sector Profitability Forecast to Rise Again in 2014," Variety, Sept. 15, 2014, retrieved from http://variety.com/2014/biz/news/media-and-entertainment-sector-to-notch-highest-profitability-in-7-years-report-1201304744/ on Feb. 26, 2015.

2. Coursera, retrieved from https://class.coursera.org/contentstrategy-001/wiki/week on Feb. 20, 2015.

3. Steve Gray, "Part II – The End of the Mass Media Era," MediaReset, Apr. 31, 2012, retrieved from http://mediareset.com/2012/04/30/part-ii-the-end-of-the-mass-media-era/ on May 19, 2014.

4. Deborah Potter, Katerina-Eva Matsa, and Amy Mitchell, "Local TV: Audience Declines as Revenue Bounces Back," The State of the News Media 2013, retrieved from http://stateofthemedia.org/2013/local-tv-audience-declines-as-revenue-bounces-back/ on May 19, 2014.

5. Benji Cannon, "A Brief History of Disruptive Innovation, Part I," DisCo, Aug. 7, 2013, retrieved from http://www.project-disco.org/competition/080713-a-brief-history-of-disruptive-innovation-part-i/ on Feb. 26, 2015.

6. "Theories of Technology," Wikipedia, Jan. 22, 2015, retrieved from http://en.wikipedia.org/wiki/Theories_of_technology on May 19, 2014.

7. "Chicken or Egg: Consumer Driven or Technology Driven?" Innovation.net, Jan. 13, 2014, retrieved from http://venture2.typepad.com/innovationnet/2014/01/chicken-or-egg-consumer-driven-or-technology-driven.html on Feb. 23, 2015.

8. Vauhini Vara, "How BlackBerry Fell," The New Yorker, Aug. 12, 2013, retrieved from http://www.newyorker.com/online/blogs/elements/2013/08/blackberry-sale-announcement-iphone-smartphone-market.html on May 19, 2014.

9. Jesse Holcomb, "NBC Makes a Bet on Getting User-Generated Content From Citizen Videographers," Pew Research Center, Aug. 20, 2013, retrieved from http://www.pewresearch.org/fact-tank/2013/08/20/nbc-makes-a-bet-on-getting-user-generated-content-from-citizen-videographers/ on May 19, 2014.

10. Peter Marsh, "5 Things to Know About Content, Advertising and Trust," News-Cycle Solutions, Feb. 27, 2004, retrieved from http://www.newscyclesolutions.com/5-things-to-know-about-content-advertising-and-trust/ on Feb. 20, 2015.

11. "Broadcast TV Advertising Revenue in the United States from 2004 to 2013 (in Billion U.S. Dollars)," Statista, 2015, retrieved from http://www.statista.com/statistics/183366/ad-revenue-in-us-broadcast-television-since-2004/ on Feb. 20, 2015.

12. "'Magazine Media 360' Explained, The Mr. Magazine™ Interview With Mary Berner," Mr. Magazine, Oct. 13, 2014, retrieved from http://mrmagazine.wordpress.com/2014/10/13/magazine-media-360-explained-the-mr-magazine-interview-with-mary-berner-president-ceo-mpa-the-association-of-magazine-media/ on Feb. 20, 2015.

13. "Tribal Marketing," Marketing Tools, Jan. 28, 2009, retrieved from http://themarketingtools.wordpress.com/tag/tribal-marketing-definition/ on Feb. 20, 2015.

14. Larry Percy, "What Is a Behavioral Sequence Model?" retrieved from http://www.larrypercy.com/bsm.html on Feb. 20, 2015.

15. Allen Stafford, "Behavioral Sequence Model (BSM)," Marketing Binder, retrieved from http://www.marketingbinder.com/glossary/behavioral-sequence-model-bsm-marketing-definition/ on Feb. 20, 2015.

chapter 4

Newspapers

"We want to serve our readers anytime, anywhere and anyhow they want to get their content."

—Michael Rooney
The Wall Street Journal

BENEFITS

- In this chapter, we see that while newspapers overall in the United States are struggling, innovation and the ability to seize opportunities have some organizations beginning to resuscitate.
- We learn how newspapers are adapting to change forced on them by digital news consumption and how they're rethinking and realigning business models.
- And we look at the possibility of "Mom and Pop" operations being the future for small, community papers.

STATE OF THE MEDIUM

Since the end of 2007, when the deep recession began, there hasn't been much to be optimistic about where newspapers are concerned. But, organizations dependent on print media are now experimenting with new avenues to bring in revenue and are redesigning their operations with a digital emphasis.

Gannett Co., for example, has expanded its presence in both broadcasting and digital products. The company purchased enough television stations to nearly double its broadcast portfolio in the space of two years. Gannett has also begun offering digital marketing services, helping advertisers with social media planning and audience targeting at the local and national levels. Other publishing companies such as E.W. Scripps, The New York Times and Journal Communications Inc. are also trying to adapt their revenue-generating strategies.[1]

PHOTO 4-1 Smart journalism companies are not allowing the decline of print to control their futures. New models of distribution and revenue concentrate on the value of content.

One of the most widely discussed adjustments is the move to pay walls, which can be defined as a system of restricting content to users who have paid to subscribe.

According to the Pew Research Center, digital pay plans have been adopted at 450 of the country's approximately 1,380 dailies and appear to be working not just at The New York Times, but also at small and midsize papers.

Stan Tiner is executive editor and vice president of the Sun Herald newspaper (46,598 daily circ.) in Biloxi-Gulfport, Mississippi. The McClatchy-owned newspaper put up a pay wall on its website in 2012. Tiner says the paper's timing was strategic.

"The decision by the Advance newspapers in Pascagoula, New Orleans and Mobile to go to a three-day-a-week publication schedule was a wake-up call for our readers and customer base," Tiner says. "It drove home the fact that newspapers were experiencing financial challenges, and there was something of an outpouring of support around the fact that we were maintaining a seven-day publication commitment. Also, I believe in part because of the Advance moves, there was virtually no pushback when we instituted a pay wall."

Pay walls, combined with print subscriptions and single-copy sales, have helped some companies begin to reverse years of decline in revenues and may

PHOTO 4-2 The Sun Herald's pay wall offers subscribers both digital and print options.

SunHerald+
SunHerald.com

All the local news and information you want.
All the ways you want it.

SunHerald+ gives you more ways to get your news. And in our busy world, we give you the convenience of instant access to news and information on your computer, your tablet, your mobile phone, as well as in print. Breaking news, more information, photo and video galleries: you get it all with **SunHerald+**.

Android App   iPhone App   iPad App   Digital Replica iPad App

A SunHerald+ subscription includes:

• SunHerald.com (South Mississippi's local news website)
• SunHerald Mobile (free apps for your mobile phone and tablets)
• SunHerald E-Edition (electronic replica of the Sun Herald)
• Sun Herald home delivery

Download your free SunHerald app here, or install direct to your phone or tablet from your Apple or Android app store.

Already a print subscriber?
Activate your digital account here.

Already have a digital account?
Sign in here.

Not a print or digital subscriber?
Check out our digital and print offers!

Helpful Links

• Frequently Asked Questions
• Activation tutorial
• Forgot my password
• Change my password
• Put my paper on vacation hold
• Restart newspaper delivery
• Report a delivery error

http://www.sunherald.com/plus

be rebalancing the industry's outdated and overwhelming dependence on advertising. We'll talk much more about these revenue-generating strategies in Chapter 10.

How Do Consumers Connect With Newspaper Media Today?

The Newspaper Association of America had the base total of newspaper readership – both in print and online – at about 164 million in March 2013,[2] but the percentage of people reading the printed product has been trending downward for more than a decade.

Some of those losses have been offset by increases in mobile consumption of newspaper content. That same survey found that the mobile newspaper audience is growing fast: up 58 percent from 2011. About 34 million adults regularly read newspaper content on a mobile device.

Another bright spot can be found in the income levels of newspaper readers. Nearly two-thirds of Americans at the highest income levels still read a printed newspaper at least once a week. Advertising remains a significant factor in monetizing print media, and newspapers can deliver a high-end consumer.

Billy Morris, CEO of Morris Communications, which owns 11 daily newspapers around the country, says newspapers are clearly still filling a critical need, and that bodes well for their future.

PHOTO 4-3 William (Billy) Morris III, chairman and CEO of Morris Communications, led his company from a one-newspaper company to a major multimedia company that includes 11 newspapers, hundreds of magazines, radio stations and digital media.

Courtesy of Billy Morris III

"We are a free people in this country, and we need lots of information. We make all of our own decisions, and in order to do that we must have information – information on the small items like what movie to go to tonight and what to buy at the grocery store and infinite information on the bigger items like what house to buy or what car to buy," says Morris.

He adds that newspapers are even more necessary when it comes to providing content that keeps our communities and the country in business: "And then there's the more important decisions which we make about our democracy: who to vote for and what to do with those important issues. So we have a real calling as journalists to provide information to a variety of different people on a variety of different subjects and for a variety of different reasons and purposes."

Leadership Report – Stan Tiner

PHOTO 4-4

Courtesy of The Sun Herald

Executive Editor, The Sun Herald

Stan Tiner has been, since May 2000, the executive editor and vice president of the Sun Herald newspaper in Biloxi-Gulfport, Mississippi. He previously served briefly as the executive editor of The Daily Oklahoman in Oklahoma City and as editor of the Press-Register in Mobile, Alabama. The Sun Herald under Tiner's editorship won the 2006 Pulitzer Prize for public service because of its coverage of Hurricane Katrina.

How has the role of media changed today?

In my 40 years as a news person, the role of media has never stopped changing. But the speed of change is much faster now and the consequences of those changes more profound.

How do you balance that with your revenues and profit pressures? Can you make money with headlines?

My impression is that no one who is a media player, certainly not those in the mainstream or traditional media (newspapers, television, radio and magazines), has been exempted from the digital revolution. Revenue and profits have been reduced for almost everyone; therefore the business model for all is quite different, which means fewer resources.

So you feel your relationship with your audience, your readers, your customers and your viewers is better today than it was five years ago?

In some ways I do believe the relationship has changed for the better in that time frame. Immediately following Katrina, the newspaper's relationship with our audience and our communities was almost unheard of from the perspective of appreciation and support. Gradually that evolved back toward a more normal relationship. I believe that papers of our size generally have a very fine relationship with their audience, and ours was very good.

We're living in a sea of change, where the waves are constantly tossing and turning us. Do you see a day when we'll go back to those calm seas, where change is not an ever-present constant, or are those days gone for good?

I have learned that it is unwise to try and predict the media landscape, but I do not anticipate seeing any calm seas.

What management theories do you subscribe to now?

Much of our thinking is derived from initiatives within the McClatchy company, and on the news side this is an editor-driven effort – we are currently quite involved in a major initiative to rethink our news operations as we transition to a digital future. This is also supported by a terrific partnership with Poynter, which offers everyone in our newsrooms the latest in training that allows for constant learning in all of the meaningful aspects of technology and technique to engage audiences while migrating the best values of our profession to the new world.

Most media organizations used to be creators of news. Now we're doing more curating. Do you see a shift in the paper? Are you doing more curating now? And do you feel "news" and "paper" is an oxymoron?

I believe we will grow our curation capacity, but we currently see our role to continue as the leading provider of local news content in South Mississippi. There certainly may be a day when we no longer publish on paper, and in truth we stopped describing ourselves as a "newspaper" a number of years ago. Our masthead used to proclaim we were "South Mississippi's Newspaper," and now we describe ourselves as "South Mississippi's News Leader." We provide information on a number of platforms, including growing emphasis on video. All of our reporters are also capable mobile journalists with video skills.

INNOVATION NEEDED

That is not to say that the industry as a whole is on solid footing. The Pew Research Center's Project for Excellence in Journalism conducted a yearlong search to identify newspaper successes in the hunt for new business models. The subsequent report analyzes four dailies – the Naples (Florida) Daily News; Santa Rosa, California's Press Democrat; Salt Lake City's Deseret News; and Columbia, Tennessee's Daily Herald.

Their leaders volunteered, in detail, the strategies and provocations behind the experimental practices and shared the data with Pew. Innovations included restructuring the sales force, rebranding the print product and Web consulting for local businesses:

- **The Naples (Florida) Daily News** (weekday circulation 44,876). After the publisher and his managerial team overhauled the composition of the sales force and its operating philosophy, the paper saw overall revenue growth in 2011 and 2012. In Naples, protecting print revenue proved to be a significant part of the success story.
- **The Santa Rosa (California) Press Democrat** (circulation 53,292). As part of a revamped business plan, the paper developed the Media Lab, a sophisticated digital agency that provides a full range of online marketing services to merchants. In its first year, the lab accounted for roughly 25% of the paper's digital revenue and is expected to grow revenue by about 60% in 2013.
- **The (Salt Lake City) Deseret News** (circulation 91,638). Former Harvard Business professor Clark Gilbert engineered a major reorganization of the Deseret media properties, building a digital company, creating a new – and more narrowly focused – editorial identity for the newspaper and unveiling a weekly national print edition. Digital revenue has been growing at over 40% a year since 2010 while daily and Sunday circulation jumped about 33% and 90% respectively from September 2011 to September 2012.
- **The Columbia (Tennessee) Daily Herald** (circulation 12,744). This small but aggressive daily in an economically hard-hit Tennessee community rolled out more than a half dozen new revenue ideas in 2012 alone, some in print, but most in digital. The resultant growth in online revenues allowed the paper to keep overall annual revenue losses well below the national average – about 2% in 2012.[3]

The increase in profits created by the changes is certainly promising, and the report went on to offer several specific lessons learned:

- **Manage the digital and legacy businesses separately (Deseret News).** Deseret News Publishing Co. CEO Clark Gilbert has a theory of media evolution. The legacy business is the crocodile, the prehistoric creature that will shrink, but can survive. The digital business is the mammal, the new life form designed to dominate the future. And they need to be managed apart. So the company created Deseret Digital Media to capture future growth, shrunk the Deseret News newsroom and reoriented the paper's editorial mission.
- **Keep developing niche editorial products (Daily Herald).** In recent years, the Daily Herald management has rolled out a successful

monthly health magazine and a new men's lifestyle magazine and plans to introduce a real estate product early in 2013 – keeping many of the costs in-house. It seems an ambitious enterprise for a small operation with modest resources, but publisher Mark Palmer says the health magazine has been "very profitable" and initial results from the new publication are quite positive.

- **Decentralize decision-making power (Daily News).** Under the sales restructuring plan, ad directors and account executives now have far greater authority to negotiate contracts on their own and the bureaucracy is more streamlined. That may sound logical, but it's not easy, according to one ad director. "It takes an incredible amount of courage and trust from the head of your business," he says. "So if someone is trying to replicate this and they don't have the courage and the trust to pass that along, it's not going to [happen.]"

- **Establish the digital agency as an independent business (Santa Rosa).** A key decision was to set up the Media Lab digital agency as a separate entity with a separate staff to operate it. While it traded on the Press Democrat's brand as a trusted news source in the community, the idea was to make the lab an incubator for innovation. In that vein, digital director Greg Retsinas says, it was absolutely crucial to the success of the Lab that it "have a start-up feel to it and not be swallowed by the older Press Democrat brand."

- **Rebuild your editorial philosophy around what you do best (Deseret News).** The News, which is owned by the Mormon Church, made the crucial decision to shift its editorial mission from general interest to coverage of topic areas such as faith and family. It's not likely many newspapers would or could focus around those particular issues, but Gilbert believes diminished newsroom resources should be allocated to unique editorial strengths that offer added value. You "have to be differentiated," he says. "Invest where you can be the best in the world . . . The failure to choose is a choice to be mediocre."

- **Don't give up on print (Daily News).** In Naples, where the print franchise is comparatively healthy, the publisher is bullish, saying "we are going to reinvent print" and envisioning a future where the print product could be customized for the individual consumer. At many dailies, where print revenues continue to plummet, that may seem overly optimistic. But the lesson from Naples is that in communities where conditions are favorable, a substantial bet on print can still pay off.[4]

Yet, the news business is clearly one that asks, "What have you done for me lately?" So, the continued success of the companies profiled depends on their leaders' abilities to continue reinventing the business and the product over and over again.

The 4 C's Strategy: Change

Change is often difficult to adapt to or to implement within an organization. The Chinese define insanity as doing the same thing over and over and expecting different results. Smart newspapers realize they are no longer in the business of simply delivering the news. They have to be in the business of showing their customers WIIFM ("What's in it for me?"), as well as delivering high-quality journalism.

The biggest resistance to change in the newspaper business is the people in the newsroom. As much as they love to talk about change, in reality they're not willing to do so. The strategy of change should be evident in the evolution of the way that we cover the news in print and in the acceptance that we have to surrender news to the electronic and digital devices and focus more on the analytical. Today's newspaper must become a weekly on a daily basis. If that doesn't happen, no amount of change in design, format, size or printing methods is going to help the newspapers. This should be a wake-up call that newspapers have to be more involved in the analysis of information while devoting daily news delivery to websites and digital. That is why the strategy of change is vital to newspapers, because they are becoming the most disposable print entity.

Focus on Local

Realizing that there are new ways of doing business is vital to reviving the newspaper industry, and community papers especially are rethinking their strategies. Small, and sometimes locally owned, publications are conceding the impossibility of chasing "breaking" news with paper. Before you can pull the ink-on-paper off the press, a digital resource has already reported the headline.

Recognizing that fact, smaller papers have begun to see their strong suit is in reporting the stories that the national papers won't: namely, their own hometown news. The Sun Herald's Tiner says the paper is currently the leading provider of local news content in South Mississippi and says it needs to stay that way, regardless of the platform.

"The future is still bright, I believe, for our company, if we keep focused on being the major news and information source for our region," says Tiner.

Morris, too, says that this continued emphasis on meeting audience needs is what will keep his company in business: "And what we do both in our newspapers and in our magazines is essentially important to the people who live in our communities or the people who have the interests that we serve. And we cherish the opportunity to serve them, and we hope to be able to have the highest possible standard that we can accomplish to do that for them."

Research from the National Newspaper Association offers support for the approach taken by Tiner and Morris. In 2012, the organization surveyed people living in small U.S. towns and cities where the circulation size of the local newspaper was 15,000 or less. In those communities, more than 70 percent of people read the local paper at least once a week. Among those readers, more than 80 percent said they relied on that paper for local news and information. Perhaps even more important to the success of locally focused newspapers, 94 percent of the readers said they paid for their newspaper subscriptions.[5]

©iStockphoto.com/ Devonyu

Leadership Report – Scott Coopwood

PHOTO 4-6

Courtesy of Coopwood Communications

Founder, Coopwood Communications

Scott Coopwood started business journal newspapers in Jackson and Cleveland, the latter being the first of its kind in the Mississippi Delta. He is the founder of Coopwood Communications, a full-service advertising, marketing and public relations firm with offices in Cleveland and Ridgeland, Mississippi. In July 2003, Scott started Delta Magazine. Since then, Scott started Cypress Web Design, a website design and hosting firm, and The Cleveland Current, Cleveland's Sunday morning newspaper (3,000 circ.).

How has your company adjusted to declining profits in the newspaper industry?

We run a pretty tight sales team. We are very demanding, and we constantly think of ways we can bring in additional revenue – from selling special sections in our paper, to holding events, to publishing special publications periodically during the year.

What management theories do you subscribe to now?

In this day and time, we make up management as we go because we never know what is around the next corner. I think basic management practices will always be in place

(Continued)

(Continued)

and newspapers have to use those, but that is just the beginning. New problems arise each day, and you have to be flexible in your management procedures in order to move forward and adapt.

You say your relationship with your audience – your readers, your customers and your viewers – is better today than it was five years ago. Why?

Yes, mainly because over the course of our five years in business we have established ourselves, and that has brought us much credibility and more readers. Because of our digital formats, we are better connected to our readers, and that has also strengthened our relationship. We are most always the "first" with the news via our paper or our digital products, and that has also brought us many readers.

How do you view the future? Five years from now, will we be sitting here discussing the same or completely different topics?

I think all of the hype about the Internet putting the hurt on newspapers is mostly hype. Sure enough, the big-city newspapers have been hurt by the Internet; however, look carefully as to why. Mostly it has been the content of these papers; an enormous portion of their news can also be found on iPhones and everything else. Take the Memphis newspaper – why in the world would they feature stories on the Middle East when readers can find that news on cable, their phones, computer, and so on? Instead, a paper like that should be concentrating entirely on its own community; you can't find that news on the Internet.

So, the big newspapers are losing readership because of how they are being run – mostly by lazy people. Hold those readers with excellent content, and those ads will stay in place. At least that is what is happening in the rural newspapers throughout the country. The big-city newspapers experienced over-the-top profits for way too long. That made them lazy. Now they really have to work for their profits because of the Internet competition. Most of the people that run the larger newspapers, I have found over and over, are absolute idiots and as lazy as they can be. Give the readers some super content, and they'll stay with you. That will force advertisers to stay with you, and advertisers will have to buy both newspaper advertising and Internet advertising.

Rethinking Frequency

However, as Tiner mentioned earlier in the chapter, some local papers have felt compelled to go from a daily to a tri-weekly, or even a weekly, publication schedule to save money.

In May 2012, news broke that the only daily newspaper in the metropolitan New Orleans area would go from a daily to a tri-weekly publication. The powers-that-be at Advance Publications, which owns The Times-Picayune through its subsidiary NOLA Media Group, announced that, in an attempt to combat the industry's decline, they had chosen to target their market with digital news reporting. This announcement sent more than half of the paper's reporters home to deal with sudden unemployment.

A May 2012 article published in The New York Times quoted Ricky Mathews, president of NOLA Media Group, with an explanation of the motivation behind the decision: "After the experiment with decreased frequency in Ann Arbor and a string of small daily newspapers in Michigan, the company decided that it was the best, and perhaps only, route to ensure the long-term survival of its newspaper in New Orleans. Beginning in the fall, The Times-Picayune will issue print editions on Wednesday, Friday and Sunday, in part because those days are the most valuable for advertisers, said Ricky Mathews, who will become president of the NOLA Media Group."[6]

The move garnered a great deal of criticism from local citizens and was the topic of numerous discussions among media watchers. The (Baton Rouge, Louisiana) Advocate took this as an opportunity and began publishing a New Orleans edition. Eventually, The Times-Picayune began producing a second print product called TP Street, which publishes on the days The Times-Picayune does not.

By the end of 2013, results were interesting. Average Sunday circulation of The Times-Picayune had risen 12 percent, and The Advocate reported a 24 percent rise.[7] Perhaps the intense focus – locally, regionally and nationally – on what was happening with the New Orleans newspaper market was enough to convince residents that they needed their local paper.

Other experiments in reduced frequency are ongoing in Detroit, Cleveland, Syracuse and Portland, Oregon. Depending on your perspective, these are gambles grounded in desperation or a necessary part of what newspapers need to do to stay in business.

The Wall Street Journal Model

Few papers have had as much success as The Wall Street Journal (1.4 million circ.), the largest of the three national newspapers in the United States, which also include The New York Times and USA Today. Michael Rooney is a former chief revenue officer at the Journal and now chief financial officer for Tribune Publishing; when he spoke to us before changing jobs, he said the headline-driven nature of today's news business has forced a change at the paper.

"Now we have this concept of liquid edit, or liquid content. So, we're in the news business, and it flows continuously and rapidly. We sit in our news hub, and by the way, it's a very dynamic place where people are working on stories and the editors get to decide: This is a headline and something that I have got to get out immediately, and I'm going to put it out on my mobile device to get people excited. Or it's going to require a little analysis, and I can do it by the end of the day, or it's something I can put in the paper tomorrow where I need to be more in depth," Rooney said. "So we have the luxury of having all the different platforms in order to deliver a story, whether it's a headline or a long-form feature. And I think that's what keeps our readers and users close to us because they don't have to go to different places to get their information. We are not afraid of any platform."

Rooney said that the relationship with the Journal's readers is better today than it was five years ago: "There are some who questioned us going into the consumer business and launching a weekend product and a luxury magazine, but they found we haven't given up an inch of financial, economics or business coverage; instead, we've just added. So if your local newspaper has shrunk or has gone away, we now think that we're the full meal. The only thing we're not giving you is your local sports, and ESPN can't even do that."

Many have posited that the Journal's hyperfocus on providing unique and specialized business-related content is what makes the company so successful. Rooney, who started with the Journal in 2007 before making the move to Tribune Publishing, said it's actually been relatively easy to convince readers of the paper's value.

"We've raised subscription prices 75 percent since I arrived here, and have not seen a significant drop in our circulation, so we know that readers are willing to pay for it. And we've given them more value as a result of that. So we raised the prices, but we added more pages, more international, political and consumer coverage," Rooney said.

What has been more challenging, he added, is dealing with advertisers.

"We've held our own on advertising rates. And that's been very, very difficult to do because of the climate that we're in," said Rooney. "It's becoming harder and harder to do that because the weaker titles are doing whatever they can to maintain their page levels to look healthy. And I've seen proposals from my competitors, and I just shake my head and wonder how they're staying in business."

Rooney also said the industry cannot avoid the fact that brands are becoming content developers, something we'll discuss in depth in Chapter 10.

"It's really shaking up the business. We're in the game of special advertising sections and always have been. But when a client comes and suggests to me that they have a better idea for my technology coverage, I know there's a problem out there in the marketplace. And that's happened."

PHOTO 4-7 There are two major sources of revenue for magazines and newspapers: advertising and circulation. While the majority of revenue is coming from advertising, newspapers and magazines are always looking to beef up their numbers by using low-price subscription offers like this one to help sell more advertising.

Source: Retrieved from http://online.wsj.com/public/page/news-business-us.html.

Rooney was taking about native advertising, which involves placing ads within online content such as a product promotion alongside search results on Google or promoted tweets, trends and people on Twitter. It can also include content marketing, in which sponsor-funded content is highlighted alongside editorial content. Rooney thinks the future may bring a total breakdown of the advertiser-supported media model.

"And the whole clients-becoming-publishers will finally come full circle," he said, "and they'll realize, 'You know what, Kraft? You make the cheese and I'll make the content, and let's stop all this nonsense. If you have a good recipe, get it out there, but I'm not your distribution arm for that; go figure that out on your own.'"

Rooney may or may not be right about the future, but The Wall Street Journal's strategy of super-serving its very specific audience is one that has clearly paid off for the property.

LOOKING BACK – TECHNOLOGY CHALLENGE

It's easy now to say that newspaper companies should have recognized the revolutionary impact of digital technology, but until 2007 and 2008, newspapers were still experiencing healthy profit margins.

"I wish we would have started on the pathway to digital by a pay-as-you-evolve basis, but newspaper industry leaders, like those in many industries, did not foresee the road to the future quite as well as we would have hoped," says Tiner.

Even those who were eagerly embracing technology had some missteps. Industry watchers suggest that companies like Knight Ridder, for example, may have actually adopted too much technology too soon. The company invested heavily in Viewtron videotext service in the '90s, but that was before there was enough infrastructure – bandwidth, devices, consumer capabilities and interest – to help make it a viable business.

Morris says his company focused its technology investment on the back end of the business: "The technological changes that occurred first in the newspaper business through the use of computers to hyphenate and justify type – we were the second or the third newspaper company in the country to use the IBM 513 computer to do that, which greatly speeded up and made more efficient the process of setting type.

"We were one of the first companies in the country to connect our three newspapers – Augustus, Savannah and Athens – to one computer located in Augusta over telephone lines – this was back in the '60s – to use that one machine to hyphenate, justify type for three different newspapers in three different communities."

Morris says efficient production has been one of the keys to his company's success.

"It has given us good profit margins, which has enabled us to reinvest in the product side – the product side, the content side and the editorial side of our business – and to do a better job there."

Leadership Report – Michael Rooney

PHOTO 4-8

Courtesy of Michael Rooney

Former Chief Revenue Officer, The Wall Street Journal

Michael Rooney, former Dow Jones & Co./The Wall Street Journal chief revenue officer, had a very successful 35-year magazine and newspaper publishing career. Rooney helped early on in his career to launch Men's Health (1987) and was also publisher of Discover (1991) and Field & Stream/Outdoor Life (1994) and the founding publisher of ESPN The Magazine. In 2014, he was named Tribune Publishing's first chief financial officer.

How has the role of media changed today?

It's all headlines now, snippets of stories and content. Unfortunately, people think they're getting a full meal from it, but they're not. And you can't stop it. That's the reality of the business today: It's all about headlines. And very few are going in depth.

Do you see a day when change in the industry is no longer a constant, or are those days gone for good?

I think we're in an extreme era of experimentation, brought on by digital innovation and social media. It's fantastic, but it's also creating chaos as everybody just sort of tries to hold onto what they have. And that's going to go on for a while longer.

Does that make your job more difficult?

I run an ad agency here, is what I do. I mean, I sell a little bit of advertising, but I have a marketing department downstairs that does what ad agencies used to do. And that's really hard because we have to be very smart on calls now and really listen to our clients beyond just running their ads and cashing their checks and telling them how great our audience is. We come up with incredible programs that you never would have dreamed of 10 years ago.

Can you expand a little bit on that?

Citibank has a program with us called "City of the Year," and they're all about innovation and investing in infrastructures, much like IBM has done with their building each city [the Smarter Cities program]. So we did this whole campaign picking the city of the year – in Tel Aviv, in Medellin, Colombia – and New York City won and we ran the whole thing for them. We were more than just an ad agency; we were a promotion and events company and an ad agency all at one time. And at the end of the day, it's still the ads that pay the checks around here and the bonuses.

It required us to really get into bed with Citi, and it was global, and we're all over the world with them. So that was a huge one.

There are conferences that the energy category has; for example, we sent people to the energy conference in the Middle East to help Chevron create a unique position for themselves among their competitors. We spent a fortune sending people there to help them position the company as a leader in technology within the energy category. I didn't learn to do that when I got into the business, and now I'm signing checks for thousands and thousands of dollars to help a client get something done.

What management theories do you subscribe to now?

I think the fundamentals are still very sound. And that's get to know your clients' business, listen to what they have to say and help them solve their problems; all of those are still fundamentals that existed when I got into the business.

Why didn't the industry take its cue from cable? Leaders in the TV industry said no one would ever pay for TV, but they did.

I worked 10 years at ESPN. I watched those buildings go up and those salaries go up, and it was fantastic.

But we've charged for content on WSJ.com since the beginning, and we did that because it's part of our DNA; we have a newswire service, and we charge for content. I remember when this happened; the Web became added value for advertising too. Not only was the content free, but the advertising was free also. It was as if people didn't really believe it was going to take off.

Most of the money comes from print right now, but we're going to be a lot more efficient when we're more digital. The margins are just much better. We don't have the printing plants, we don't have the trucks and we don't have the paper and the ink. We'll be much more efficient.

But I'm just shocked that people didn't see the opportunity on the digital side of the business when it comes to paying for content. I'm just shocked by it. And, of course, now everyone is conditioned to get Web content for free.

We created a welfare information society.

Yes, I know. It's crazy. So we're lucky that we've been charging. And I watch others get two or three stories and start to charge, and it annoys people when it shouldn't at all.

Will The Wall Street Journal ever be involved in e-commerce?

Yes, we talk about that a lot, and we're experimenting in that. From an ad seller's point of view, I want to be careful, because we're all caught up in the "clicks" thing now anyway. They say 80 percent of the clicks come from 8 percent of the online audience. CEOs and business decision makers don't click on ads. So are they going to start buying products? I don't think so, not that way.

And the other part is, I don't want to get into a competition where I'm selling one product for one advertiser, versus another one.

If we were in the sports business, ESPN could sell jerseys for Ole Miss and things like that, and nobody would be bothered by that. But if I start getting into selling automobiles or even clothing for one versus another, then they're measuring the success of that, and then I'd just become a retailer or an e-tailer. And I'd rather not be in that business.

(Continued)

(Continued)

Most media organizations used to be creators of news. Now we're doing more curating. Do you see a shift in the Journal? Are you doing more curating now?

Not for us. We have 2,000 journalists around the globe who are creating news. And they are digging into stories and are damned proud of it, and they're working for the readers. We break news all the time.

We had a series called "What They Know" which was all about online privacy, and it upset a lot of people I do business with, but it was fantastic. And it was breakthrough. God help us if we stop doing that.

But you're right. There are a lot of curators out there, stealing my content and others' and trying to spin it in a different way. I think that's part of the experimentation, too. That will go away, and people will start to dig where they know they can find the truth.

Theory in Practice – Contingency Theory

Is there one set theory that could help define the path a newspaper company should take in today's digital world?

The answer would have to be no. In the 21st century, digital information media sources aren't going anywhere. That's a given, while the future of print newspapers seems to be a bit unclear. However, within that uncertainty, the best news media managers are making decisions based on the very particular set of factors that affect their publications. This approach to management and organizational structure is based on contingency theory.

The crux of the theory is that there really is no one correct way to do things when it comes to organizational business practices or leadership. Instead, decisions are influenced by various aspects of the environment: the contingency factors.

Contingency theory was first developed by researchers at Ohio State University in the 1950s and refined several times in subsequent decades. In the book *Images of Organization*, Gareth Morgan lays out four main principles of the theory:

1. Organizations need careful management to satisfy and balance internal needs and to adapt to environmental circumstances.
2. The appropriate form for the organization depends on the kind of task or environment.
3. Good managers must focus on achieving alignments and good fits.
4. Different types of organizations are needed in different types of environments.

For example, the Sun Herald instituting a website pay wall at the same time nearby papers were cutting back on publication frequency is a good example of an external factor influencing a managerial decision. The Wall Street Journal operating as a promotion and events company and an ad agency all at one time for Citibank in response to changes in the advertising sphere is another example of leaders making decisions based on contingency factors. As technology and other digital developments continue to disrupt the ecosystem of printed products, strong news media leaders will develop organizations that can adapt to as many contingencies as possible.

FOCUS ON THE FUTURE

From the information gleaned in this chapter, we've substantiated the claim that the only constant in the media business is change.

But we've also seen that stalwart change produces results – some good, some bad. The strategies being experimented with and implemented at newspapers across the country may or may not be long-term solutions to the problems newspapers have in today's digital world, but it is innovation that will always keep media moving forward.

Rooney points out that one of the world's richest men seems confident enough to invest.

"Warren Buffett is buying local newspapers," he says.

But beyond just a few national powerhouses like The Wall Street Journal, his confidence is reserved for the community-based daily news business.

"There are hyperlocal news communities that are still really important to people," he says. "And that's never going to go away. And I think print will always be a part of that, but big national print – probably not, certainly not that. That's not going to be around. It's too late."

Rooney and others believe that, whether it is the picture of your son scoring a goal in soccer or a story about an increase in home break-ins for the area, those newspapers that concentrate on hyperlocal content will continue to serve the purpose of connecting the audience with their community regardless of what other new platforms exist.

PHOTO 4-9 Newspaper delivery systems will continue to undergo change, but the more important revolution is in content. Journalism companies must produce content designed for the end user.

PHOTO 4-10 Arizona Republic Print Edition

Source: Retrieved from http://www1.newseum.org/today
sfrontpages/hr.asp?fpVname=AZ_AR&ref_pge=lst.

Though news managers who focus on hyperlocal content likely feel they already know their audiences pretty well, they must be sure that they have excellent strategies in place to maintain or expand that audience relationship. They must continually ask what types of local news will connect best with their readers and determine how the audience wants that news presented. Success for newspapers, and every other news organization, depends on identifying what existing and potential readers want and how they want it.

EXECUTIVE SUMMARY

In today's digital world, the only constant is change. And newspapers have hit a tsunami of change, in part, because it's no longer feasible to chase news with paper. With one click of a mouse or tap of the finger, stories from every corner of the world are available to our audience. The Internet has made the word "newspaper" an oxymoron. Breaking news with print is impossible in the cybernetic world we live in. National papers, such as The Wall Street Journal, have managed to reach their audience through all platforms and charge for all content – print and digital – and continue to see a profit. But there is hope for hometown newspapers by providing something that nationals, such as The Wall Street Journal, can't: hometown news. A fortuitous concept many are beginning to realize.

THINK AND DO

Some papers are changing the kind of coverage provided in the print product, focusing less on breaking news, which the Internet is much better suited to deliver, and more on analytical or contextual stories.

For example, compare the front page of the print edition of the Arizona Republic with the home page of azcentral.com, the Arizona Republic's online site. Answer the following questions:

1. What evidence do you see that news managers have considered the audience specific to the delivery platform?
2. Based on what you see on the front page of each, how might you sell each of the products differently to advertisers?

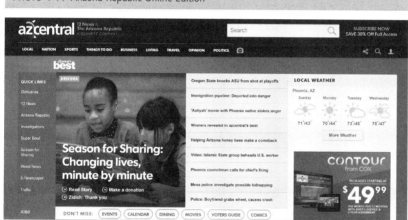

PHOTO 4-11 Arizona Republic Online Edition

Source: Retrieved from http://www.azcentral.com/Retrieved on November 16, 2014.

NOTES

1. Zacks.com, "Gannett to Expand Its Broadcasting Footprint – Analyst Blog," NAS-DAQ, May 15, 2014, retrieved from http://www.nasdaq.com/article/gannet-to-expand-its-broadcasting-footprint-analyst-blog-cm353557#ixzz32AN75sTY on Feb. 24, 2015.
2. "Across Platforms, 7 in 10 Adults Access Content From Newspaper Media Each Week," Newspaper Association of America, March 25, 2013, retrieved from http://www.naa.org/Trends-and-Numbers/Readership.aspx on Feb. 21, 2015.
3. Mark Jurkowitz and Amy Mitchell, "Newspapers Turning Ideas Into Dollars," Pew Research Center, Feb. 11, 2013, retrieved from http://www.journalism.org/2013/02/11/newspapers-turning-ideas-dollars/ on Feb. 21, 2015.
4. Ibid.
5. "Survey: Community Newspapers Still Tops for Local News," National Newspaper Association, Feb. 25, 2013, retrieved from http://nnaweb.org/article?articleTitle=survey-community-papers-still-tops-for-local-news--1361822263--02--1top-story on Nov. 16, 2014.

6. David Carr, "Times-Picayune Confirms Staff Cuts and 3-Day-a-Week Print Schedule," Media Decoder, The New York Times, May 24, 2012, retrieved from http://mediadecoder.blogs.nytimes.com/2012/05/24/new-orleans-times-picayune-to-cut-staff-and-cease-daily-newspape/?_r=0 on Feb. 26, 2015.

7. Andrew Beaujon, "USA Today's Circulation Up 67 Percent? Newspaper Industry Makes Comparisons Increasingly Difficult," Poynter, Oct. 31, 2013, retrieved from http://www.poynter.org/latest-news/mediawire/227958/usa-todays-circulation-up-67-percent-newspaper-industry-makes-comparisons-increasingly-difficult/ on Feb. 21, 2015.

chapter 5

Magazines

"Unbound is our corporate philosophy and our positioning. We don't believe it's a zero-sum world that in order for us to win in digital somehow print must pay, or vice versa. The principles of unbound are strong core belief in the magazine media today, as well as all the new forms of expression that will follow in the future. And that's the magazine, and not only the digital products that we've been discussing, but it's also new forms of revenue."

—David Carey
President, Hearst Magazines

BENEFITS

- In this chapter we explore what has been done to adapt to the changes forced on the magazine media world in a digital-focused marketplace. Example: niche content and new products.
- We ponder what can be done and what has already been done to build audience relationships.
- And we continue to delve into strategies magazines are using to bring revenues back to acceptable levels.

STATE OF THE MEDIUM

Is print dying? Not really a fair question. Of course, everything dies; it's the cycle of life. But everything is also reborn. So it is with print.

The old ways of the magazine print world are dead, no question about it. No more do people flock to the newsstands to find out the latest (and we do mean the latest) on their favorite celebrity's love life. If they want to know who X, Y or Z is dating today, all they have to do is go online and – poof – the information is at their fingertips.

FIGURE 5-1 The Pew Research Journalism Project found, based on information from the Alliance for Audited Media, that circulation for consumer magazines overall rebounded in 2012, but then fell off again in 2013.

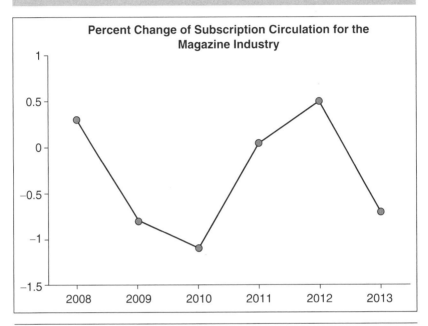

Source: Alliance for Audited Media, Snapshot reports for consumer magazines. Pew Research Center, http://www.journalism.org/media-indicators/subscriptions-circulation-for-the-magazine-industry.

Note: Data represent circulation numbers for magazines that they reported for the last six months audited for each year, ending December 31.

Overall magazine circulation (including single-copy sales and subscriptions) has been a bit of a roller coaster, though the number of print ads has been falling every year in recent memory. Subscription numbers are hard to read because they are often propped up by magazines offering deep discounts or special offers. Suffice it to say that after a couple years of increases, circulation fell again in 2014.[1]

Newsweeklies

When it comes to magazine journalism, America's newsweeklies have long been among the standard bearers. Yet, Jeffrey Cole, director of the Center for the Digital Future at the University of Southern California, predicted that newsweeklies would be the first magazine category to die out in the print-to-digital shift.[2] The evidence to support this view is not difficult to find. For example, TIME is now the only major American newsweekly that still publishes a print edition with nearly 3 million copies weekly.

Rick Stengel, former TIME editor, says newsweeklies can survive, but they need to rethink print: "I think the paper product will never go away. I think it simply becomes a more premium, more lux, and even more desirable, more expensive product that is a part of this total brand of TIME."

He also backs an a la carte pricing plan that lets consumers buy one, or all, of TIME's content across media platforms.

"So for a digital subscription," he says, "you might also get a paper subscription, for a higher price that is, but again, I just don't think print is going away, particularly for upmarket, upscale publications that people like to have on their coffee table and like to have in their home and like to be able to carry with them."

But Stengel realizes print can be just one part of a magazine's strategy going forward.

"I think everything we do revolves around the brand's center, and one of the spokes of the wheel is the print product, like the iPad product, like TIME .com, like what we do for mobile and what we do for phones," he says. "And you can have just one, or you can have them all."

PHOTO 5-1   In what started as an afterthought in 1927 when TIME magazine failed to cover Charles Lindbergh's flight across the Atlantic, the editors decided to dub him as the "Man of the Year," on its cover. The Man of the Year, later renamed Person of the Year, is now one of the most iconic brands in magazine publishing. Here former TIME magazine Managing Editor Richard Stengel discusses the selection process on NBC News' "Today." Every year audiences from all over the world engage in a competition to try to guess who is the next Person of the Year. Audiences are invited to submit their nomination, and once the decision is made the Person of the Year is revealed on the morning shows on television and social media before the magazine hits the newsstands and mailboxes.

Virginia Sherwood/NBC NewsWire via Getty Images

Despite Stengel's faith in the future of print magazines, the Alliance for Audited Media reports that sales of newsstand copies for news magazines, the measure most accepted by the industry, fell 2% on average in 2013, following years of declining numbers. . . . The Economist was the hardest hit, losing 16% of its newsstand sales, after a 17% decline in 2012. The Atlantic and The Week were also hit (down 12% and 7% respectively). The New Yorker enjoyed a 16% increase, one of the highest reported in past years. TIME posted some significant gains too, up 6% from the year before. Since 2008, when Pew Research started tracking these figures, the news magazines have lost 43% of their single-copy sales on average.[3]

Still, it's important to note that newsstands represent less than 5 percent of the total distribution of newsweeklies. Newsweeklies traditionally are subscription driven and have long had very limited sales on the single-copy front.

Audience Relationship

In order to compete in this changing, on-demand digital world, newsmagazines have had to become more creative when it comes to audience engagement, and some have begun to concentrate on offering cultural curation.

"That's what The Week's service is all about," says Michael Wolfe, former publisher of The Week, "not just aggregating, not just curating, but formatting, but narrating, but creating a context in which, on my terms, my time-conscious terms, I'm now able to digest interesting opinion but in a manner that suits my needs and my time and that gives me more than I could possibly digest with the time that I have by reading the hundreds of sources that this comes from."

Wolfe emphasizes the service aspect of the magazine's approach – the focus on audience.

"That's being more than just a magazine brand," he says. "That's hitting on a life challenge that I have and helping me solve it; that's what a smart brand does in a difficult media culture. It hits at the heart of a challenge, and it answers it."

The 4 C's Strategy: Customers

The magazine industry has changed entirely since 1980 when there were about 2,000 magazines sold on newsstands and in other ways available for the customer; now we have more than 10,000 magazines circulating, each trying to survive and thrive. The marketplace changes reflect a dramatic shift; for example, in 1980 we had magazines like TV Guide selling 18 million copies or Reader's Digest selling 17 million, but those mega numbers are no longer there.

The new reality has forced a change in strategy from counting customers to looking for customers who count. No longer should magazines be targeting only the big numbers to sell to advertisers; rather, now there is an emphasis on looking for specific, qualified customers whose values and lifestyles meet and intersect with the values and needs of the advertisers.

Nancy Gibbs is TIME's managing editor. She says the "sense maker" role of newsweeklies has never been more necessary: "We've gone through enormous economic transformation, enormous technological transformation, and people understand that making sense and understanding what's at stake in the midst of all this change requires sources of information that you can trust."[4]

Leadership Report – David Carey

PHOTO 5-2

Courtesy of Hearst Magazines

President, Hearst Magazines

David Carey was named president of Hearst Magazines in June 2010. As one of the world's largest publishers of monthly magazines, Hearst Magazines has more than 300 editions around the world, including 21 U.S. titles and 19 magazines in the United Kingdom, through its wholly owned subsidiary, Hearst Magazines UK. The company operates more than 28 websites and a variety of digital applications. Carey is also a senior vice president and director of Hearst Corp.

Why are you optimistic about the future of magazines?

Magazine brands have billion-dollar awareness footprints. Successful monthly magazines, the good ones, have a hundred million dollars of revenue, some a little bit more, some a little bit less. So, the opportunity is to capture the value between the billion dollars of awareness and the hundred-million-dollar businesses.

This is best expressed through our exciting new relationship with NBC, which we've announced, and the creation of the Esquire channel. NBC totally understood and recognized the instant cache and reputation of Esquire. But those that admire Esquire, who look at the brand favorably, and would be interested in the network, are many multiples of those who read the magazine.

That is the eternal opportunity as well as the challenge: to capture the distance between the current size of the business and the readership that looks favorably upon the brand.

When it comes to media companies now and the creating and curation of information and content, are you finding media companies, specifically Hearst, acting more as curators or media creators?

I think that the tilt is very much in creation, although a part of the Web strategy has to be curation. The magazines create original content. Those are the things that in the print form make magazines great: this content that is carefully edited and reported over a period of time, photography that has a lot of thought and care put into it. And that's what the core magazine media is.

(Continued)

(Continued)

The next opportunity for the industry is going to have to be in consumers and in being able to harness them in a more intelligent way than simply commentary on the sides. The Forbes contributor model, a thousand people contributing to the site – this is an evolution of the Huffington Post model, not all of them fully paid – these are people who work for the associated benefits of that – that's a very interesting model.

Let's take our automotive books. There are people who are just total savants of 1960-era Corvettes. They know far more than anyone at our magazine; they have this narrow window, and this is what they know. So how can we access that sort of intelligence? There's a world of people who love 1965 Corvettes. They know everything about them; they can spot how one might be modified, and they just have an eye for it. How do we bring them into our content creation as well? Every sector has that opportunity.

With all the technological changes and challenges of today, what are the expectations you have for current and potential employees?

People have to be masters of many things. If you think about the skills of everyone from senior to entry-level, you have to start with an enormous curiosity about the world and the way that your content and your brand can be expressed in different ways. You need people who can really be adept at personally engaging with all the platforms and to have the imagination to think about how Cosmopolitan's social media strategy is different from what we're doing with the tablet and different from what we're doing with the magazine. Yet it's possible that all those things can come out of one person's mind.

NEW REVENUE STREAMS

With traditional forms of revenue under attack, industry leaders are coming up with new moneymaking ideas or expanding on traditional approaches.

High-priced bookazines are one potentially lucrative revenue stream for the industry. Bookazines are print publications that combine elements of books and magazines. They are sometimes so niched that they're about one subject – say, "The Duke," John Wayne. Yet, they are much meatier and photo-oriented than your average magazine.

Condé Nast will be publishing a growing number of them, reports the company's president, Bob Sauerberg. "I think this is going to be a big piece of the sales potential over the next few years," he says, "and I think the better we get at it, the better the sales and profits."[5]

Skip Zimbalist, chairman and CEO of Active Interest Media (AIM), agrees that bookazines are very important. He says they demonstrate consumers' willingness to pay high prices for high value, and are a great way to test ideas for new magazines.

Bookazines are one form of special interest publications (SIPs) that Steve Lacy, chairman and CEO of Meredith Corp., says his company has been publishing since 1938. He says these offer the advantage of being able to be expanded or reduced in number based on economic circumstances. When the economy was very robust, home remodeling and decorating interests drove Meredith up to about 200 SIPs per year; in other years, that number might be as low as 130.

Hearst is using SIPs in a variety of ways, reports Carey, including as a tool for accessing new markets. For example, the frequency of Cosmopolitan for Latinas was increased from two issues to four, after its initial success. He also notes the success of the premium-priced Esquire Big Black Book.

"'With the high price point and longer shelf life, [bookazines] have very good economics for us,' and have gotten strong retailer support, particularly in airports," Carey says.[6]

Beyond Printed Products

Zimbalist has said that while it's early days, "there's got to be a way for us to partner with retailers to sell digital copies and digital subscriptions" generated by a consumer's interest being spurred by seeing a magazine in-store.

He also said that events that AIM partners on with retailers, such as clinics in an outdoor store that help customers put a backpack together, bring the magazine to life in the eyes of the consumer and generate substantial sales for the retailer.

Carey said that it's time that publishers put aside some of the old orthodoxies, when it comes to promotions. "The goal is to move product, and as we partner and use our own covers as promotional tools, we have to continue to push the boundaries," he said, noting that select retail copies of an upcoming issue of Cosmopolitan will have a visible discount QRC [Quick Response Code] in the "belly button" area of the model.

He also said that publishers should be looking to find ways to do even more to help the retailer tap into the power of the magazine readers who are retailers' most profitable customers.

Sauerberg stressed that retailers, as well as publishers, should be embracing and pushing to leverage big data/data partnerships on an industrywide basis, to achieve the scale needed to target efficiently to consumers. . . .

He said that he believes that magazines will continue to be very attractive to retailers from a profitability perspective. "But there are a lot of efforts that need time and support from all channel partners," he said. "We need to work together to set priorities, create some wins, talk about these and get retailers excited, and make [initiatives] work financially for all parties. [As a publisher], we're going to do all we can with content, innovation and putting digital assets on the table, but we're all going to have to [collaborate] to think about the potential we have, rather than just manage decline."[7]

Leadership Report – Donna Kessler

PHOTO 5-3

Courtesy of Morris Media

President, Morris Media Network

Donna Kessler is president of Morris Media Network (MMN), a division of Morris Communications Co. in Augusta, Georgia. She is an 18-year veteran of the media industry, having served previously as vice president of operations for travel publishing firm Guest Informant and then as president of Morris Visitor Publications. As MMN president, she oversees affinity units for travel, lifestyle, regional interests and the outdoors.

Morris Communications has been actively acquiring media properties in addition to its 11 daily newspapers. It has 30 nondaily publications and 150 other printed products including magazines and specialty publications. How easy was it taking all these different titles and bringing them in one way or another to Augusta, Georgia, the company headquarters?

Part of that entire process was establishing or staying true to the philosophy of "What needs to be local stays local" because we have 35-plus markets outside of Augusta and we have a strong local presence.

So we wanted to make sure that the editor stayed local because it's very important to make sure we have our finger on the pulse and we are reporting timely, accurate curated content. We wanted the salespeople to stay local because it's very important for them to touch their customers on a regular basis. And we wanted the circulation to stay local because they needed to be able to see where the product was going and have a relationship with our distribution partners.

What advice would you offer somebody about the print aspect of the business in this digital era?

Well, I think first and foremost given where we are right now, you can't only focus on print. Print obviously is what pays the bills, and I think print is a very important part of what we do, but if I had to give somebody advice, I don't think it would necessarily be dollar-and-cents advice. I think it would be "Stay true to your passions."

Be true to your readers, be true to your advertisers, be dedicated and committed to providing the best possible content, the most usable content, to the people who have these passions. And also be prepared in any way, shape or form that they want to receive that content. So I think if you are true to that and know who you are serving, then the rest kind of falls into place as long as you can offer that in a variety of different ways.

You have a print background. You came from a print production background. How easy or hard was the adjustment from this print background to this digital era that we're living in?

It was a difficult adjustment for me, and I think if you would have asked me two years ago or three years ago, I probably would have said, "Oh yeah, I get it; I get the fact that we need to make the change." But it took me about another year to truly understand what that meant. And I think once I truly embraced it, then I was able to communicate that to the team. People say it all the time: If you as a leader don't believe that this is inevitable and this is happening, then no one in your organization is going to believe it.

What advice would you give others?

I think it goes back to what I said to the answer that I gave the question before. Again, if you focus on the content, if you focus on the passion, if you focus on the needs of the person who is consuming your content and then take that – that's where you start. And then take that and say, "How can I serve that person, that passionate person in whatever way – print, digital, e-commerce or events? I think as long as you focus on that, it leads you down the right path.

Where is now, in the current Morris Media Network, the manifestation of the content? Can I find it on the Web, can I find it on an app and can I find it in print?

Yes, and it depends upon which title you're talking about. The plan of course is to analyze each title and each passion – we've done some of this already – and see what adjacencies, if you will, make sense. If you look in the travel space, we just launched a new website. We are in the process of also getting ready to launch by the end of the first quarter a native app. If you take a look at some of the more traditional publications, some of them have Adobe DPS [Digital Publishing Suite] versions, some of them just have replica versions and some of them have apps. Some of them have really, really strong social media presences, depending on the product's type and the passion. Some of them are aggressively going into the events space. Again, it goes back to what is the best way to deliver content to those people.

Mobile: Pros and Cons

The mobile phenomenon has also created new challenges and new opportunities for the industry.

Hearst's David Carey says one of the toughest problems is the "mobile blinder" syndrome, wherein consumers use their mobile devices rather than notice products displayed at checkouts. "'We have to co-opt that experience at the front of the store' with magazine content and promotional innovations that employ digital and mobile technology," he says.[8]

One approach involves push messaging, or sending information (SMS/MMS), directly on the consumer's mobile phone under the condition that his or her acceptance has been given.

Active Interest Media (AIM) is doing a lot of push messaging through smartphones, because mobile is driving virtually the entire growth of its Web traffic, according to Zimbalist. He points out those phone location devices will enable sending promotions about a new issue available for purchase in a retail store when a prospective or existing reader is in the store. "You can't fight mobile, but you can use it," he says.

Sauerberg said that within five to 10 years, there will be massive programs offering all kinds of ways to target and promote to consumers in-store, and the magazine business needs to be prepare to leverage these capabilities.

Carey added that, in addition to using mobile messaging, it makes sense to try to design store promotions that reach consumers in parts of the store where they're likely to be shopping (and attentive to what's around them) rather than using their smartphones.[9]

Steve Lacy, chairman and CEO of Meredith Corp., pointed out that Meredith's recently acquired all-digital brand AllRecipes is an eye-opener, because about a quarter of the 25 million unique visits per month are generated right in store aisles, as shoppers look for recipes and ingredients information. As a test, Meredith took one of its food special interest publications and put the AllRecipes logo on the cover. This yielded a 40% retail sales lift, he reported.

PHOTO 5-4 In the last few years, digital companies have been discovering the power of print. More digital-only entities are launching new magazines. WebMD, CNET, Politico and Allrecipes are but a few. Following the mantra "No customer left behind," media companies are recognizing the need for being platform agnostic while acknowledging that their audience may still be platform specific. The Allrecipes.com website and Allrecipes Magazine is a great example of how a digital-entity-first platform offers similar content to a different audience throughout its network of mobile, Web and print.

Digital Format

No need to tear out pages! The same great content delivered straight to your mobile device. Get the digital version, instead.

Subscribe

Source: Retrieved from http://www.smartappsforandroid.com/2014/11/start-planning-holiday-meals-with .html.

"This is a digital consumer, and she's also very interested in the print that ties this all together. Our greatest corporate lesson in the last year has been to figure out how to connect those dots and help our advertisers sell product to her when she's right there in the supermarket. Everything that we're seeing is that Gen Y is very engaged in these brands on every platform, from mobile to print," said Lacy.[10]

Leadership Report – Steve Kotok

PHOTO 5-5

Courtesy of Steve Kotok

Former General Manager, The Week

Before taking on his role at The Week, Steve Kotok worked on the Maxim magazine launch as Dennis Publishing's business manager. He then helped launch Dennis Interactive as its executive producer, managing the team that produced award-winning websites and interactive projects for clients such as Mercedes-Benz and Art.com. Kotok joined The Week six months after its 2001 launch as business and circulation director, where he grew circulation 400 percent in five years to 500,000 paid subscribers.

It feels like we are living in a sea of change. If you want to put your future cap on, are we ever going back to the time when we do our business, we find a model and we continue doing it like we did in the previous 50 or 60 years?

Look at TV shows versus TV networks; you know what I mean? ABC has been around for a long time or NBC or CBS longer, but their shows will come and go. I think magazines maybe should've been doing that, but didn't because they were able to prop themselves up, and maybe they should've come and go a little more than they did. But they had means to prevent that with subscription agents and stuff like that.

I think the Web and digital and all these other things – digital video and watching your TV through your computer and all that stuff – you may get some stability on platforms, but I think it will be more like TV shows coming and going.

How does the fast-changing media environment impact the people you hire and the way you do business with people?

You're less likely to hire someone and put them in a slot and say, "This person is good at this, and they can do this for 20 years, and we're good." You're hiring more on talent and ability. You see in sports where there will be trends where it goes from specialist-type players to players who can play multiple roles. It's the same in business. I think the player who can play multiple roles and adjust to whatever is coming next is more valued now than kind of the player who has this one thing they're great at – you can't count on that thing still being important five years from now.

(Continued)

(Continued)

How are you fostering innovation within the company?

You really want people who don't look at the future in fear but look at it as an opportunity. That's not too different than how we did things 10 years ago as a company that was launching brands and whatnot, but it's more of a cultural thing. The company culture has always been a "tackling challenges" culture, not a fearing culture. We've never felt that happy – even the few years we were fat and happy with Maxim. I think culturally you want to have the hungry culture.

LOOKING BACK

The magazine industry, like others, now realizes it underestimated the impact of the Internet and other digital technologies.

"There are probably very few things in life that the industry regrets, but one thing has to be that we gave our Web content away for free right from the very start. Backing up on that now is a very difficult thing. The Times has done a good job as a newspaper, but I think for magazines it's a challenging thing to re-gate your content," says Carey.

Some magazines are experimenting with pay walls; for example, The Atlantic began packaging a selection of free online articles in an ad-free weekly

PHOTO 5-6 Like newspapers, magazines were slow to understand the potential revenue opportunities beyond print. Digital revenue is now a top priority, although the majority of the revenue is still coming from print.

Creatas/Creatas/Thinkstock

Theory in Practice – Leadership Theory

The magazine industry has long been a place where individuals can have a dramatic effect on the quality of the publication. The right leader can save a struggling entity, just as the wrong type of leader can destroy a previously strong product.

Transformational leadership theory was initially introduced by leadership expert and presidential biographer James MacGregor Burns. According to Burns, through the strength of their visions and personalities, transformational leaders inspire followers to work toward common goals.

Later, researcher Bernard M. Bass expanded upon Burns' original ideas to develop what is today referred to as Bass' transformational leadership theory. According to Bass, transformational leadership can be defined based on the impact that it has on followers. Transformational leaders, Bass suggested, garner trust, respect and admiration from their followers.

At Hearst, Carey is considered one of those transformational leaders, whether he likes it or not.

"That's something that I groan about: when I get any personal credit for the organization's success and the things that we're doing, because it's the team that does the work. The first rule of leadership is that you pass out the credit and you take the blame for the things that go wrong. And the people who flip that around don't find that they can get their organization to work very hard for them," he says.

The transformational leader is often contrasted with the transactional leaders, who focus on the "give and take" between themselves and those who work for them. This sort of "you scratch my back and I'll scratch yours" approach is sometimes seen as antithetical to the transformational style.

Carey says his leadership style is focused on staying out of the limelight: "See, I don't do the heavy lifting. I might give them the permission to do it, but they do the hard work, not me. And they should get the credit and not the person who sits in the corner office."

magazine it makes available on iTunes. Others, like TIME, are relying on apps with downloadable digital editions for which they charge a fee.

In addition, the whole approach to subscription pricing is one the industry may regret. By charging so little for subscriptions, magazines increased their dependence on advertising to an extent that's likely unsustainable in the digital age.

FOCUS ON THE FUTURE

In the future, magazines will have to change to survive, and those changes will need to permeate the core print products, digital outgrowths and additional revenue- or audience-generating initiatives. Gibbs believes that the survival of TIME and other news-oriented publications depends on creating a valued experience for the audience.

"I think that the need to make sense of the world for people, and to tell stories in a way that they remember, that moves them, that is powerful, I think that's something that TIME has always believed in, and I certainly do as well," she says.[11]

Carey agrees, but says magazines must also do a better job of leveraging their ready-made advantages.

"Historically, magazines have inspired people to buy lots of things. To this day people rip out pages and go into the store and say, 'I want one of these,'" he says.

The challenge for magazines is to leverage the economic value they've created for themselves, and increasingly they'll do that through digital products.

"Our tablets will be e-commerce enabled because that will be easiest of all," Carey adds. "You're in a reading environment, and you see the mixing bowl in Good Housekeeping. You should be able to touch and to buy it, with as little consumer effort as possible."

Carey also says there's an urgency for magazines to get this figured out: "Is it easier for commerce companies to add content or for content companies to add commerce? I come down to that it's easier for commerce companies to add content. I do think that that equation is more difficult for us than it is for the commerce companies. That's not to say that we can't master it, but I think that it's harder for us to go upstream than for them to go downstream. But it's something that we have to solve."

EXECUTIVE SUMMARY

Magazine media publishing has undergone a major change since the beginning of the digital invasion. Establishing business partnerships, instead of traditional advertising relationships, and, in some instances, taking on the role of ad executives when it comes to handling clients' accounts are both part of the industry's evolution. Add to that the effort to produce innovative and interactive print content, and you can see how magazine publishing is competing with instantaneous, on-demand news and information. It's been a harrowing, but strength-building, experience – something magazines have withstood, albeit not without repercussions.

Revenue's down, circulation's down, yet audiences are still faithful – to a certain extent. For managers, the goal is to become even more innovative and determined to see this through to the end – "this" being the magazine's journey through the bleak wilderness in search of the savior.

THINK AND DO

Magazine industry leaders believe their products have some unique characteristics that will help keep them viable in the future.

For example, TIME decided to launch Red Border Films, a new documentary filmmaking unit and interactive digital platform on TIME.com. According to the announcement, the enterprise will feature "deeply reported films by TIME journalists and photojournalists."

Based on your reading of the chapter, answer the following discussion questions:

1. What are the assets available to an organization like TIME that might lead you to believe this effort will succeed?
2. Name at least two ways that success might be defined for the documentary unit.
3. What might be the downside to creating a documentary-producing unit within the TIME company?

NOTES

1. Neal Lulofs, "Top 25 U.S. Consumer Magazines for June 2014," Alliance for Audited Media, Aug. 7, 2014, retrieved from http://auditedmedia.com/news/blog/2014/august/top-25-us-consumer-magazines-for-june-2014.aspx on Feb. 26, 2015.
2. Emma Bazilian, "After Newsweek, Is Writing on Wall for Newsweeklies?" Adweek, Oct. 18, 2012, retrieved from http://www.adweek.com/news/press/after-news week-writing-wall-newsweeklies-144549 on Feb. 24, 2015.
3. "Key Indicators in Media and News," Pew Research Center, March 26, 2014, retrieved from http://www.journalism.org/2014/03/26/state-of-the-news-media-2014-key-indicators-in-media-and-news/ on May 19, 2013.
4. "'There's Always Going to Be Time for a Newsweekly,' Nancy Gibbs, TIME's New Editor, Tells Samir Husni. The Mr. Magazine™ Interview." Mr. Magazine, Sept. 25, 2013, retrieved from http://mrmagazine.wordpress.com/2013/09/ on Feb. 24, 2015.
5. "Newsstands and Retail: What's on the Mind of Top Magazine Executives? A Panel at the MPA/PBAA Retail Marketplace Provides the Answers," Mr. Magazine, June 13, 2013, retrieved from https://mrmagazine.wordpress.com/2013/06/13/news stands-and-retail-whats-on-the-mind-of-top-magazine-executives-a-panel-at-the-mpapbaa-retail-marketplace-provides-the-answers/ on Feb. 24, 2015.
6. Ibid.
7. Ibid.
8. Ibid.
9. Ibid.
10. Ibid.
11. "'There's Always Going to Be Time for a Newsweekly,' Nancy Gibbs, TIME's New Editor, Tells Samir Husni. The Mr. Magazine™ Interview." Mr. Magazine, Sept. 25, 2013, retrieved from http://mrmagazine.wordpress.com/2013/09/ on Feb. 24, 2015.

TV

> "The audience has become our partners in a way; they're acting as our ears and eyes and participating in the process in a way that they never did before; we rely on them and ask them to help. The key now is to make it genuine; don't ask them to engage if you don't care or won't use their stuff. Your interaction has to be authentic."

> —Donna Reed
> Former Vice President of Content, Media General

BENEFITS

- In this chapter, we explore strategies for building audience relationships, especially through social TV and mobile applications.
- We consider the redefinition of television news stations as video news and information providers.
- And we look at localism as integral to the success of local media companies. It may be their greatest weapon to combat disruptors like Google and Yahoo.

STATE OF THE MEDIUM

More people get their news from television than from any other medium, according to the Pew Research Center. When it comes to television programming in general, the average American over the age of 2 spends more than 35 hours a week watching live TV, says a Nielsen report – plus another 3 to 6 hours watching time-shifted programs. Yet, television companies producing news and information are uneasy.

Overall, local TV advertising has been trending down (except for intermittent boosts related to political and Olympics coverage). Local TV news viewership, a major revenue driver for stations, is also declining. Though nearly half of Americans say they watch local TV news regularly, younger demographics appear to be less interested in watching newscasts on TV. According to Pew, the number of adults under 30 who are regular local news viewers has already had one precipitous drop from 42 percent in 2006 to just 28 percent in 2012 – and, unfortunately for those in the traditional TV business, that decrease is expected to continue.[1]

For years, local news stations responded to the declines in audience by adding more newscasts, often early in the morning or at 6:30 or 7 p.m. to give consumers more options for news viewing. Yet, despite those efforts, TV news viewership continues its overall downward trend.

"I'm worried about the business," says Donna Reed, former vice president of content for Media General. "News managers should be in that conversation with their sales and marketing folks every day; they need to be talking about audience and reach and numbers. It's tough – I feel like we try more now, but for years we didn't push the envelope enough."

Many television stations have moved aggressively in recent years to step up their digital media initiatives. They're beefing up websites, creating mobile apps, integrating social media and offering cross-screen advertising opportunities. However, declines in traditional television revenue have not yet been offset by gains in digital profits. BIA/Kelsey predicts that digital will continue to grow, but to only 4 percent of total station revenues in 2016.

Add that to the fact that disruption of the core business will continue and is likely to accelerate, so today's TV managers have more than a station to run – they have an imperative to build out their digital offerings and to experiment with new business models while traditional revenue streams are still relatively strong.

Getting Social

One of the newest audience-generating strategies revolves around what's called social TV. If you've ever posted a comment to social media about a favorite TV show or character, you've been a part of social television. According to the Digital Marketing Glossary, social TV usually refers to "the use of social media platforms to enrich the experience of consuming a TV program and to possibly extend its audience."[2]

The 4 C's Strategy: Choice

If you were watching television in the 1970s, you had the three networks—CBS, NBC, and ABC—and in some areas PBS. Every time you were watching anything then, there were millions more watching the same thing with you. As cable and then satellite came into the marketplace, the number of channels available for the general public exploded. Instead of sharing a news and information meal with so many others, now we have a cafeteria where people can select whatever they like from whichever channel they want.

As choice changes our society and puts more focus on customization and personalization, smart news managers have to learn how to adapt to an environment where their organization is just one of many possible choices.

Social TV can encompass promotion of TV content, offer a way to incorporate interactivity into a TV program or help keep the conversation about a program going after the program airs, through the use of a Twitter hashtag, for example. Twitter has been the dominant force in social TV, capturing much of the traffic about television viewing, though Facebook also generates a great deal of interactivity around TV programming.

Local television stations have been trying to capitalize on this trend to grow audience and revenue. For example, hundreds of local TV news stations signed up to use ConnecTV to get their social TV conversation ramped up. ConnecTV is one of multiple "second-screen apps" that allows the user to interact with hundreds of programs – syndicated shows, prime-time fare and live programming, such as sporting events and newscasts.

Media General is one of the major news companies using the app. Former WCMH-TV President and General Manager Dan Bradley says his station is offering interactive elements on the screen during a newscast.

"A little basic at first, but we hope to get to being able to offer PDFs of documents related to the story, interactive maps and graphics, and so on," says Bradley.

Chip Mahaney, senior director of local operations at E. W. Scripps Company, another ConnecTV partner, says a lot is riding on stations being able to figure out social TV.

"A huge challenge for us in a 24/7 multi-screen, always-connected world is creating 'must-see' reasons to watch local, live TV news," he says. "Second-screen engagement, with its potential for instant interactivity and community engagement, is one of those opportunities to meet that huge challenge."

One of the most attractive things about second-screen apps is the potential for advertising dollars. Bradley says in the ConnecTV app, there is a frame dedicated to ads.

"It has the ability to interact with commercials playing on the TV. For instance, if there is a Ford F-150 ad on TV, it will show up in the app with a link to a site for more detailed info, maybe build your own model and set an appointment with a local dealer. This feature would work during any type of programming, local or network," says Bradley.

Mahaney says these second-screen apps are ripe places for advertisers who want to be engaged, but says his first priority is to build a social media community surrounding his company's newscasts.

"We want to create loyalists – people who come back night after night – [and] creating community is one way to build a loyal audience," says Mahaney.[3]

The Social Audience

This strategy of attracting audience first and relying on the lure of that audience to attract advertisers has been at the heart of broadcast management for decades. Alternatively, there are stations that have chosen to forgo the second-screen app approach to engagement and are relying on Facebook and Twitter, Instagram and other social media networks as a bridge to new audiences. They use

PHOTO 6-1 When WHSV-TV in Harrisonburg, Virginia, had a big snowstorm on the way, the station managers wanted to capitalize on the social media audience to help in their coverage. They worked with a local hospital to sponsor a photo contest on Facebook and Pinterest. User-generated pictures were displayed on air and the station's social media sites. The contest generated likes for both the station and the sponsor.[4]

Source: Retrieved from: https://www.facebook.com/WHSV.TV/timeline on November 3, 2014.

social media to drive traffic to their websites or to their on-air programming, and they are experimenting with ideas for monetizing the social media audience itself. For example, some news organizations are experimenting with "sponsored" tweets and other forms of paid content, which they feed to their existing social media audiences. These broadcast managers are banking on the idea that by offering relevant interactivity through social media, they can convert that audience into additional revenue, by selling advertisers on the idea of a more engaged consumer.

Mobile Moves

It's tough to talk about the importance of social media without immediately thinking about the impact of mobile as well. More often than not, the second screen in use for people watching television is a mobile device.

Additionally, mobile devices are growing in popularity as a way to watch programming itself. A Council for Research Excellence survey found that 15 percent of smartphone usage was spent viewing video news, compared to 11 percent of tablet use.[5]

The study also found that mobile viewers are not significantly motivated by a desire to avoid seeing advertisements; instead, they like the convenience of the mobile viewing experience. For example, if someone in the home is already watching TV, a mobile device can be used to view something different.

Leadership Report – Donna Reed

PHOTO 6-2

Courtesy of Donna Reed

Former Vice President of Content, Media General

Donna Reed led efforts to improve the quality of Media General's broadcast journalism at 18 television stations owned by the Richmond, Virginia-based company. She was previously the news leader for Media General's Publishing Division and was managing editor of The Tampa Tribune.

What do you think the media's role in society is now?

I'm not sure that it has changed significantly from when I first started working in this business. What have changed are the delivery mechanisms for our news and information. Fundamentally, our role is not different; we still play a role in supporting and defending democracy. Our role always has been acting as a voice for the voiceless, informing the public about the things that they need to know to live their lives. We are a significant part of how our country operates; they don't call it the Fourth Estate for nothing. So, even with all the technological changes, we have the same responsibility to seek out the truth and help people manage their daily lives. We give them what they want and need to know, and every once in a while, we try to surprise them with a story about good people doing good things. What's changed is what news and information looks like and how it's consumed, not its purpose. At the heart of it – and I have to come to the same conclusion for broadcast and print – is good storytelling.

How do you balance that against revenue and profit pressures when it comes to gaining an audience?

That's the heart of today's challenge: How do we make the business profitable and sustain journalism? It's far more difficult today with the vulnerability of the economy and the fracturing of audience; we don't enjoy the big numbers that we used to when we were one of a handful of sources for news. Today's news managers should be thinking of gaining new audiences, new demographics. Part of our job now is to help the sales side of the business, but it is harder and harder to simultaneously keep key demos while attracting others.

With the Web, social media and mobile, the audience is now coming in through a side door that used to not be there. It's a constant struggle to be sure you're delivering what they want on the platform they want it. In television, we've lost the numbers we used to have, and now the question is, are we ever going to get back there, or are we just going to try to get a little piece of all of it – a piece of the audience on as many platforms as possible?

Define your organization's relationship with your own audience.

We're already changing our thinking on social media. It's gone from purely promotion to being a news delivery system in its own right. On Facebook our target has gone from

(Continued)

(Continued)

being number of fans to amount of engagement; now the metrics we're interested in are "shares." We're now using it as a news delivery vehicle for an audience that you would have never reached in the past, even outside your DMA [Designated Market Area].

The effect is that we're much closer now to our audience. We're not talking at people; we talk with people. This all started out with story commenting; remember all those arguments about whether we should allow comments on our websites? We had a hard time dealing with the idea that the audience was talking back to us – and sometimes not in a nice way. They're telling us what they think of us? Oh, my! Before, we told them what we wanted to tell them and signed off. We've gone from policing audience interaction to embracing it. They're telling us what they think and what they know; they're sending us photos, story ideas, et cetera. We've gone from fearing the audience to talking with them.

All of this has made us better, but our job is now harder, too. We have to sort through truth from fiction and get to the heart of the story, especially on the local level. We have to help them understand what the information means to them.

How does it need to change to remain in business going forward?

The answer to your question might depend on what comes next with technology. We've tried some of that real-time interaction with services like ConnecTV. That may be the precursor to how we engage in the future. The public wants us to be a gatekeeper of truth, to curate the news for them, to bring the interesting important news to them, and they want it more real-time.

Television is still a mass medium, and now we're talking to even more people. If a video goes viral, you could be talking to millions. Yet, it's a fractured market, and the viewership numbers individual stations used to enjoy aren't going to come back, but the audience is still there – the appetite for news and information is still there. Unfortunately, we still measure audience in the old-fashioned way. Companies like Rentrak are trying to get in the game to measure audience for your content in a more accurate way.

The researchers emphasized how important it is for media managers to understand that mobile devices are having a "screen multiplier effect within households." That means more television is consumed, not less, thanks to mobile.

At CNN, mobile is already central to the company's overall news strategy.

"We can reach people on mobile and circulate them from online to TV," says Louis Gump, former vice president of CNN Mobile. "If we do it well, we shape and enhance the brand."

Along the way, CNN is finding opportunities to make money.

"Take video. We have a ton of awesome video that we can monetize through mobile ads. Online display inventory may go unsold, but we can sell all the video inventory we have on mobile," says Gump.

Mobile is also bringing in younger demographics. The Reynolds Journalism Institute survey on mobile media consumption found that two-thirds of mobile device owners ages 18 to 34 spent an average of five hours per week accessing local, national and international news on those devices. Those least likely to consume news on mobile were device owners ages 55 and older, and they averaged four hours a week.

"Mobile presents revenue opportunities similar to what we had 50 years ago when radio was transitioning to TV," Gump says.

He suggests that local news organizations also have a chance to sell advertisers on some of the unique features of mobile delivery, such as the targeting capabilities of geolocation.

"Local content providers will excel if they deploy location strategy well. Targeting is always in demand by advertisers, and it's one of the most fundamental points of rolling out mobile," Gump says.

What's challenging for local broadcasters is coming up with strategies for customized mobile advertising that are cost-effective for both the television station and the advertisers. Without that piece of it, making significant money from mobile is more theoretical than practical at this point.

According to the Project for Excellence in Journalism, just 1 in 100 mobile news consumers pays for an app to access the content.[6] As we'll discuss in Chapter 8, until media organizations are able to retrain the audience to pay for something they've generally received for free, advertiser support for mobile content will remain critical to any efforts to monetize mobile.

Gump says figuring all this out may ultimately just take courage. He says you can't wait until all the data are available and the path is entirely clear. Instead, he says, you should gather all the information you can and forge ahead: "Mobile will be the dominant delivery platform for many media businesses. The extent to which they succeed will be how well they succeed in mobile."[7]

Watching the Web

In many markets, mobile viewing of TV content has overtaken website use, but news organizations have an opportunity to grow their Web audiences as well, thanks to a move by many newspapers to construct pay walls, as we discussed in Chapter 5.

According to The State of the News Media 2013, stations in Albuquerque, New Mexico, Tulsa, Oklahoma, and Des Moines, Iowa, have capitalized on newspaper pay walls in their markets to become the dominant local news sites. The changes in the newspaper industry and the push to the Web from social media may already be having an impact on website traffic for TV stations.

The Radio Television Digital News Association's annual TV and Radio News Staffing and Profitability Survey found that just under 40 percent of TV station websites reported making a profit in 2012 – the highest percentage in the 14 years of the survey question. Of course, many digital naysayers are quick to point out that website profitability often fails to take into account the cost of gathering the information presented online, a burden carried by the legacy news operation – in this case, the television station. However, it is significant that the Web is now generating additional dollars for TV stations, often enough to pay for website-specific expenses, such as infrastructure and personnel.

PHOTO 6-3 WCPO-TV, the Scripps-owned station in Cincinnati, Ohio, created the first-ever local TV pay wall for a website called the WCPO Insider. The company won't say how many subscribers it has paying $7.99 per month, but the idea is that people will pay for unique news content that they can't get anywhere else.[8]

Source: Retrieved from http://www.wcpo.com/subscribe on November 3, 2014.

Today's Bottom Line

Traditional TV viewing is declining, but stations are growing off-air audiences for their content. What has been challenging for stations is measuring the impact of the social, mobile and online audience as it relates to the reach of a local TV station.

Leon Long is a vice president for Raycom Media's television stations. He says the industry is getting close to finding the right metric.

"We can clearly quantify what people look at on our sites or how many people are exposed to a message. What we don't know is whether they're actively consuming that message, but I think that's going to change dramatically over the next few months, maybe years," Long says.

In fact, Nielsen and other companies are working on perfecting technology that already captures and measures online and mobile viewing, and Long, like many other media managers, is confident that the data will be available and saleable.

"There's a way to measure," Long says, "but what we really have to figure out is what that value exchange is, and once we get that value exchange figured out, I think the barriers that are holding back that wave of digital money will fall away. We'll figure it out – we're getting close; it's not that far off."

LOOKING BACK – COMPLACENT PAST

Though most television stations are better situated than many local newspapers, it hasn't always been thanks to good management. Consider a case in point by traveling back in time with us.

It's 2003, and the Project for Excellence in Journalism has invited about a dozen news directors to meet in the District of Columbia. The purpose of the meeting is to talk about audience declines and how broadcasters might change their approaches to the newscasts to reverse those losses. At one point during the meeting, one of the participants asks what role the Web should play in their strategies. What is the universal response? "We can't worry about the Web. We have newscasts to produce."

And that was the prevailing attitude in many television stations throughout the early to mid-2000s. Some industry experts believe it's a case of organizations being "trapped by revenue." Stations were so afraid of losing existing revenue and ratings that they were risk averse when it came to the Web, letting newspapers become the dominant source of online news in most markets.

Still, there were some outliers, organizations that embraced digital delivery of content from the get-go. Capitol Broadcasting Co. owns WRAL-TV in Raleigh, North Carolina, and Steve Hammel is the station's general manager.

"I'm familiar with when websites at a TV station were an afterthought," Hammel says. "A station would grudgingly have one or two people working on the website – maybe no one on the weekend. From an industry standpoint, the industry sort of went kicking and screaming into understanding there is value in the digital world, but it took a while, and those who understood it earlier had the edge."

In the 10 years since that D.C. meeting of news directors, it's a much different world for TV station managers. Stations quickly embraced social media as a promotional tool and subsequently began to use it as a way to engage audience. Mobile delivery of news content took off in 2008 as most news organizations, including TV stations, began to develop mobile apps to give audiences access to their content. Part of the reason is that it's typically not until a business is faced with death, or at least a significant challenge, that it begins to innovate.

The radio industry is the classic example. By the late 1930s, radio dominated in-home entertainment in the United States and was hugely profitable. But by the 1950s, television had destroyed the old radio model, so the industry reinvented itself as a local community service. In the 1970s, when in-home use of radio evaporated, radio once again reinvented itself as an in-car FM stereo music provider. When AM radio died in the 1980s, it was reinvented as news talk.

Television is in a period of reinvention and innovation, but one of the biggest obstacles it faces is the culture inside individual television stations. At WRAL, changing the culture is the task of an entire group of people.

"We have a whole division called new media. They are constantly looking at new revenue opportunities," Hammel says. "It's important for us to be thinking beyond what's on the TV screen; any successful business looks beyond today and next year to see what other revenue opportunities might be next."

PHOTO 6-4 WRAL-TV in Raleigh, North Carolina, is known as a station that is unafraid to experiment with new technologies that might help them better connect with the audience. They had their morning show team wear Google Glass on the air to take the viewers behind the scenes of the newscast.[9]

Source: Retrieved from http://www.wral.com/wral-tv/video/13379681.

Leadership Report – Leon Long

PHOTO 6-5

Courtesy of Leon Long

Vice President, Television, Raycom Media

Prior to joining Raycom, Leon Long was vice president of operations for Liberty and general manager of WLOX-TV. Long is a past chairman/president of the ABC Television Affiliates Association, served as the chairman of the National Association of Broadcasters 100+ Committee, is a member of the board for the Mississippi Association of Broadcasters, and was selected by TV Business Confidential as one of "America's Best GM's."

How do you foster innovation within your organization?

Stay out of the way. You just wait for the young kids to give you their ideas and try not to say, "Forget it. This is the way we do it." If you can not do that, if you can just embrace the ideas they bring you and realize a lot of them will be clunkers, there are going to be a few good ones in there that you can capitalize on and run with.

How does your organization's relationship with the audience need to change going forward?

Our job is to keep them connected, and we can do that in various ways, through the Internet and over the air. Our responsibility is great.

It used to be a very linear world that we lived in – we fed programs, and we expected you to change your life around watching the 6 o'clock and the 10 o'clock news programs because that's when we put it on. Then the DVRs came along, and we allowed you to time shift, but I don't think that's enough.

Today viewers want more flexibility; they want to consume your products on their terms, conditions and timetables. It's not about us; it's about them, and they want to see us publish all this content we aggregate every day called news, and they want to see us publish all that on the Internet, so they can jump in when they want and jump out when they want; they can consume little pieces of it or huge volumes of it, so it's a very nonlinear world that we live in today.

Theory in Practice – Innovation Management

The push for change and reinvention describes a theory called innovation management. This discipline can be used to develop new products or to make an organization itself more adaptable. It helps those involved create a common understanding of the company's objectives and makes the process more efficient.

When innovation management is implemented properly, it involves workers at every level of the company who may contribute creatively to everything from the company's overall development, to specific product development and manufacturing, to the company's marketing.

For example, WXII-TV in Winston-Salem, North Carolina, went directly to its employees, sharing the station's need for more innovation in the digital space. One of the most innovative ideas came from a newscast director – a technical job that involves executing the on-air look of a news program.

The director said she had an intense interest in weddings, so the station created a wedding business on the Web. The site included everything from video of the news anchors' weddings, to ads for local photographers and limo services, to special wedding weather forecasts.

The focus of innovation management is to allow the organization to respond to an external or internal opportunity, and use its creative efforts to introduce new ideas, processes or products.[10]

According to Paul Trott and his book, "Innovation Management and New Product Development," innovation processes can be either pushed or pulled through development. A pushed process is based on existing or newly invented technology that the organization

(Continued)

(Continued)

has access to, and tries to find profitable applications to use this technology. This is where it seems most media organizations tend to focus; they come up with new applications for emerging technologies, such as the early use of social media as a tool to promote news content.

A pulled process tries to find areas where customers' needs are not met, and then focus development efforts to find solutions to those needs.[11] This is where the focus of more media organizations needs to shift – instead of waiting for two guys in a garage to develop the next big thing in news and information sharing, station managers must do a better job of leveraging the creative power of their employees through a system of shared goals and entrepreneurial spirit.

Leadership Report – Steve Hammel

PHOTO 6-6

Courtesy of Steve Hammel

Vice President and General Manager, WRAL-TV, Capitol Broadcasting Co.

Steve Hammel became vice president and general manager at WRAL-TV in November 2008. He previously held the same position at the CBS affiliate in Phoenix. While at KPHO, Steve initiated and developed the Meredith-Cronkite Fellowship and the CBC-UNC Diversity Fellowship Program. He also started the first-ever-in-Phoenix Hispanic Advisory Board. Steve oversaw newsrooms in the District of Columbia, St. Louis and Dallas, as well.

What do you think the media's role in society is now?

I think the role of the news media is to provide relevant, compelling and necessary information to individuals and to a company. Technology has changed; the way people get their information has changed and will change and evolve, but people still need to know if school is open or closed, or if there is an evacuation of an area or if the water is drinkable or not. I don't think human nature will ever change – we all want information about life, health, family, our livelihoods – that's the news that it's the media's role to provide.

How do you balance that against revenue and profit pressures when it comes to gaining an audience?

If you don't provide the necessary information – relevant, compelling news – then you will butt up against those revenue and profit pressures; you will have fewer people watching, and you'll have advertisers who will pay you less. Advertisers will pay you more when you are being relevant and compelling, providing terrific journalism.

"60 minutes" has a great formula, if you will. The first two stories are exactly what I explained – necessary, relevant, compelling information – but the third story might be about a great entertainer; it's enjoyable or fun to watch. There can easily be a good mix of necessary, relevant, compelling information along with a sprinkle of "Bruce Springsteen is in town."

Define your organization's relationship with your own audience. How does it need to change to remain in business going forward?

I think we have an intimate relationship with the audience; we are welcomed or not welcomed into someone's home or the palm of one's hand, and we have to earn that invitation on an hourly or daily basis by what we do for the audience. We need to know the audience as well as we can, whether that means the old-fashioned way with anchors and reporters getting out in the community and going to events or we do research. We ask viewers in an organized, systematic way what the type of things are that they're interested in.

What we do here, in addition to TV – we have a very active website and we're very involved with mobile and digital and apps, but the most important relationship between us and our audience continues to be with the information we provide and how we act toward our community. What changes is the technology; I don't see the need for the information to change, just the delivery method.

How has the competitive landscape changed? Who do you view as competitors now versus 5 or 10 years ago?

We compete with anything that takes eyeballs or time away from us; that can be as nontraditional as an Xbox and video games because, if someone is playing a video game, they're not watching us or reading our website. If someone is watching Netflix or Roku or Apple TV, those items take time or eyeballs away from us. Again, not to sound like a broken record, we need to be compelling and relevant to get them to spend time with us. We need to help them live their lives better informed, even if that's just information about which street not to turn down because of traffic.

In the face of continual technological changes within the media industry, how do you manage people who can no longer count on their job duties remaining the same for any significant period of time?

Let me talk about the newsroom; there was a time when a reporter was a reporter, a photographer was a photographer, a producer was a producer, but not only with all the technical changes, but also with the ups and downs of the economy, we have and will continue to cross-train people. We have a lot of people who are really good at multiple things, and they're more valuable because of that.

I also challenge our folks; I make sure that people are reading about things that are going on in the industry outside of Raleigh. We were the first station in the world to go high-definition, we were the first to have a newsgathering helicopter, but none of that happens unless you are hiring terrific people and you challenge them.

Earlier this year, I noticed a station in Rochester was using Google Glass to partially cover the Super Bowl. I said, "Let's get one of those newfangled things and see what we can do with it that's different, unique, interesting, compelling." After a bit of

(Continued)

(Continued)

brainstorming, we took a week of our morning show and let the audience look behind the scenes through Google Glass. We got to see what the anchor was seeing on air and during breaks, for example. It was streamed live, side by side with the newscast on the Web. It was just another interesting way to utilize new technology and to get our own people and the viewers interested in it. We're constantly looking for things to do that might lead to the next best approach.

How do you foster that innovation within your organization?

I think people have to understand that, if you never fail, you're probably not trying things. If you fail here, it's OK, as long as it happens occasionally, not all the time. We have to encourage creativity, people trying things, and by definition, if something hasn't been done before, there's probably a reason, but it's OK to not always be successful. At the same time, if we keep the status quo, we know we'll get behind. I don't know of anyone who has stock from a year ago that says, "Well, it did so well last year; it doesn't have to do better this year." We have to build on what was successful last year. The fostering of innovation, of doing better, starts with the premise that the status quo is unacceptable.

Are there management theories that you subscribe to, or are you essentially reinventing the approach of managing your business as you go?

I guess I took a management course in college; I can't recall it, but I suspect at Syracuse, I did take one. I wish I made the time to read a lot more management books, but the fact of the matter is that I try to use good old common sense in terms of what I believe motivates people, what I believe motivates co-workers. I think people get motivated by positive reinforcement and not by yelling and screaming, though at times that might be necessary.

What role do you see curation of content playing at WRAL?

The thing that continues to allow us to thrive is being the original generators, the first responders, the people who come up with the interesting story ideas, put it on the Web and on TV. The thing that allows us to stand out in our community is making sure that we are generating real news, enterprise stories; I certainly see us as generators more than curators.

What's on your list of issues that today's news media manager has to consider and be informed about?

Don't just focus on today's newscast or today's story, or merely the job you've been assigned to do; understand how things outside of that can impact you as a manager. If you are a little more worldly, if you understand how everything around you impacts your business, that can help. For example, if your city has a number of hospitals, if medicine is a big deal, get to understand how that affects your community. Ultimately, it's everything else outside the newsroom that will impact the newsroom, so the more informed they are, the better managers they can be as they look ahead.

> **Television audiences are declining; how do you react to the audience falling off?**
>
> I view it as a challenge, one that's both personal and professional. I'm going to provide a viewer the most compelling information possible. If I do that, I'll have a fighting chance not to lose and maybe gain audience. If I do the lowest-common-denominator journalism and do things that aren't relevant, then that trend of audience loss will continue.
>
> I realize that I am one human being and cannot change the world, but within our community here we have to do what we think is right, and that's providing terrific material that viewers will respond to. What we have to do is to be the best we can be to stem the tide, turn it around – whether you're a producer, reporter or teleprompter operator, each of us has to say, "I'll do whatever I can to make it better." Then there's a fighting chance.

FOCUS ON THE FUTURE

Throughout this text, we've been urging media managers to continually ask themselves, "What do customers want?" and television stations have a history of doing this pretty well.

It's clear the audience still wants news, information and entertainment, and that puts companies like Raycom, which owns dozens of local TV stations, in a position to succeed.

"In TV specifically, and media in general, our function is both to entertain and to inform – if we do those two things, we kind of fulfill our mission statement. Today the landscape is changing, so we're working on growing our company of 53 television stations, another 100 or so multicast channels and another huge cluster of assets in the digital space. We're working on a way to take a broader media focus," says Long.

That broader focus includes the social, mobile and Web media we've already discussed, but it also entails sub-channels or D2 as it has commonly come to be called. By using data compression techniques, the TV station can use its single TV signal to broadcast more than one program simultaneously, a practice that is also called multicasting. TV stations are running additional programming on these sub-channels at very little additional expense and with tremendous opportunities for revenue.

The future of television and video news distribution is still in flux. Television stations now make a significant amount of money from cable companies that are paying them retransmission fees, so each local cable system can carry the local TV stations' programming in the market.

However, the cable TV model itself is fragile, according to Hammel and others, especially with a growing number of consumers choosing to "cut the cord" – dropping cable to take advantage of over-the-air (OTA) free broadcast through antenna or over-the-top (OTT) broadcast over the Internet. Companies in the TV business are also creating mobile apps that allow for free, live streaming of programming on a smartphone or tablet.

What media organizations cannot do if they wish to remain viable is to get hung up on a single delivery system, and local TV stations have a powerful tool to help them remain relevant to their audiences.

"The best thing local television stations do for their communities is produce strong journalism that is unique, enlightening, revealing and very local. Local news is No. 1. That, I believe, is our greatest strength and carries the greatest value to viewers," Reed says.

Hammel agrees and says that it's imperative that TV companies continue to monitor the technological landscape to be sure that they're always able to deliver content on the platform the customers choose, and they must also take some calculated risks by investing in innovation. Without that, TV stations will not be able to unleash the creative power of their own staffs or discover that yet-to-be-revealed, innovative solution to the consumers' needs.

EXECUTIVE SUMMARY

Television news has weathered the media storm more easily than newspapers, in part, because it has been researching audience desires and responding more directly to those desires for much of its history. In addition, even after the Internet began eating into the profits of the print industry, for years, slow connection speeds for consumers and other technical obstacles prevented online sites from offering a comparable video viewing experience. That's certainly not to say that the explosion of digital delivery systems hasn't affected the television industry; however, television companies have advantages in the digital age that, if managed properly, can keep them viable into the future.

THINK AND DO

You're managing a local news station and hoping to take advantage of the social TV trend. Examine the following set of facts to come up with a relationship-building initiative involving social TV and original news programming.

The Background

Your station, in a tech-savvy town with several universities in the area, has produced a documentary about the influence of money on college athletics and features some big names, including the basketball coach at a premier school in your market, the commissioner of one of the top conferences in college sports, several sports TV analysts and former college athletes.

The Goal

You want to engage existing audience and build new audience by capitalizing on the social TV phenomenon. As a station leader, how will you achieve this goal? Be sure to draw on what you've learned about branding and audience power in previous chapters.

Describe how the theory of innovation management could be used to help guide your efforts.

NOTES

1. "In Changing News Landscape, Even Television Is Vulnerable," Pew Research Center, Sept. 27, 2012, retrieved from http://www.people-press.org/2012/09/27/in-changing-news-landscape-even-television-is-vulnerable/ on Feb. 25, 2015.

2. "What Is Social TV?" The Digital Marketing Glossary, Aug. 1, 2013, retrieved from http://www.digitalmarketing-glossary.com/What-is-Social-TV-definition on March 2, 2015.

3. Deb Halpern Wenger, "Social TV May Mean Money, Viewer Loyalty, for News," RTNDA, Jan. 29, 2015, retrieved from http://www.rtdna.org/article/social_tv_may_mean_money_viewer_loyalty_for_news on Feb. 25, 2015.

4. Retrieved from https://www.facebook.com/WHSV.TV/timeline on Nov. 3, 2014.

5. Council for Research Excellence, "Following the Mobile Path of TV Content," TV Untethered, July 24, 2013, retrieved from http://www.researchexcellence.com/files/pdf/2015-02/id102_tv_untethered_presentation_7_24_13.pdf on March 2, 2015.

6. Patrick Goldstein and James Rainey, "Survey: Love of Mobile News Does Not = Pay for Mobile News," The Big Picture, Los Angeles Times, March 13, 2011, retrieved from http://latimesblogs.latimes.com/the_big_picture/2011/03/survey-love-of-mobile-news-does-not-pay-for-mobile-news.html?utm_source=feed burner&utm_medium=feed&utm_campaign=Feed%3A+PatrickGoldstein+%28 L.A.+Times+-+Patrick+Goldstein%29 on Feb. 25, 2015.

7. Deb Halpern Wenger, "Will the 'M' in Mobile Stand for Money?" Quill, July/August 2012, retrieved from http://digitaleditions.walsworthprintgroup.com/article/will_the_%27m%27_in_mobile_stand_for_money%3F/1132105/120451/article.html on March 2, 2015.

8. WCPO Cincinnati, retrieved from http://www.wcpo.com/subscribe on Nov. 3, 2014.

9. "Dual View: Newscast, Google Glass," WRAL.com, retrieved from http://www.wral.com/wral-tv/video/13379681/ on Nov. 4, 2014.

10. Patrick Kelly and Melvin Kranzburg, "Technological Innovation: A Critical Review of Current Knowledge," San Francisco: San Francisco Press, 1978.

11. Paul Trott, "Innovation Management and New Product Development," Essex, U.K.: Prentice Hall, 2005.

Online

> *"It's a mindset; you either understand and embrace changes and you're excited about that, or you satisfy yourself with the dwindling opportunities you have now. They may still be good for several years, so some companies will worry about later later, but there are very few that refuse to acknowledge that information is ubiquitous, so you have to make your content essential, and if the information is that good, the delivery method becomes less important."*
>
> —Chip Mahaney
> Senior Director, Local Operations, Scripps Digital

BENEFITS

- In this chapter, we explore strategies for adapting to change. Today's media companies have to be adept at adaptation, much more nimble than ever before.
- We explore the redefinition of websites as platforms offering people the opportunity to create and distribute and consume content.
- And we look at the challenges of monetizing digital media and strategies to reduce dependence on advertising.

STATE OF THE MEDIUM

If you look at Internet usage, there's never been a better time to be distributing content digitally. More than three-quarters of Americans have Internet access; that's about 250 million people in the United States alone.[1]

Though TV is still the medium of first choice for Americans, online is in second place with at least 26 percent of total media consumption time spent in front of a desktop or laptop computer, Internet-connected TV or another nonmobile connected device.[2]

And people are interested in getting news online – most often from traditional news media companies. Well-known news brands – the websites of newspapers, cable and network news – account for 20 of the 25 most popular news sites listed by comScore.[3]

With so many people going online and the interest in news and information so high, the Web should be a bonanza for news media, right? However, legacy media websites currently generate a fraction of the revenue earned by the print or broadcast products. Bill McCandless, former vice president of video programming and production for the Bleacher Report digital sports media network, says it's inevitable that news media companies would find themselves in this position.

"There's the audience curve and the revenue curve. The revenue curve always trails the audience curve; they never cross. Great revenue leaders know that and turn to their content crews to say, 'You go get it – get the audience and then we'll get the revenue.' We never say, 'Get those dollars and then we'll get the audience,'" McCandless says.

FIGURE 7-1 **Overall spending on advertising is growing, fueled by digital ad sales.**

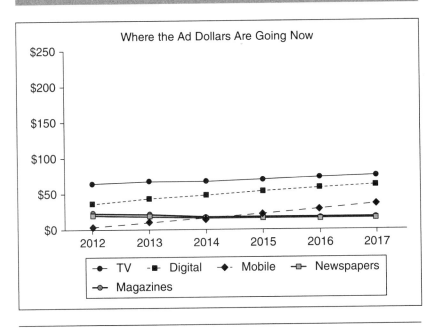

Source: eMarketer. "US Ad Spending Forecast." 2013. Adapted from "U.S. Advertising by Media," from the Pew Research Journalism Project. Retrieved from http://www.journalism.org/media-indicators/u-s-advertising-by-media/ on November 6, 2014.

Note: Mobile is a subset of digital. Y-axis values are listed in billions of dollars.

Online Revenue

The good news is, the digital ad dollars are there. Worldwide, digital advertising spending (including mobile) is estimated to account for more than one-quarter of all ad spending by 2016.[4] In the United States expenditures on digital ads surpassed newspaper advertising for the first time in 2011, and by 2018, eMarketer projects digital will surpass TV, making up more than 37 percent of the U.S. ad market.[5]

The issue is that most of that money is not going to traditional media companies. Google alone gobbled up nearly a third of the billions companies took in from digital advertising worldwide in 2012. Coming in second was Facebook – its share for that year was 4.1 percent.[6]

One big reason for Google's dominance is that the company gets the lion's share of search advertising – a method of placing online advertisements on Web pages that show results from search engine queries. That leaves news media companies and others fighting for the dollars spent on the other seven categories of digital advertising, including well-known forms such as banner ads, classifieds and video.

All this means is that digital dollars will continue to be important to news media companies, but media managers may have to work harder to capture their share of the revenue. Chip Mahaney, senior director for local operations at E.W. Scripps Co., says their relationship with local advertising customers is what should give them an advantage.

"Now, we have to be smarter and more connected to these people than even before. They can go to Google to buy targeted ads, so we have to be better than that with our products; we have to prove that we provide the best solutions, whether that's time on TV, impressions on the Web, sponsorship on mobile – or selling through a network of sites. If a customer is really looking to hit a gender or geo-targeted location, we can use audience extension products. That helps us compete with the big players – helps us operate with the precision of someone like Google," says Mahaney.

Leadership Report – Bill McCandless

PHOTO 7-1

Courtesy of Bill McCandless

Vice President of Video Programming/ Production, Bleacher Report

Bill McCandless spent much of his career in senior news producer roles with TV affiliates on the East Coast before joining NBC/CNBC in 2000. After CNBC, McCandless joined TheStreet.com as general manager/ executive editor where he built out TheStreet's digital video content creation business and award-winning mobile apps. McCandless also helped HuffingtonPost. com establish digital video operations.

(Continued)

(Continued)

Define your organization's relationship with your audience.

Bleacher Report is a platform – it gives people the opportunity to create and distribute and consume content. We're evolving more into a content creator.

We provide information that's different from what traditional media tell you that you should care about; for us, the definition of news is still what people talk about. We're just very honest about what they are or would be talking about.

If you assume that you are smarter than your user, you're done. That's why a lot of media dies. It's built on big-J journalism, and it's all very ivory tower.

What will role will advertising dollars play in the future of media?

Advertising will always be a primary source of revenue for a media company. Advertiser-supported content is never going away. I've been part of two major media acquisition deals – AOL's purchase of The Huffington Post and Turner's purchase of Bleacher Report – both of those properties were purely ad supported.

Why did Yahoo buy Tumblr? They see an opportunity to push audience at giant advertisers – these companies are buying pools of people; they're trying to get on all the right screens to keep selling audience to advertisers.

How has technological change affected the way you manage people and your business?

In our office, we have all kinds of cool posters because we work in sports, but two posters are very important. They feature the George Costanza character from "Seinfeld" in black socks and underwear with his George Costanza glasses and his hairy chest, and they illustrate the Costanza Rule. Remember the episode where George walks up to the girl in the café, the gorgeous model, and he decides he's going to do the opposite of what he would usually do? He tells her he's bald and unemployed and lives with his parents and she loves it, so he creates "Opposite George."

That's what I tell people my age and younger down to about age 33 or 34. Everything you thought that worked, everything you thought you knew about how content comes together, from the way you pick stories to the way you write stories – everything you've been trained to do is wrong.

We thought the audience loved the way we thought about things and that they were coming to us for our great selection of content – wrong. They're not here for us at all – it's very ego deflating. Our job is to get them what they want.

What does the future hold for media managers?

There will be some other kind of revolution like mobile. Right now we're working in derivatives of screens everywhere, and content needs to be screen agnostic. We need to be understanding the differences – to produce different content based on the size of screen – and we need to figure out how to monetize mobile better. That search is going to lead to things that I don't know about yet, but I know I'm going to be a part of it.

Pay Walls and Other Products

At the same time that news media companies are shoring up relationships with advertising customers, they're also looking to increase and diversify other revenue streams.

When it comes to making money from digital circulation, pay walls or some sort of metered payment plans are in place at approximately 400 of the 1,350 daily newspapers in the United States.[7] Despite fears that only major newspapers such as The New York Times or The Wall Street Journal could make pay walls work, Gannett's 80 community newspapers appear to have come up with a successful strategy as well. In the fourth quarter of 2012, Gannett said circulation revenue growth from digital-only subscriptions had more than made up for print advertising losses for the same period.[8] The various forms of pay walls and metered payment plans are explored more fully in Chapter 10, but suffice it to say that many media companies are trying to figure out exactly what content people will pay for online. Some are focusing on creating specialized content that the audience can't get anywhere else.

"Look at The Wall Street Journal; they understood the unique value of their content and began monetizing it. They said, 'We have a highly educated and highly competitive audience, and we're providing information for those building their fortunes. We won't get everyone to pay attention, but the people who do pay attention to us will pay.' They figured out their audience," says Mahaney. "Really, that's the most personal connection you can have with your audience – you ask them to pay for what you do, and they do it."

Other companies like national magazine The Atlantic are no longer thinking of themselves as a single media product; they're thinking about themselves as brands, a concept we explored in Chapter 2. For example, to expand the company's digital footprint, the magazine created Atlantic Books to produce and market e-books. The company already had expertise in editing, built-in marketing channels and an established audience, so the goal is to leverage those assets with this new type of product.[9]

Mahaney says it's important for companies to remember what they're good at, as well as their core values when it comes to creating new products. Within that framework, he says Scripps is expanding efforts to serve its communities, especially through mobile apps.

"Our Storm Shield app is doing really well for us. The technology allows us to provide weather based on where you are; the alerts are finely targeted to those specific areas, so it's not just a TV weathercast or a Web story. It's an app targeted to the severe weather–focused audience," says Mahaney. "Now, that's not a full pivot from our traditional content, but we recognize that opportunity won't come if we concentrate solely on serving a broadcast- or newspaper-like audience. The challenge will be in identifying viable communities that we can provide content, information and engagement."

PHOTO 7-2 Years before Fox, CBS or HBO began offering on-demand streaming video, the business news–oriented cable channel Bloomberg was already available online. In 2014, the service recorded 9.2 million unique viewers for video content, more than double its number from the previous year.[10]

Source: Retrieved from http://www.bloomberg.com/now/2013-12-11/another-bloomberg-first-delivering-live-business-news-to-apple-tv/ on November 13, 2014.

Streaming Video

For news media managers, streaming video may offer another audience- and revenue-building opportunity. According to Pew's Journalism Project, about 6 in 10 U.S. adults watch video online, but only a little more than a third (36 percent) say they consume news video that way. On the plus side are data that show about half of those aged 18 to 29 say they watch online news videos, something that encourages organizations that have struggled to reach younger audiences.[11]

The online news site Vice Media, for example, seems to be targeting younger demos with hip, irreverent video reporting on important topics, such as the riots in Ferguson, Missouri. Long-established newspapers like The New York Times have also invested in the production of original news video, along with start-ups like NowThis News, which aggregates video reporting done elsewhere.

Of course, one of the reasons it's taken media organizations so long to develop strategies for online TV has a lot to do with money. As late as 2014, it was nearly impossible to accurately measure people viewing programming online, or more importantly, to translate online viewership stats to the industry's standard ratings for traditional TV. Now, Nielsen, the premier measurement service for TV viewing, has partnered with Adobe to start developing reliable and sellable ratings for online viewership. As these and other players help monetize online viewing, that portion of the news media business is inevitably going to grow in importance.

Leadership Report – Warren Webster

PHOTO 7-3

Courtesy of Warren Webster

Co-Founder, Patch.com

Warren Webster began his media career in 1997 at Morris Communications, where he held various executive positions, including group general manager of nine local newspapers, magazines and websites between Aspen and Vail, Colorado. Since then he has been vice president of material media; publisher of niche content sites, including Babble.com; and director of magazine publishing for Gannett in Westchester, New York, where he was responsible for 40+ local and regional titles.

What role does the curation of content play in the news media landscape?

Someone, somewhere has to create the content, and the people who do that hold an extremely valuable asset. That said, the digital world is a cluttered one, and there is equal value in curating experiences for the user. The companies who do both of these things well will be the winners.

Are there management theories that you subscribe to, or are you essentially reinventing the approach of managing your business as you go?

Many of the same theories have made fast-moving, innovative start-up companies successful in recent years (Apple, Google and Facebook to name a few). I could write several chapters on this, but to sum it up quickly: strong vision and mission behind everything we do; transparent, open communication with all employees; only create bureaucracy when absolutely necessary, and challenge each other to make things easier and faster; collaborate and don't be afraid to fail. Most importantly, think about the resident of the town or the local business who is interacting with our site and what we can do to make that experience better and more successful.

In the face of continual technological changes within the media industry, how do you manage people?

Great technology coupled with great people is what will fill the void in local information. One cannot be successful without the other. The technology is evolving rapidly, allowing us to do new things every day that will help communities and residents. To manage this constant evolution, we look for tech-savvy, entrepreneurial people who also have a relevant specialty like journalism, and who share our enthusiasm for building something entirely new versus tinkering with the same old model.

Beyond Legacy Media

In fact, one of the great promises of the Web was that it offered a lower barrier to entry for anyone interested in creating his or her own media outlet, and in fact, we've seen some amazing examples of digital media companies growing out of the passion of one person or small groups of people. Whether it's Matt Drudge of Drudge Report or Arianna Huffington with The Huffington Post, the Web has facilitated disruption of the media landscape in an unprecedented way. One of the most profound effects is that audiences have more options than ever before.

"For the user, so much choice is fabulous. You get to figure out what you want to consume and from whom," says McCandless. "The fragmentation of content started a change in consumption and a change in expectations. In the same way a department store became a thing of the past, having a place where you went for all your news became a thing of the past."

Bleacher Report is another good example of how the Web facilitates the creation of new news and information outlets. Bleacher Report was founded in 2007 by David Finocchio, Alexander Freund, Bryan Goldberg and David Nemetz – four friends and sports fans who thought there was a better way to superserve a segment of the sports news audience.

"What we said was, we know you have a very particular interest in sports. You might like baseball, but you really only care about the Texas Rangers or the Tampa Bay Rays or the Boston Red Sox. If you go to the sports department store called ESPN, you may never hear about those teams, so you're left with a lot of work to do as a consumer if you want to get all the news you can about your favorite team," says McCandless. "Now, we don't care if the information comes from Major League Baseball or a lawyer who blogs about your team after he gets home at night. We seek all that information, and we curate it."

This hyperfocus on niche audiences is something that has been a challenge for traditional media companies to master. Their focus has been on serving mass audiences for so long that they often don't have the mindset that allows them to identify these narrow but lucrative audiences, or they may not have the expertise to develop the products that will engage these audiences. Often, big media will purchase successful online entities as Turner Broadcasting did with Bleacher Report in 2012. In the five years leading up to the purchase, Bleacher Report had figured out there was an audience that wanted a different type of sports coverage.

"When we cover the NBA, we don't cover games until the playoffs. We cover style, the way the players live, how they interact with other media – that's what the audience tells us they want. They say, 'I'm super interested in why LeBron James is wearing his pants too short or why all these players are wearing brown shoes,'" says McCandless.

Bleacher Report has been criticized for its content, which has used unpaid contributors for a significant portion of what's on the site, as well as content designed specifically to drive clicks, sometimes at the expense of quality. However, the founders argue that their success in engaging with audience speaks for itself.

The 4 C's Strategy: Change

Today's news media managers have to be adept at adaptability. The upheaval to the news industry brought on by consumer use of the Internet and other digital technology is unlikely to dissipate anytime soon. What that means for those overseeing online media is that they have to become experts in that adaptability. If we glance into the past of online, from the days where we referred to it as desktop publishing to the days where it became instant delivery of information via all kinds of devices, from laptops to desktops to the tablet, online news has witnessed ongoing transformations, racing toward the future, while legacy media experienced change at a much slower speed.

And it's essential that those news media managers realize how their audience is adapting to this extremely fast-paced change and to stay in tune with their customers throughout it all.

This tension between traditional or legacy media and digital news start-ups is widespread. When Patch.com Editor-in-Chief Brian Farnham resigned in April 2012, he said, "I've never worked for a company that has been as scrutinized, criticized, and coal-raked as this one . . . You'd think we were creating toxic waste, instead of, you know, free useful information."[12]

By the time Farnham resigned, Patch, too, had been acquired by AOL, but the local news and information platform was founded in 2007 by Tim Armstrong, Jon Brod and Warren Webster as a way to fill a need for local information online.

"Patch is not a one-way conversation like many news outlets," says Webster. "We facilitate conversation between journalist and resident, resident and resident, consumer and business. My hope is that these conversations only increase and that we continue to have a deeper relationship with our audience and advertisers."

The stated goal at Patch has been to aggregate content about local communities that is already available online; to invite people in the community to contribute information, including local businesses; and to generate some new local content through freelance reporting and the efforts of a local staff editor or two. Mainstream media has again been critical – citing a low pay scale and low-quality content as being detrimental to journalism, while others question the business model. In 2011, Patch reportedly lost $100 million for AOL.[13] However, in 2014, AOL handed over a majority stake in the company to the Hale Global investment firm, which reports Patch.com is now making a profit. The new company's approach included eliminating some sites, going after national advertising and sharing more content among individual Patch sites.[14]

The story of Patch is one that news media managers should heed – not every product that's facilitated by technology comes with a ready-made path to profit. Learning from what happens with a company like Patch is just as important as watching a company that goes from start-up to the stratosphere in a just a few years.

Leadership Report – Chip Mahaney

PHOTO 7-4

Courtesy of Chip Mahaney

Senior Director, Local Operations, E.W. Scripps Co.

Chip Mahaney heads up digital strategy and initiatives for E.W. Scripps Co.'s television stations in 13 markets. His mission is to grow the stations' online audience and business via multiple platforms, including Web, mobile, apps and social media.

Chip is a former local TV news director and a longtime TV news manager, working for stations in the FOX O&O, Raycom, Gannett and Belo groups. He has 30 years of experience covering local news, sports and extreme weather, and managing newsroom technology. He's won an Emmy, and he's led a newsroom to an Edward R. Murrow Overall Excellence award. Over 20 years, he has trained thousands of journalists in new technologies and the leadership skills to implement them.

How has the competitive landscape changed for your company?

In terms of audience, our biggest local competitor might be Yahoo, even for local news. They can customize for a local market, and that's where a lot of people get their news, from Yahoo. People get their news from Facebook, and they make an assumption – if it's important enough, it will find me; people will share it, and that will elevate the content enough so that it gets to me.

The other issue is that people are spending time with smaller, more specific interests. Whether they've purchased an app that provides information about their particular hobby or some other demographic-based service, it's challenge for us to compete from the mega to the micro.

What is difficult about managing such rapid technological change?

The biggest challenge is getting people in our organizations to evolve and adapt to the changes. The journalists who have the best chance at future success are those who can demonstrate that they understand and appreciate technology.

How do you know which tech to embrace?

I work closely with local digital directors; we have a collaborative group, and we try to make people feel free to experiment and learn and then share best practices. If they try something out and it really works, then we have 25 others interested in figuring out the same success. You can't force it; it won't happen if someone tells you to do it. You have to hire people with a sense of curiosity and who just want to explore.

If you had to predict the future, when would you see us reaching a period of stasis where the evolution of the media slows?

The evolution of media is not going in just one direction; it's really cool that there's innovation at every turn. Nothing will slow down. More and more people are creating ideas, concepts and tools in a wildly diversified marketplace.

There's change in technology, content and the audience's needs, wants and expectations – it only gets crazier, but it gives you more and more opportunity, too.

However, it makes it more difficult for people who think they can be everything to succeed. The same thing happened to stores like Montgomery Ward long ago – those juggernauts that sold everything are largely gone. The stores that survived today have found niches, and the media are no different. As these technologies emerge and then mature, you have to stake out specific spots; you will struggle if you try to be everything to everyone. It's too hard to be good at anything that way.

How do you foster innovation within your organization?

By telling them to start doing it. And when there is a success, you champion it – you make a big deal of it. And when there's a failure, you acknowledge it and show you can accept it. You make them feel like it was a success that they did it in the first place. You have to reward risk; your words can only go so far; you have to demonstrate those values of innovation and taking risk.

It goes to hiring the right people: hiring the curious, the people who know where to look for what's happening around you and apply critical thought. They may take something existing and try to add one more step and create and innovate that way.

You spend time looking where front-line thinking is occurring. Most innovation probably begins with a small idea that you start working on as it evolves and adapts, and you decide if it's worth the time and effort – if it is, you invest more or you pack up and move on to next idea.

You have to realize that change is going to be part of your environment. I'm not the first one to say it by any means, but the best way to predict the future is to create it, and the best way to be at the forefront of change is to put yourself there. That involves reading, learning and networking, trying and being part of the discussion.

Are there management theories that you subscribe to, or are you essentially reinventing the approach of managing your business as you go?

Few of us got an MBA before we became managers. Increasingly, though, I admire those who seek out entrepreneurial experience. You can build a business for yourself if you have some basic skills.

I put myself in the best position possible to learn from other people. Sometimes that means seeking formal training, even if that means paying for it myself. Sometimes it's reading the right books and subscribing to right magazines or blogs. You learn what people are talking about, and then you figure concepts out for yourself. Connecting and networking, attending conferences and meeting people who are doing innovative things: That's an investment in yourself and your career.

LOOKING BACK – HINDSIGHT IS EASY

It's hard to believe that the first public Web page first appeared on April 30, 1993. It was text only with a few links taking the user to nearly everything available online. Fast-forward 20 years to a media landscape where some estimate that the Web grows at a rate of 7.3 million pages per day.[15]

PHOTO 7-5 The first public site on the World Wide Web – a rudimentary text-only primer on its use – was first posted April 30, 1993, by CERN, the European science laboratory where the Web was born.[16]

World Wide Web

The WorldWideWeb (W3) is a wide-area hypermedia information retrieval initiative aiming to give universal access to a large universe of documents.

Everything there is online about W3 is linked directly or indirectly to this document, including an executive summary of the project, Mailing lists , Policy , November's W3 news , Frequently Asked Questions .

What's out there?
    Pointers to the world's online information, subjects , W3 servers, etc.
Help
    on the browser you are using
Software Products
    A list of W3 project components and their current state. (e.g. Line Mode ,X11 Viola , NeXTStep , Servers , Tools ,Mail robot , Library)
Technical
    Details of protocols, formats, program internals etc
Bibliography
    Paper documentation on W3 and references.
People
    A list of some people involved in the project.
History
    A summary of the history of the project.
How can I help ?
    If you would like to support the web..
Getting code
    Getting the code by anonymous FTP , etc.

Source: Retrieved from http://www.w3.org/History/19921103-hypertext/hypertext/WWW/TheProject .html on November 13, 2014.

From our vantage point today, it's all too easy to say that traditional news media companies should have anticipated the impact of the Web and capitalized more rapidly on the opportunities created. McCandless says the critics are forgetting too much about the online environment 15 or 20 years ago.

"People sit in old media companies, or they used to be part of them, and they say the media gave away the revenue stream and gave away the content and they lost control of the customer and blah-blah-blah. In 1996, would you have entered your credit card into a website? We were dealing with dial-up at that point – would you have paid to watch video on dial-up, really? There's just no way to say they should have done it differently – nobody saw what was going to happen back then."

Yet, John Huey, former editor-in-chief of Time Inc., says that, in some cases, media companies may have just moved too quickly to embrace the Web. Huey is one of the authors of a Shorenstein Center–sponsored project called "Riptide," which explores the digital history of the last 30 years.

"I did not realize till we did this how thoroughly forward-looking Tribune and Knight-Ridder were. And, of course, the reason nobody realizes that today is because they both crashed on the rocks and had very unhappy endings, so everybody tends to think, 'Oh, well, they just slept through the digital revolution.' Au contraire! They were out in front of it," says Huey.[17]

What Huey says is that technology creates new opportunities for distribution of information and for new business models to sustain that distribution. When the distribution too rapidly outpaces new revenues, the results are seldom good for the company. However, Huey says this is a pattern that repeats itself, and media managers need to recognize that fact.

"There are two things that aren't going to happen: One, there is not going to be some stable island where everyone lands and says, 'OK, here's the new model, here we are. We loved that old model, now here's the new model, this is going to last 50 years like the old model.' This is going to keep changing and changing and changing. And the other thing that isn't going to happen is the erosion of the old model is not going to just suddenly stop for some reason and we can say, 'This is the floor. This is the bottom. We've hit rock, now we can go from here,'" says Huey.[18]

So, how can news and information companies respond now? Deseret News and Deseret Digital Media CEO Clark Gilbert advocates something called "dual transformation." This approach preserves and continues to invest in the core business while building an entirely new, disruptive business to attack new revenue opportunities. With this approach, Deseret operates its digital business separately, while it continues to invest in and grow its traditional broadcast and newspaper properties. According to the American Press Institute, the approach appears to be working – U.S. newspapers overall derive an average of 17 percent of their revenue from digital; Deseret News and Deseret Digital Media average 45 percent.

Theory in Practice – Dual Transformation

Desert Digital Media CEO Clark Gilbert developed his theories on media management as part of his work with Harvard's Clayton M. Christensen, the author of "The Innovator's Dilemma."

Gilbert's approach involves two transformations. One is the evolution of the legacy business; the second is the birth of a new business. At Deseret, that new business encompasses digital advertising, e-commerce, marketplace services, digital consulting and other emerging revenue streams in which tablets, mobile and social are integral parts. This new unit has separate staff, a separate physical space, a separate balance sheet of profit and loss, its own management structure and distinct content and product teams. Gilbert says the people in the new business think differently, talk differently and see technology as an unrivaled opportunity.

The evolution of the legacy business – the print newspaper in the case of Deseret – involves cost cutting and a redefinition of what the newspaper will cover. Gilbert and others argue that the Internet rewards sites that are superb at one thing, so the community newspaper must redesign itself around that principle, as well.

At Deseret, Gilbert and his team identified six core subject areas where they felt the news division could not just improve but become world class. He says that any publication should be able to go through a similar process of uncovering natural advantages and unmet needs in the marketplace. Differentiated coverage then allows the organization to distinguish itself and to allocate enhanced resources to those targeted areas of coverage.

Gilbert says the two businesses meet to share resources and an overall vision, but those interactions are limited. The tendency is for A to "suck the life out of B," Gilbert says, so top managers have to take great care to let each organization work independently.[19]

FOCUS ON THE FUTURE

For news and information companies, success online is going to require a ramped-up focus on understanding audience and the ability to analyze data generated about media use and preferences.

"The audience is in charge, and that can take many forms. On a management level, in terms of digital, you have to surrender to the data. You need good data, and you need to be good at analyzing it," says McCandless. "If you can't surrender to data, you're doomed. That's the hard part; media types don't want to surrender to audience."

Those data should allow online news and information outlets to better serve audiences and to offer them content that is essential to their lives. John Borthwick, CEO of Betaworks, which created Bitly and Chartbeat to help companies track sharing data, says media companies of the future need to focus on helping the audience with "discovery, saving, slow reading and fast reading."[20] Eventually, he sees media companies leveraging tools that can figure out exactly when and where someone wants to read an article or watch a video and then deliver the content directly to the individual at that time.

Data analysis will also be essential in helping news media deliver the more personalized level of interaction people have come to expect.

"That's a challenge," says Mahaney. "On social media everything is personalized. Facebook innovated this concept with the news feed. Facebook is a gate; it's an engine with the primary goal of customizing an experience for each user to get people to stay there longer. Facebook knows what you want based on what you click on or engage with. We have to rapidly adjust our mindsets and our products to compete."

McCandless says if media companies don't get in the data game, someone else will – and will end up making big money.

"Everybody votes with their hands now – with the click of a mouse or a thumb scrolling across a screen," he says. "That data is sold to the Fords of the world who are buying audience, reach and engagement. If you have those, you win."

EXECUTIVE SUMMARY

When the news media went online, few could imagine what it would mean for the industry's future. Most treated technology as a capital expense, not as a key component in the creative process of connecting with audience in new ways. Though today's news media managers are now well aware of the far-reaching impact of online delivery, many have not yet embraced the idea that ongoing media disruption is inevitable. In addition, new technologies for creating and disseminating content require new business models, as the role of the Web is changing again in a world populated with mobile devices.

THINK AND DO

Understanding analytics is an important part of any news manager's job. Review the following data from a small, online-only local news site, and then answer the related questions.

Page Views

A **page view** is the number of times a web page was accessed. For example, if a web page was viewed 45 times, that page has 45 page views. You can also use analytics to see which pages or articles were popular and which, because of low page views, were not.

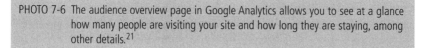

PHOTO 7-6 The audience overview page in Google Analytics allows you to see at a glance how many people are visiting your site and how long they are staying, among other details.[21]

Source: Google Analytics. Retrieved from https://www.google.com/analytics/web/?hl=en#report/visitors-overview/a35535656w63365892p65008914/ on November 13, 2014.

Unique Visitors

The number of **unique visitors** represents the number of individual visitors who accessed a particular web page. For example, if a page was viewed 45 times by 25 different Internet users, those 25 people represent the number of unique visitors.

Time on Site

Analytics tools can also calculate the amount of time the average visitor spent on a particular page. The average **time on site** for a news site is usually about 1 to 2 minutes – meaning the average person spent 1 to 2 minutes looking at the site before they clicked away.

Bounce Rate

The **bounce rate** is the number of visitors who left the site after viewing a single web page or article. A high bounce rate percentage means many visitors left the website after accessing just that page or article. A low bounce rate means many visitors accessed other pages on the same site before they clicked away.

Sources

It's also important to know how visitors arrived at your site. **Sources** of a site's traffic are the websites that referred visitors to your site or web page. Information about sources can help you target or build a rapport with sites that deliver traffic to your website.[22]

PHOTO 7-7 News managers need to be well versed in their site's best sources for traffic in order to make good decisions on where to deploy resources.[23]

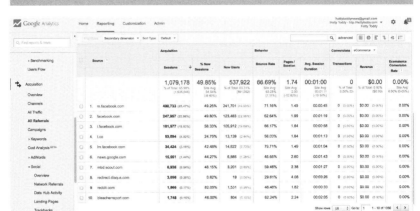

Source: Google Analytics. Retrieved from https://www.google.com/analytics/web/?hl=en#report/traffic-sources-referrals/a35535656w63365892p65008914/%3F_u.date00%3D20140101%26_u.date01%3D20141112/ on November 13, 2014.

1. Looking at the Google Analytics overview in Photo 7-6, what do you see in the data that leads you to believe that this site is doing some things well, and what may be areas of concern?
2. Checking in on sources of the site's traffic in Photo 7-7, how would you approach social media efforts for the website? Where do you see strengths, and where do you see opportunities?

NOTES

1. "Statistics," ITU, 2015, retrieved from http://www.itu.int/en/ITU-D/Statistics/Pages/stat/default.aspx on Feb. 26, 2015.
2. "eMarketer: Consumers Spending More Time With Mobile as Growth Slows for Time Online," Oct. 22, 2012, retrieved from http://www.emarketer.com/news room/index.php/consumers-spending-time-mobile-growth-time-online-slows/ on Feb. 26, 2015.
3. Jane Sasseen, "Digital: As Mobile Grows Rapidly, the Pressures on News Intensify," The State of the News Media 2013, retrieved from http://stateofthemedia.org/2013/digital-as-mobile-grows-rapidly-the-pressures-on-news-intensify/20-top-sites-2012-comscore/ on Feb. 26, 2015.
4. "Digital to Account for One in Five Ad Dollars," eMarketer, Jan. 9, 2013, retrieved from http://www.emarketer.com/Article/Digital-Account-One-Five-Ad-Dollars/1009592 on March 2, 2015.
5. "Total US Ad Spending to See Largest Increase Since 2004," retrieved from http://www.emarketer.com/Article/Total-US-Ad-Spending-See-Largest-Increase-Since-2004/1010982 on March 2, 2015.

6. "Google Takes Home Half of Worldwide Mobile Internet Ad Revenues," eMarketer, June 13, 2013, retrieved from http://www.emarketer.com/Article/Google-Takes-Home-Half-of-Worldwide-Mobile-Internet-Ad-Revenues/1009966 on Feb. 26, 2015.

7. Rick Edmonds, "The Case for Paywalls: Gannett Gains While Digital First Experiments," Poynter, Feb. 5, 2013, updated Nov. 25, 2014, retrieved from http://www.poynter.org/latest-news/business-news/the-biz-blog/202897/the-case-for-paywalls-gannett-gains-while-digital-first-experiments/ on Feb. 26, 2015.

8. Ibid.

9. Dena Levitz, "10 Secrets of Successful Meters, Paywalls and Reader Revenue Strategies," American Press Institute, Sept. 24, 2013, retrieved from http://www.americanpressinstitute.org/en/Training/Transformation-Tour/10-Secrets-of-Successful.aspx on Feb. 26, 2015.

10. "Another Bloomberg First: Delivering Live Business News to Apple TV," Bloomberg, Dec. 11, 2013, retrieved from http://www.bloomberg.com/now/2013-12-11/another-bloomberg-first-delivering-live-business-news-to-apple-tv/ on Nov. 13, 2014.

11. Kenneth Olmstead, Amy Mitchell, Jesse Holcomb and Nancy Vogt, "News Video on the Web," Pew Research Center, March 26, 2014, retrieved from http://www.journalism.org/2014/03/26/news-video-on-the-web/ on Nov. 6, 2014.

12. Kelly Faircloth, "AOL's Patch Editor-in-Chief Leaves, Does Not Go Scorched Earth," Observer, April 12, 2012, retrieved from http://betabeat.com/2012/04/patch-editor-in-chief-leaves-does-not-go-scorched-earth/ on Feb. 26, 2015.

13. Nicholas Carlson, "Exclusive: Now We Know AOL's Patch Revenue – and It's Tiny," Business Insider, Dec. 16, 2011, retrieved from http://www.businessinsider.com/weve-gotten-a-good-look-at-aols-local-ad-revenues-and-they-are-tiny-2011-12 on March 2, 2015.

14. Leslie Kaufman, "Patch Sites Turn Corner After Sale and Big Cuts," The New York Times, May 18, 2014, retrieved from http://www.nytimes.com/2014/05/19/business/media/patch-sites-turn-corner-after-sale-and-big-cuts.html?_r=0 on Feb. 26, 2015.

15. "Internet – Summary," How Much Information? 2000, retrieved from http://www2.sims.berkeley.edu/research/projects/how-much-info/internet.html on Feb. 26, 2015.

16. "World Wide Web," retrieved from http://www.w3.org/History/19921103-hypertext/hypertext/WWW/TheProject.html on Nov. 13, 2014.

17. "John Huey, Former Time Inc. Editor-in-Chief: Research Chat," Journalist's Resource, Shorenstein Center, May 16, 2013, retrieved from http://journalistsresource.org/skills/reporting/john-huey-former-time-inc-editor-in-chief-research-chat# on Feb. 26, 2015.

18. Ibid.

19. Excerpted from Dena Levitz, "6 Principles Clark Gilbert Used to Transform Deseret News," American Press Institute, Sept. 24, 2013, retrieved from http://www.americanpressinstitute.org/Training/Transformation-Tour/Six-Principles-Clark-Gilbert-Has-Used-To-Transform-The-Deseret-News.aspx on Feb. 26, 2015.

20. Seth Fiegerman, "Betaworks Vision for the Future of Online News," Mashable, May 7, 2013, retrieved from http://mashable.com/2013/05/07/betaworks-future/ on Feb. 26, 2015.

21. Google Analytics, retrieved from https://www.google.com/analytics/web/?hl=en#report/visitors-overview/a35535656w63365892p65008914/ on Nov. 13, 2014.

22. Excerpted from "The Journalists' Guide to Analytics," 10,000 Words, Fishbow lNY, Aug. 3, 2010, retrieved from http://www.mediabistro.com/10000words/the-journalists-guide-to-analytics_b875 on Sept. 28, 2013.

23. Google Analytics, retrieved from https://www.google.com/analytics/web/?hl=en# report/trafficsources-referrals/a35535656w63365892p65008914/%3F_u.date00%3 D20140101%26_u.date01%3D20141112/ on Nov. 13, 2014.

8

Mobile

"We have wised up; eyes are now completely open to what's going on, but we're playing with tools, not owning and creating the tools. To be part of the game, we have to decide if we are going to be the bat boy or if we're getting up to play."

—David Cohn
Executive Producer at AJ+, Founder of Circa and Spot.US

BENEFITS

- In this chapter, we offer the industry's best thinking on how news media companies can integrate existing platforms successfully with mobile and avoid the mistakes made with the Web.
- We explore the role mobile will play in the development of the next business models for news media.
- And we look at the development of news apps and some who are trying to create an experiential platform that takes the audience beyond simply browsing legacy content.

STATE OF THE MEDIUM

Approximately 80 percent of Americans say they have used one or more mobile devices in the past seven days, and more than half say they have used a mobile device to keep up with the news.[1] When it comes to daily use, other surveys have found that more than a third of people use their mobile devices to consume news every single day.[2]

Attracting Younger Demos

What's particularly encouraging to those in the news industry is the demographic breakdown of the mobile news user. As you can see in Figure 8.1, according to research by the Reynolds Journalism Institute, nearly three-fourths of those ages 18 to 24 use their mobile devices to access news – that's the highest percentage of any demographic surveyed. News organizations have long looked for avenues to reach younger demographics, and mobile appears to be one of the best options yet.

Bill Tallent runs Mercury Intermedia, a company that focuses on developing mobile solutions for news organizations, and one that has created apps for Fox News, USA Today and other media clients. He says smart news companies will focus their mobile strategies on those younger consumers, and that focus will be reflected in the people they employ.

"We tell our customers to develop media apps that are in tune with the way that 18 to 39 demo wants to see content. We urge them to hire passionate, innovative people in that age range and listen to them," says Tallent.

Tallent, who is in his 70s, says companies ignore at their own peril the need to do things differently for a new kind of news consumer in a new medium.

"Let me say something about developing a mobile philosophy because this is really important. Most of the people who run mobile aren't as old as I am but in my age group; they do not understand how younger consumers operate, how they work and how they think," he says.

Tallent adds that lack of understanding means that new forms of information presentation aren't taking off fast enough.

"What we advise companies to do is to present the news in ways that younger people are consuming it," he says. "For example, if you're working for the lifestyles section of USA Today's mobile app and you're writing a story about a new singing group, what you need to do is embed audio in that story to listen to and to buy in the iTunes store, and you need to be able to let the user see reviews of the music by other people. Younger consumers expect a very different experience."

Despite Tallent's concerns that the industry isn't adapting quickly enough, mobile traffic is driving an increasing amount of the overall visits to news sites. Many news outlets report half or more of their traffic is coming from mobile, and the visitors are bringing advertising dollars along with them.

Advertising Opportunities

As we've said earlier in this text, mobile advertising is growing faster than any other form, though the revenue generated by mobile is still a fraction of what advertising on other media is bringing in the door. However, that could soon change.

Mary Meeker, a Kleiner Perkins Caufield & Byers partner, reported in her 2013 Internet Trends Report that more than nine times more money was spent on Internet advertising than mobile advertising. However, if you look at the time consumers spend with each of those media, by Meeker's calculations, there's huge opportunity for those in the mobile space – that's if you assume Internet and mobile ad spending should be proportionate to the amount of time consumers are spending with those media.[3]

FIGURE 8-1   **The Reynolds Journalism Institute found that younger demos in particular are relying on mobile devices to access news and information. For journalism organizations, that means mobile may hold the key to reaching a younger audience.**

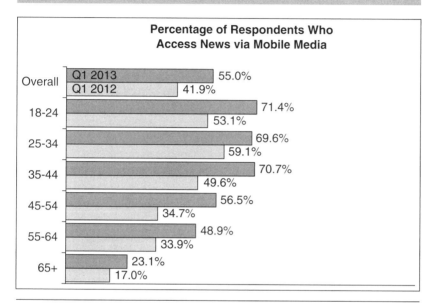

Percentage of Respondents Who Access News via Mobile Media

	Q1 2013	Q1 2012
Overall	55.0%	41.9%
18-24	71.4%	53.1%
25-34	69.6%	59.1%
35-44	70.7%	49.6%
45-54	56.5%	34.7%
55-64	48.9%	33.9%
65+	23.1%	17.0%

Source: From "News Consumption on Mobile Media Surpassing Desktop Computers and Newspaper," from the Donald W. Reynolds Journalism Institute.[4]

The 4 C's Strategy: Control

Mobile devices have nearly become attached to the human body; iPhones live next to hearts inside pockets, and tablets are always within arm's reach on nightstands and coffee tables, so subsequently, personal location is no longer important when it comes to content delivery; if you're the consumer, information is mobile, and you have control of where and when it finds you.

Having this powerful technology traveling with your audience daily is a heady thing, so it becomes paramount that you're on target and know your customers' habits when it comes to their mobile devices, such as how often they're on their device and what they're doing when they are. Armed with that information, you can create a better experience for your customers.

Of course, what remains to be seen is how much of the mobile ad dollar opportunity can be snagged by news organizations. Already companies like Google and Facebook are aggressively pursuing and capturing mobile money. In the second quarter of 2013, Facebook reported that mobile advertising made up 41 percent of its total ad revenue and predicted that it would surpass desktop-sourced ad income by the end of the year.[5]

PHOTO 8-1 In 2014, The Economist implemented a new strategy to bring in more digital ad dollars. The publication guaranteed those buying space on its apps and website that readers would spend a certain amount of time with their ads. They're trying to sell "reader attention" rather than clicks.

Still, some media companies are making aggressive mobile moves with some measure of success. As we mentioned in Chapter 6, mobile is a major part of CNN's overall business strategy. Ironically, before Jeff Zucker took over as president of CNN, he was credited with coining the phrase "trading analog dollars for digital pennies" – wording he used back in 2008 to describe the challenge faced by companies built around content distribution and advertising. He now has a new perspective.

"We're much further along than pennies, and we're further along I think than dimes, and we're probably a little north of quarters. You know, I don't know that there's 50-cent pieces, but somewhere between that," he says.[6]

For local news operations, revenue from mobile is also a growing part of the overall package. According to Gary Vogel, digital sales manager for WCMH-TV/nbc4i.com in Columbus, Ohio, mobile is outpacing other digital formats currently being sold, and he expects that to continue.

"Local businesses seem more interested in mobile campaigns than any other form. With the emerging mobile trend and interest, we foresee much more demand on the horizon," says Vogel.

Borrell Associates' analysts report similar findings – more than a third of small and medium businesses that had not yet tried mobile advertising said they were likely to do so within the coming year, and a vast majority of those who had actually engaged in some sort of mobile campaign said they were likely to do so again. The Borrell research indicates that mobile ad spends are expected to increase dramatically in every market analysts studied.[7]

Additional Revenue

Mobile may also be opening up additional revenue streams beyond traditional advertising dollars. To some extent, mobile audiences have already been trained to pay for content since it's a rare mobile device user who has not downloaded at least one or more paid apps, and news media companies have hoped to use that tendency to their advantage.

However, paid news apps have not yet become the hoped-for bonanza. According to Journalism.org's "Future of Mobile News" research, only about a fifth of mobile news users in the United States had some kind of digital news subscription – often bundled with the print edition.[8]

Some of that may be due to the relatively small number of U.S. news organizations that require payment for their digital products. In countries where it's more common, the percentage of those willing to pay is somewhat higher. For example, nearly a quarter of those surveyed in Brazil say they've paid for digital delivery of news content, and in Italy it's 21 percent, according to Reuters' Digital News Report 2013.[9] The survey also found that, across the nine countries surveyed, once again the youngest demographic, those ages 25 to 34, were most willing to pay for digital delivery.

Traci Hogue is the multimedia marketing director for WCMH-TV/nbc4i .com. She says a unique value proposition is essential if local news stations are going to be able to monetize paid apps.

"The consumer expects to get their news and weather for free. However, there are opportunities that exist at the local level where the TV station is in unique partnerships with community organizations wherein paid apps could be marketed," Hogue says. "Ideas may include developing a local food finder tied directly to station food critics or local farmers' markets and co-ops; editorial travel features tied to one-of-a kind unique traveler experiences around the state; or local sports insights into high school recruiting and scouting."

The challenge for media managers is to identify apps that offer unique, highly valued local content that can provide their organizations another stream of revenue.

Smartphones vs. Tablets

According to various studies, tablet users may be a better target both for mobile ads and for paid apps and digital subscriptions.

Among all weekly tablet news users, mobile advertisements appear to be having some success in engaging audience, especially younger demos. A quarter of 18- to 29-year-old tablet news users say they touch or click on ads.

In the Reuters survey, when the respondents were broken down by device type, about a quarter of tablet owners had paid for digital news content or accessed a paid digital news service, compared to just under a fifth of smartphone users. The outlook gets even brighter when you look specifically at those who use both tablets and smartphones in the United States. The survey found that group to be four times more likely to pay for digital news than the average American.[10]

Revenue Challenge

Even those who are most optimistic about the digital news future say media companies will likely need to create and maintain a number of simultaneous revenue streams that will likely include advertising, paid content options and other profit generators.

"Unfortunately for media's traditional role, the new business models probably won't generate as much revenue as has been the case in the past," says Mercury Intermedia's Tallent.

At the same time revenue is harder to come by, competition for the mobile audience is also quite fierce. David Cohn is the founding editor of Circa, a free mobile news app. He says the nature of the mobile medium is such that an app for The Atlantic may easily sit right alongside one for Angry Birds.

"That's where real competition comes in," he says. "How can they command our attention? We have a wealth of information at our fingertips. What's to stop someone from watching Netflix versus reading our story? They're both on the same device, so there's less of a mental space now."

Cohn says it's vital that media companies focus on specialization, providing something unique. For example, Circa calls itself "the first born-on-mobile news experience." It's designed to break down a news story into core elements: facts, stats, quotes and media such as images or maps. Readers can check the origin of a piece of information by clicking on the embedded links.

"At Circa, we're mobile first and mobile-centric," Cohn says. "We're picturing people on a commute – on a bus or a subway – we're picturing that person who has very little time and wants to catch up on the news of the day. We're focusing 100 percent on that user and picturing that user because we know a lot of people have that problem, so we're offering a solution to that one problem. We're consciously not trying to be everything to everyone, or we'll end up being nothing to nobody."

This focus on content specialization is a recurring theme for media companies as they work to target user niches. The goal is to offer unique content, developed specifically for the device on which it's offered.

LOOKING BACK – MOBILE MOVES QUICKLY

Of course, compared to a medium like print, mobile has a rather brief history to look back upon. Since the launch of the iPhone in 2007, news organizations have moved relatively quickly to understand and monetize mobile, something Cohn says he didn't see happening when the Web first became a factor in the distribution of news.

"A lot of opportunities were missed by organizations not understanding that journalism is in the information business, not the paper business," says Cohn. "Journalists should have been all over the Internet from Day One."

Leadership Report – David Cohn

PHOTO 8-2

Courtesy of David Cohn

Executive Producer at AJ+, Founder of Circa and Spot.US

David Cohn founded the nonprofit Spot.US in 2008. This innovative crowdsourcing and crowdfunding organization was designed to bring citizens, journalists and news publishers together online. American Public Media bought the company in 2011, and Cohn went on to create Circa, a news app, which Cohn calls "the first born-on-mobile news experience."

What do you think the media's role in society is now?

It offers a way for society to have a conversation with itself. There is no "the media" anymore as a result of technology. I think now it's less "the media" and more "many media" – a more intricate media.

If you picture the golden age of newspapers, you have to ask, "Golden for whom?" I don't think we're lamenting that there aren't better and more robust conversations going on; the lamenting is purely from the business side of journalism. Journalism as a process, a human activity, is stronger today than ever in human history; there are simply more acts of journalism occurring.

The journalism industry is much weaker, though. People like to complain about Craigslist, saying it killed journalism. Ask your average person 35 and under – if they had a choice between the robust newspaper of 1970 or today's paper plus Craigslist, what would they choose?

Define your organization's relationship with your own audience.

My entire career has been online, so there is an implicit understanding that my readers know more than I do. Our understanding of the audience is that they have the ability to inform what we're doing, to correct and to guide. We're serving them and their information needs.

Your app relies entirely on aggregation or content curation. What role do you see curated content playing for news media organizations in general?

Curating content is an integral part of how regular people will get their information. Certain users during the Boston Marathon bombing, for example, stayed glued to Twitter watching every single moment fly by. Conversely, others will stay glued to TV and listen to reporters for 24 hours repeating the same thing over and over again; the second one fits more people than the first one, so curation plays a really important role. Especially in a slow-moving story, people need someone to collect information, filter and distribute it – most journalists do it without thinking about it.

(Continued)

(Continued)

You've been a journalism entrepreneur and innovator – why is it so hard for news companies to spark innovation?

I've been really lucky – it's easier because we've been smaller organizations dedicated to pushing boundaries. What we're doing with Circa is different, but we're not supergeniuses; it's not like we've gone to the future and come back; we just have less legacy concerns than other organizations.

We don't have to worry about putting out a paper or risking 500 employees' jobs. Yes, we're risking our own hides, but if you run The New York Times, that would be much scarier to do something, as far as fostering space for innovation. You can't realistically expect as much innovation when you're facing those kinds of legacy concerns.

What sources do you rely on to stay on top of current trends that affect your profession?

I started out as a technology reporter, which was one of the saving graces of my career. All journalists should follow technology blogs, as well as media sites and blogs like Poynter and Nieman Journalism Lab that are covering the technology of journalism. You need to be anywhere these two topics collide.

What are your biggest fears about what's happening in the news business?

I'm very confident journalism will continue. It's part of the human endeavor to go out and find out what's happening and tell someone else about it.

My biggest fear is whether or not people who identify themselves as professional journalists will be able to find their home; we have a little bit of a diaspora going on right now.

It makes me think of the story of Moses and the Jews in Egypt. God sends the 10 plagues, and then Moses takes the Jews, parts the Red Sea and gets them on the other side. But what happens next? They wander in the desert for 40 years. So, God does all these crazy miracles, and he can't whisk them away to somewhere with air conditioning? Instead he leaves them in the desert.

The idea is you had a generation of people who only knew life in Egypt; before their tribe could get to the Holy Land, they had to live and die in the desert. Apparently, they wouldn't have been able to understand their new world without that period.

Journalism is currently in that desert phase; there's something we're all hoping to get to. My biggest fear is that we wander the desert aimlessly for too long.

However, Cohn says most news media organizations have moved more rapidly to embrace mobile. Dan Bradley, former vice president/general manager of WCMH-TV/nbc4i.co, agrees. He also says there are good reasons why companies don't pounce on every new communications trend.

"Large media companies try to be nimble, but given the huge amount of technological change they have been dealing with over the last 10 to 15 years, it takes time to shift capital investment from one new thing to the next," Bradley says. "They need to have a degree of certainty that the next new thing is going to gain support of consumers."

In the relatively short period of time that mobile has been a factor in the news business, answers to some important questions have begun to emerge. For example, the big debate on whether apps or responsive design creates the best user experience has led some news outlets to conclude that both have their place in the mobile environment.

Responsive design reshapes itself to fit all screens – that makes developing a digital presence across a myriad of devices cheaper and helps organizations avoid having to get apps approved in the Apple App Store. However, "native apps" seem to work best when organizations are creating products that solve specific problems, such as a local entertainment app might do. The benefit to a well-done app is that when news organizations create utility for the user, their brands become a part of users' daily lives.

In addition, news organizations now know that people want different kinds of content at different times and on different screens. For example, videos that people watch on their smartphones during the day tend to be shorter than what they watch at night at home. Tablet users tend to spend more time per session than smartphone users when it comes to browsing the Internet, researching products and watching videos.

Despite all that we've learned about mobile, however, efforts to address it as a unique medium are still inconsistent within individual news media outlets, and much remains to be determined when it comes to developing best practices.

Leadership Report – Bill Tallent

PHOTO 8-3

Courtesy of Bill Tallent

CEO, Mercury Intermedia

With a career that spans mainframe computers, minicomputers, personal computers and the Internet, Bill Tallent says he believes mobile computing will be the biggest of all. He is the CEO of Mercury Intermedia, which specializes in creating applications for next-generation mobile devices. The company has worked to develop apps for USA Today, Sports Illustrated, Golf Magazine and the NFL.

(Continued)

(Continued)

Do you think print and broadcast companies made a mistake in their approaches to the Web when it first became a platform for news and information? Are they handling mobile differently?

They blew it totally. They didn't know what it was. Back then it was "check-a-box" – do we have a website? Check. That's versus intentionality. The mentality was check-a-box – "Man, I've got a website, and it's gotten 1,400 hits." Nobody knew what the Web was or where it was going. I don't want to be too critical, but it seems to me they just figured they had to have something out there on the Web, but they didn't think it through – how it was going to be designed, the impact on the business model – a lot of the same things are happening in mobile. I'd like to say we learned from the Web, but we didn't learn much. The people following the check-a-box mentality, they lose against those that develop apps that people really want, and then they damage their brands – intentionality is critical.

Why is it so important for news organizations to study how the audience uses their products?

Let me say something about user experience. Newspapers and magazines always obsessed about the user experience; they constantly experimented with what to put in the front section, the subject of the second section and so on and so forth – that becomes even more critical in the mobile field. You have less real estate to look at – the biggest screens start at 12 inches and go down to 1 inch. When you have a smaller screen and less real estate, you have to be much more adept at user experience design – because of the dimensions of the screen, the successful mobile apps are those that have elegant user experiences.

How do you foster innovation within your organization?

I think the answer is a very short story. We hired a new designer last night – yesterday afternoon, we were trying to make a decision between two people. What made the final choice for us was passion; we hire people who are passionate about what they're doing – it's what's important to them. The paycheck is there, but avocation and vocation are in alignment, and they get to do what they want to do while they're at work. The guy we hired is absolutely passionate about design; it's not a job to him.

We have a whole company full of passionate people – they learned the media business hands down, and they are passionate about media; when you have passionate people, they innovate endlessly.

Tallent says we've all seen this before.

"I think it will follow the traditional pattern – you have a big new medium, like the Internet, which brings on a period of relentless exploration. That took 10 years to settle down; mobile will take another 4 years. After that, the rate of change for mobile is going to slow, but then there will be something new," offers Tallent.

FIGURE 8-2 **Certain computing technologies have tended to dominate for about 10 years before something "better" comes along. But the speed of technological change is increasing and news organizations must now continually monitor tech trends that affect their ability to reach audiences.**

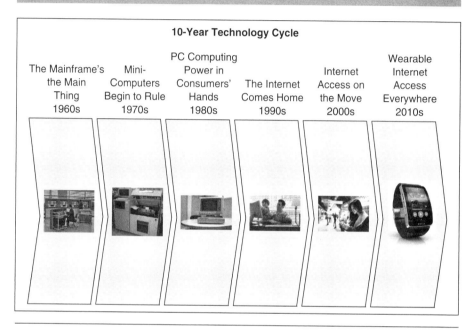

10-Year Technology Cycle

The Mainframe's the Main Thing 1960s	Mini-Computers Begin to Rule 1970s	PC Computing Power in Consumers' Hands 1980s	The Internet Comes Home 1990s	Internet Access on the Move 2000s	Wearable Internet Access Everywhere 2010s

Source: Adapted from Internet Trends D11 Conference presentation by Mary Meeker and Liang Wu, slide 49. Retrieved from http://www.kpcb.com/insights/2013-internet-trends on Oct. 29, 2014. Photos from: ©iStockphoto.com/HultonArchive; ©Flickr.com/Bob; ©granata1111/iStock/Thinkstock; ©Purestock/thinkstock; ©iStockphoto.com/franckreporter; ©iStockphoto.com/scanrail.

Theory in Practice – New Product Development

A product can be either tangible – such as a new type of mobile device – or intangible – like an app that provides a new service. New product development (NPD) theory explores the complete process of bringing a new product to market.

Since NPD often requires both engineering and marketing expertise, creating what's called a cross-functional team is common. The team is responsible for the entire project from the idea stage through the product launch – a process that generally involves eight stages:

1. Idea generation.
Typically, new-product teams will research customer needs and evaluate competitive products where applicable. A SWOT analysis (identifying the organization's strengths,

(Continued)

(Continued)

weaknesses, opportunities and threats) may be a part of the brainstorming process. The goal is to generate as many ideas as possible.

2. Idea screening.
The team sifts through initial ideas to identify those most likely to succeed. They typically test the ideas against questions such as these: Is it technically feasible to produce the product? Will the product be profitable?

3. Concept development and testing.
The team prepares detailed designs and specifications for the new product, collaborating with colleagues in engineering and other areas when necessary to plan manufacturing requirements. Before the product moves into full-scale production, the team asks for potential customers' opinions.

4. Business analysis.
The team calculates optimal selling price based on such factors as customer feedback and competitor pricing. They estimate demand and costs for development, production and marketing. They also forecast revenue.

5. Marketing strategy and development.
The team determines how the product/service idea will be launched within the market. A proposed marketing strategy will set out the customer target, positioning of the product and the marketing mix required to take the product to market.

6. Market testing.
The team prepares a physical mock-up or prototype to test in typical usage situations. They ask selected customers to evaluate the product and provide feedback. Testing will either validate the product's potential or provide feedback for refinement.

7. Commercialization.
The team prepares detailed commercial and marketing plans and produces advertising and other promotions. They finalize pricing and marketing strategy, as well as brief those involved in sales and distribution.

8. Launch.
At launch, the team executes their marketing-communication strategy to raise awareness and stimulate demand for the new product. If applicable, they encourage retailers and distributors to hold stock to meet anticipated demand, and they ensure that the customer service team is trained to deal with initial inquiries.

  Of course, some of these steps are repeated and some may be eliminated, and it's not unusual for companies to complete several steps concurrently. To date, media companies have tended to operate with a reactive strategy, waiting for others to innovate before they respond with new products. Some, like Circa's David Cohn, suggest that news organizations need to become more proactive – identifying market and technological changes that will allow them to develop new product opportunities before their nonjournalism competitors.

FOCUS ON THE FUTURE

The future of mobile is clearly still unfolding, but a few trends are emerging.

Fortunately for news outlets, mobile users appear to be significant news consumers – some actually increasing their overall news consumption, thanks to the portability and convenience of mobile devices.

Advertisers are increasing their mobile expenditures, and consumers seem to be accepting of mobile ads, especially younger users – an important demographic for news outlets to reach.

Increasingly, news consumers are expecting everything a news outlet produces to be available on all platforms, which can make customizing user experiences for each device more challenging. In addition, that list of devices may soon include sensor-enabled wearable mobile devices, such as Apple Watch and others.

"I'm wearing a watch right now that talks to my phone. I have the sound off on my phone, but when I get a phone call or a new email, my wrist tells me," Tallent says. "This device is rudimentary compared to what we're going to see in the next 10 to 12 years."

Tallent's view is that the future will include a whole range of devices that tie into a global network – a massive Web that connects people.

"Mobile is part of that membrane," he says. "News media must see itself as part of this network of information that flows through a myriad of devices. Breaking news may first hit the wrist – anything beyond a Twitter-sized bite may be consumed on the phone during the day or in the evening on a tablet."

Wearable devices are already changing the way news can be gathered; for example, Google Glass helped facilitate dramatic first-person coverage of protests in Ferguson, Missouri, in 2014. Then there's the innovative storytelling made possible by Oculus Rift, a virtual reality headset that enabled The Des Moines Register to create an immersive look at the family farm, for example. Other devices, like the Apple Watch, will prompt smart media managers to consider how content might be delivered to take advantage of the hands-free, always-on, environmentally aware nature of these wearable, mobile tools.

Mobile has also expanded the competition for those in the news business. Cohn says that companies like Facebook, Twitter, YouTube and Reddit are also media companies, though not necessarily producing journalism. For him, that raises an important question.

"Should media companies become tech companies? Owning tech is not benign, accidental and happenstance. The technology platform defines the future. We won't have future if we don't have the technology platform that defines the message. It's great that we have embraced technology, using Twitter and Facebook, but we're not masters of our destinies," says Cohn.

In contrast, Bradley says that few, if any, media companies have the bandwidth to make technology development realistic.

"I think this would be a huge waste of resources. Our role is to create high-value content for distribution," says Bradley. "I also do not necessarily buy into the thinking that local newsrooms need to be on the bleeding edge point of this evolution, so long as we have plans in place to migrate to new technological opportunities when they prove to be of high value to the consumers."

However, migrating to new technological opportunities will require media managers to become increasingly vigilant in monitoring what's happening with technology and the ways in which people are using it to stay informed, connected and engaged.

Leadership Report – Dan Bradley

PHOTO 8-4

Courtesy of Dan Bradley

Former Vice President/General Manager, WCMH-TV/nbc4i.com

Dan Bradley has been a driving force in Media General's media convergence efforts, first at WFLA-TV in Tampa, Florida, and then across all of the company's stations. Bradley moved to Columbus, Ohio, in April 2009 to become director of digital journalism and content for WCMH, and before that he was vice president of news for Media General's Broadcast Division.

Is there any future in paid apps created by local news operations?

I do not hold out a lot of hope for paid apps. In our experience here in Columbus, we have created several apps that are narrowly focused on something – weather, high school football, Red, White & Boom are examples – available in both iTunes and Google's Play store. We make the apps available for free and work to sell advertising into them (the traditional model). We are having limited success in turning a profit, but see this as a work in progress.

Are there other mobile revenue streams you're pursuing?

Media General is part of the Pearl Mobility consortium, which is working to leverage broadcast bandwidth and developing Mobile Digital TV. Essentially we are retransmitting our over-the-air signal in a manner that allows it to be received anywhere within reach of the broadcast tower on a mobile device, such as a cell phone. However, the cellular companies have been resisting adoption, as streaming video data to their phones is a big moneymaker. An alternative delivery has been developed where you purchase a dongle that connects to your iPhone or iPad, and it receives the local channels – a similar device is about to be released for Android phones. This effort is being driven by an offshoot of Pearl, called Dyle.

Do you think the local news media made any mistakes when mobile first came on the scene, or moved too slowly?

The migration to mobile, which is well under way, is no different from any other significant techno-sociological change that has hit our society — local news was slow to respond, but has adapted quickly. Most newsrooms in larger markets have developed aggressive mobile strategies that are often led by the newsroom's social media initiatives, since that is the way most consumers are interacting with their mobile devices.

FIGURE 8-3 Wearable communication devices have six primary attributes. They are hands-free, always on, environmentally aware, connected to the Internet, they get attention without disruption, and they're open to third-party developers. News managers will need to stay on top of the ways in which consumers are using wearables to react appropriately when it comes to providing content for the devices.

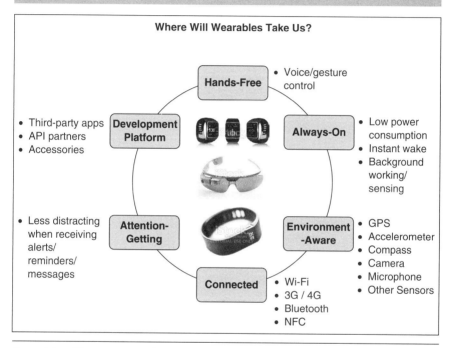

Where Will Wearables Take Us?

Hands-Free
- Voice/gesture control

Development Platform
- Third-party apps
- API partners
- Accessories

Always-On
- Low power consumption
- Instant wake
- Background working/ sensing

Attention-Getting
- Less distracting when receiving alerts/ reminders/ messages

Environment -Aware
- GPS
- Accelerometer
- Compass
- Camera
- Microphone
- Other Sensors

Connected
- Wi-Fi
- 3G / 4G
- Bluetooth
- NFC

Source: Adapted from Internet Trends D11 Conference presentation by Mary Meeker and Liang Wu, slide 53. Retrieved from http://www.kpcb.com/insights/2013-internet-trends on Oct. 29, 2014. Photos from: © iStockphoto.com/monicaodo; © iStockphoto.com/ferrantraite; © iStockphoto.com/franckreporter.

EXECUTIVE SUMMARY

Mobile news consumption offers media its next big opportunity to capitalize on the audience's ongoing desire for news and information. The medium has the ability to engage younger demographics and to provide new revenue opportunities in the form of mobile ads and the ability to sell apps as niche products. News organizations must continue to study the medium to better understand the user experience with each mobile device and should develop strategies for staying on top of technological developments that will likely require ongoing adjustments to their mobile strategies.

MANAGING TODAY'S NEWS MEDIA: AUDIENCE FIRST

<table>
<tr><td colspan="3" align="center">Times Publishing Brands</td></tr>
<tr>
<td>Tampa Bay Times</td>
<td colspan="2">TBT</td>
</tr>
<tr>
<td>This is Florida's largest newspaper. The Tampa Bay Times is a daily newspaper covering the Tampa Bay region. It has a circulation of just under a quarter million readers daily. View the website at www.tampabay.com.</td>
<td colspan="2">This weekday morning-only tabloid targets a younger demographic with what the publishers call "edgy news content." This paper focused on covering entertainment, sports and the area's social scene. View the website at www.tbt.com.</td>
</tr>
<tr>
<td>Florida Trend</td>
<td colspan="2">PolitiFact</td>
</tr>
<tr>
<td>This month magazine covers Florida business, industry, education, and leisure. It has a circulation of approximately 54,000 with a readership of approximately a quarter million. It's believed to be widely read by business executives, government officials and civic leaders. View the website at http://www.floridatrend.com.</td>
<td colspan="2">This service uses reporters and editors from the Times Publishing outlets to fact-check statements by members of Congress, the White House, lobbyists and special interest groups. They assign each a "Truth-O-Meter" rating. The ratings range from "True" for completely accurate statements to "Pants on Fire" (from the taunt "Liar, liar, pants on fire") for false and ridiculous claims. View the site at www.politifact.com.</td>
</tr>
<tr>
<td>Senior Living Guides</td>
<td>TBTwo</td>
<td>Tampa Bay Newspapers</td>
</tr>
<tr>
<td>These guides are created in both online and print versions. They offer information and advice about housing options and other support services for an older demographic living in Tampa Bay, the west coast of Florida and parts of Alabama. View the site at www.seniorlivingonline.com.</td>
<td>This free, student newspaper is distributed to about 75,000 students in two local school districts. Created in partnership with the districts, students create most of the content in this weekly. The website is at www.tb-two.com.</td>
<td>This division of the organization produces local papers for several small communities in and around Pinellas County, Florida. These include the Clearwater Beacon and Largo Leader. See the central site for the papers at www.tampabaynewspapers.com.</td>
</tr>
</table>

THINK AND DO

Imagine your company wants to explore the idea of creating a paid app to generate additional revenue. Consider what you've learned about mobile media in general and mobile apps in particular. What type of content works best in app form?

Take a look at the descriptions of the core products for Times Publishing Brands, a media company based in Florida. Review the websites for each product to get a better sense for what they do. Now, use your knowledge about the mobile audience to inform your decision about which mobile app product would be most saleable.

NOTES

1. Roger Fidler, "News Consumption on Mobile Media Surpassing Desktop Computers and Newspapers," Reynolds Journalism Institute, April 25, 2013, retrieved from http://www.rjionline.org/research/rji-dpa-mobile-media-project/2013-q1-research-report-1 on Feb. 26, 2015.

2. "News Consumption on Mobile Devices," Pew Research Center, Dec. 11, 2012, retrieved from http://www.journalism.org/analysis_report/news_consumption_mobile_devices on Feb. 26, 2015.

3. Jason Del Rey, "Mary Meeker's Internet Trends Report Is Back, at D11," All Things, May 29, 2013, retrieved from http://allthingsd.com/20130529/mary-meekers-internet-trends-report-is-back-at-d11-slides/?refcat=d11 on Feb. 26, 2015.

4. Fidler, 2013.

5. Alex Wilhelm, "Facebook's Desktop Ad Revenue Grew Only $69M in Q2, Mobile Rev to Outpace Desktop by EOY 2013," TechCrunch, July 25, 2013, retrieved from http://techcrunch.com/2013/07/25/facebooks-desktop-ad-revenue-grew-only-69m-in-q2-mobile-rev-to-outpace-desktop-by-eoy-2013/ on Feb. 26, 2015.

6. Dan Farber, "CNN's Jeff Zucker Trades Analog Dollars for Digital Quarters," CNET, July 23, 2013, retrieved from http://news.cnet.com/8301-1023_3-57595067-93/cnns-jeff-zucker-trades-analog-dollars-for-digital-quarters/ on Feb. 26, 2015.

7. "Local Mobile Ad Spend to Double in '13," NetNewsCheck, June 11, 2013, retrieved from http://www.netnewscheck.com/article/26729/local-mobile-ad-spend-to-double-in-13 on Feb. 26, 2015.

8. Amy Mitchell, Tom Rosenstiel, Laura Houston Santhanam and Leah Christian, "Revenue," Pew Research Center, Oct. 1, 2012, retrieved from http://www.journalism.org/analysis_report/revenue on Feb. 26, 2015.

9. "Paying for Digital News," Digital News Report 2013, Reuters Institute, retrieved from http://www.digitalnewsreport.org/survey/2013/paying-for-digital-news/ on Feb. 26, 2015.

10. Ibid.

From Consumer to Producer

"*Social media has allowed companies/brands to develop a personal relationship with their audience. Social helps further humanize the company, in a way, and allows for an even stronger company-audience connection to develop. This forms somewhat of an emotional tie between the two. This two-way relationship is how brands are staying relevant and 'in business.'*"

—Judy M. Stone
Executive Digital Media Product Manager, Hearst Television

BENEFITS

- In this chapter, we provide our take on the role of customer content generation in the modern media landscape. An argument can be made that there is virtually no barrier to entry in the media world any longer.
- We explore the redefinition of content value as the audience defines which sources are trusted and viable.
- And we look at how news media organizations can develop ways to curate the audience conversation. In this way, media companies get an opportunity to reach new audiences and to tap into new content sources that were out of reach in the past.

Content curation is a relatively new phenomenon, which grew out of the information glut created by the digital revolution. Rather than simply producing new and original content as they have in the past, news organizations must now develop strategies for monitoring information shared and content created by those in the audience, by newsmakers and even by competitors. In addition, news media companies must look for opportunities to leverage user-generated content (UGC) in a way that makes their work stronger and more relevant.

One of the most obvious ways to include curation in your company is through interactions with social media. Whether that's sharing a link, retweeting a quote or "pinning" a great recipe, news organizations are adding an editorial perspective by highlighting relevant and interesting content from the audience for the audience.

At a higher level, news organizations are also incorporating UGC into the products they produce. Photos and videos taken at the scenes of breaking news events often become integral to the coverage provided by news outlets. Questions of compensation for the providers and ethical use of UGC are still unresolved, though entire companies, like Storyful, have been created to help find solutions.

Outside of traditional news companies, dozens of websites have supported categorizing and sharing content with followers for years. At delicio.us, users tag and share what they consider interesting URLs, and at digg.com and reddit .com, user ratings promote or demote news articles that can then be viewed on the home page or shared. Much of the content curated on these sites, however, does originate from traditional news organizations.

SOCIAL MEDIA AND THE NEWS

Just as the news media are important suppliers of content to social media, social media has become an increasingly important distribution platform for the news media. About half of Facebook and Twitter users say they get news from those social networks, and YouTube is also a major source of news and information for the social audience. What makes social media particularly important is that it's one of the most egalitarian news platforms available.

Whether you're trying to reach men or women, whites or non-whites, those with high- or low-income levels, young or old, you can find them using some form of social media to get news.

In addition, research suggests that a significant portion of social media users would not be consuming news on any other platform. They are not avid news consumers, but they get exposed to breaking news and other incidental coverage through social networks. In this way, social media has become an important path for news organizations to reach new audiences.

At the same time, news outlet loyalists are also using social media. According to the Pew Research Center, two-fifths of Facebook news consumers also watch local television news, and one-fifth read print newspapers.[1] For this reason, social media is an opportunity to connect to existing audience in a more interactive way, as well as a way to reach the competitors' audience.

"News organizations should definitely have a social media presence on all major social media platforms – Twitter, Facebook, Google+," says Judy M. Stone, executive digital media product manager for Hearst Television. "Social platforms are an easy and quick way for news organizations to get important news in and out faster than ever before."

What Stone and others have discovered, however, is that each social media platform seems to have a particular purpose. For example, if you're trying to

PHOTO 9-1 The Pew Research Center's Journalism Project released data on news consumption habits of people who use individual social media networks. This type of research is invaluable to news managers who are keen on finding audiences for their content.[2]

Profile of the Social Media News Consumer

Percent of U.S. adults who consume news on...

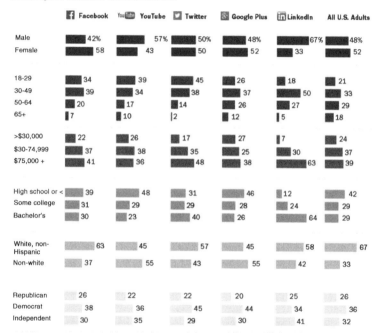

	Facebook	YouTube	Twitter	Google Plus	LinkedIn	All U.S. Adults
Male	42%	57%	50%	48%	67%	48%
Female	58	43	50	52	33	52
18-29	34	39	45	26	18	21
30-49	39	34	38	37	50	33
50-64	20	17	14	26	27	29
65+	7	10	2	12	5	18
>$30,000	22	26	17	27	7	24
$30-74,999	37	38	35	25	30	37
$75,000 +	41	36	48	38	63	39
High school or <	39	48	31	46	12	42
Some college	31	29	29	28	24	29
Bachelor's	30	23	40	26	64	29
White, non-Hispanic	63	45	57	45	58	67
Non-white	37	55	43	55	42	33
Republican	26	22	22	20	25	26
Democrat	38	36	45	44	34	36
Independent	30	35	29	30	41	32

Note: Based on Facebook news consumers (N=1,429); Twitter news consumers (N=359); Google Plus news consumers (N=194); LinkedIn news consumers (N=144); YouTube news consumers (N=456); and U.S adults (N=5,173).

Aug. 21-Sept. 2, 2013

PEW RESEARCH CENTER

Source: Pew Research Center Journalism Project Retrieved from http://www.journalism.org/2013/11/14/news-use-across-social-media-platforms/5_profile-of-the-social-media-news-consumer/ on November 18, 2014.

reach a high-income, relatively young male consumer, research suggests a Twitter campaign is going to make more sense than one on Facebook. Even more important, the more familiar a social media manager is with his particular audience, the better he is at engaging it.

"The best method for running effective social media accounts is to know your audience. Ultimately, it's how your specific audience reacts and relates to what you're pushing out that will determine the success of your social media accounts," says Lauren Zimmerman, digital managing editor at Townsquare Media.

PHOTO 9-2 Deeming its foray into Pinterest as "a visual read of the Journal," The Wall Street Journal uses Pinterest to showcase images and products correlating to stories it publishes in the paper. With about 50,000 followers, the Journal has one of the most successful "boards" on the site – engaging audiences that may or may not be the typical Journal consumer.[3]

Source: Pinterest Retrieved from http://www.pinterest.com/wsj/ on Oct. 29, 2014.

The 4 C's Strategy: Customers

The phenomenon of reader-, viewer- or user-generated content hands the power of creation and, to some extent, distribution over to the customer. In reality, online devices have made nearly every interested person a publisher or producer of content. Between personal blogs, YouTube and any number of social media sites, customers these days are contributing to the content that exists and voicing their opinions louder than ever before.

This phenomenon has moved from what some once called citizen journalism to a prominent tool for expanding news sources inside some of the most respected traditional news organizations. Those that do it right will not compete with the consumer/producer-generated content, but rather complement and integrate customers' news and information.

Audience Engagement

What Zimmerman and Stone are talking about is audience engagement, something that traditional media platforms gave little more than lip service to in the years before social media burst on the scene in the early 2000s.

"What has changed is the welcome expansion of the two-way conversation aided by social tools. Actually, the conversation expands to the social community at large," says Stone. "Newsroom staff get instant feedback 24/7. As stories are covered – or not covered – the community will voice their opinions. For example, your audience will thank you for great coverage, then turn around and quickly point out any mistakes or gaps in coverage. These voiced opinions come in the form of messages, tweets and comments, as well as more traditional email, phone calls and even in-person visits."

The key to turning the two-way nature of social media into engagement is to keep the conversation going. For example, as part of a project on "PBS NewsHour" about high school dropouts and graduation rates, the news organization used a Pinterest page to feature photos, submitted by students, that explain why they stay in school. Stone says this collaboration with the audience will only make the reporting and the news organization stronger.

"Take advantage of the channel of communication that social media gives and talk to your audience," says Stone. "Interact with them by answering their questions and commenting and liking positive comments they make."

Too often news organizations stop once they've evoked a response from the audience – they fail to answer questions or ignore comments that deserve a reply. The net effect is that they've lost one engagement opportunity and may never get another from that particular person.

For that reason, many progressive news organizations have begun to hire people with job titles such as social coordinator, social media manager or social media producer. They've realized that social media platforms have become so important to a news organization's overall business strategy that they require full-time management.

Leadership Report – Katie Hawkins-Gaar

PHOTO 9-3

Courtesy of Turner Broadcasting

Former Editor, CNN iReport

Before becoming The Poynter Institute's first Digital Innovation faculty member, Katie Hawkins-Gaar led the editorial team for CNN iReport, the network's global participatory news community. Hawkins-Gaar joined CNN.com in 2007 after graduating from Georgia State University. She worked as an associate producer with the interactives team for a year and joined iReport in early 2008.

How has social media changed the news media's role in society, if at all?

Social media has significantly changed news media and its role in society. Reporting the news is now much more about two-way communication: delivering the latest headlines and stories to your audience, of course, but also listening to what your readers have to say and paying attention to what content they're sharing. Listening is key; not only will readers tell you what kinds of stories they do and don't like, but they also often have their own interesting stories to share, which can add an entirely new layer to existing news coverage.

(Continued)

(Continued)

Because social media moves so quickly and practically everyone has access to it, misinformation is also rampant. This makes the news media's responsibility to report factual, objective information more important than ever.

How has the competitive landscape changed? Who do you view as competitors for the news media now versus 5 or 10 years ago?

Social media has made a major impact on the media landscape. People are less likely to be loyal to one news outlet or website; instead, sites like Facebook and Twitter offer a variety of news stories from various places depending on what your friends are sharing and commenting on. This is both a challenge and an opportunity for news outlets – there's now more competition, but also more opportunity to share content with wider audiences.

In the face of continual changes related to communication platforms and technologies, how does that affect your management strategies?

As a manager, I encourage my team to experiment with the latest technologies and stay flexible with the tools that we use. Team members will often suggest new apps to try out or a different platform that might boost efficiency with daily tasks. We don't always adopt every new social network or technology we try – that would be virtually impossible – but experimenting regularly does help us to stay on top of trends.

How do you foster innovation within your organization? Can you give an example of an innovative idea and how it was managed?

The iReport team goes on lots of walks. Some of our best brainstorming happens outside during casual conversations. I also try to encourage my team not to be afraid to abandon an idea for something better. For the 50th anniversary of Martin Luther King's landmark "I Have a Dream" speech, we asked people who were part of the March on Washington to share their stories. But after a tepid response, we decided to change course and instead invited our community to share stories of experiencing racism. The response was powerful and overwhelming, and culminated in a stunning interactive that was at the center of CNN's coverage of the anniversary.

Are there management theories that you subscribe to, or are you essentially reinventing the approach as you go?

I'm a fan of management books and blogs, but there aren't any specific theories that I subscribe to. I find that giving team members as much responsibility and freedom as possible helps to foster creativity and innovation, and I'm always looking for new ways to do that.

How does or should user-generated content play into a news organization's business strategy?

I'm biased here, but I believe that every news organization should invest in user-generated content. Not only do audience-submitted photos, videos and stories help enrich news content, they also help build a sense of community, which is key in today's social media–dominated world. Advertisers are often looking for innovative and meaningful ways to interact with community, so there's definite sponsorship potential for news organizations that make a commitment to soliciting and showcasing user-generated content.

What's next for user-generated content – on either the creation or the dissemination side? How does it evolve in the future?

In the six years I've worked with CNN iReport, I've seen major changes in user-generated content. As technology improves, the quality of photos and videos has improved significantly. Likewise, as social media becomes more ubiquitous, the potential for stories to spread worldwide increases. This puts less responsibility for CNN to determine which stories we select and approve for air, and more of a focus on covering the user-generated stories that resonate with a wider online audience. Essentially, the community not only shares stories with CNN, but they also tell us which of those stories they're most interested in seeing us cover.

Digital Influence

As our understanding of social media broadens, news organizations have an opportunity to use social media more efficiently and effectively. The concept of digital influence is one that is already resonating among traditional brand managers, and it has implications for all types of organizations, including news outlets.

According to techopedia.com, digital influence is "the ability to create an effect, change opinions and behaviors and drive measurable outcomes online."[4] The concept may best be described by example. Let's say you are trying to decide which new laptop to purchase; you log on to CNET.com and read all the reviews of your top two choices before buying anything. The writer of a CNET review presumably has more digital influence in this area than your brother Joe.

However, Joe may be an unparalleled expert on the local school bond issue, so his digital influence may be exactly what a local news organization wants to tap into when it's planning comprehensive coverage of the topic.

There are a number of services such as Klout or PeerIndex that measure not only "who you know, what you say and what you do, they attempt to score or rank your ability to influence those to whom you're connected," according to Brian Solis, who works for Altimeter Group Network.[5]

Social media users with high scores or ranks may have the potential to help a news organization reach more people with more narrowly targeted content. Stephanie Agresta, executive vice president and managing director of social media for Weber Shandwick, says the potential for tapping into social influence is great:

"Influence is much more than a score. This is about reaching people not just because they're connected, but because they serve a role within their online community. It's up to brand managers, marketers and communications professionals to use influence tools to learn more about the social landscapes and the people who affect their markets."[6]

The more social media managers can study their audiences and get to know who they are, the better they can leverage that audience to expand the brand and support the organization's bottom line.

Leadership Report – Judy M. Stone

PHOTO 9-4

Courtesy of Judy M. Stone

Digital Media Product Manager, Hearst Television

Judy M. Stone is a digital media product manager for Hearst Television at WXII-TV in Winston-Salem, North Carolina. Prior to that her career was focused on television production in North Carolina, Tennessee and Virginia.

In the face of continual changes within social media, how does that affect your management strategy?

Every day we are reading about the latest in social media trends to keep a pulse on other companies and brands (both inside and outside our industry) to see what is working well for them and how we can spin an idea to fit our own needs – testing new ideas accordingly and thoroughly.

That said, what is also important is not to get distracted by every shiny new social toy that comes along. As smart managers, we keep our teams focused on the social efforts that help us reach our core goals and objectives. We closely monitor workflow to ensure we focus our efforts on those that give us the highest return for time spent.

How do you foster innovation within your organization?

Hearst Corp. has a long, rich history of innovation that is alive and well to this day with an entire "Hearst Innovation" branch to the company. That branch invites and encourages collaboration between all employees, regardless of position or title or branch of the company – using a private social media website. People from vastly different areas of expertise, careers and sectors have conversations and brainstorm ideas and make contacts in the name of innovation. New business ideas can even be submitted for consideration and funding.

Do you have any recommendations for media managers when it comes to content curation?

First, social coordinators around the world cannot overlook the importance of fact checking, grammar checking and copyright law. Users and followers will lash out at any hint of inaccuracy, which in turn can affect the brand.

Second, we like to go by the rule "Quality Over Quantity." One should always ask, "Would my followers find this story important?" and "What benefit does this provide to my followers?"

Understand your social platform. You should understand your follower base and how they react to various content types. Also, it's important to have the correct message broadcast from the correct platform.

What's next for social media? How does it evolve in the future?

As technology continues to advance and integrate, it will continue to open the door for highly targeted content and marketing. We predict that companies will value the Klout Score of their followers. Followers with a higher Klout Score inherently have a larger influence on their peers. Here's how this integration could come into play:

New technology is on the horizon for smartphones in the form of higher security. This security boost gives more freedom for folks to make safe purchases with their smartphones. Imagine yourself in this scenario – you, a Starbucks regular, go up to the drive-thru in your car, and you wave your smartphone at a screen where it pulls up your most common order and your payment information. You confirm the purchase and pull up to the window. You receive a push notification from Starbucks rewarding you for a recent Instagram post of yours that promoted the Starbucks brand. Since you positively impact the brand in the digital space, Starbucks throws in a blueberry muffin with your order.

Overall, we predict a movement toward customer appreciation spawning from social media interactions with major brands.

What sources do you rely on to stay current and effective in terms of technology and the news business?

As far as keeping up with social media, we like Mashable and Social Media Examiner. Mashable, especially, is a dependable resource for news business, technology, social media and so on.

Stone says she relied on input from her digital media team to create her responses.

CONTENT CURATION

As we mentioned earlier, social media, user-generated content, social influence and content curation are all evolving, as are their uses and definitions within news organizations. At Forbes Inc., content curation plays an integral role in the business strategy, particularly on the digital side.

"Our motto is built around a notion that we are a curated network of voices," says Lewis D'Vorkin, chief product officer for the company. D'Vorkin says Forbes takes a very deliberate approach to incorporating outside expertise into the organization's content. "We have to pick you – you can't write just because you raise your hand. Content curation done in this way is valuable to both the brand and the audience and, by the way, is critical to a new kind of economic model for journalism."

At Forbes, that new economic model involves supplementing the organization's full-time reporting staff with more than 1,000 "contributors."

"Our expert voices have an opportunity to be paid for their expertise; they are paid on an incentive basis. The more audience, the more they get paid."

For D'Vorkin, curation also includes content created by advertisers. Though he makes it clear that information from "marketing partners" must be identified and labeled, D'Vorkin says customers want the "insights" that advertisers can provide.

Leadership Report – Lewis D'Vorkin

PHOTO 9-5

Courtesy of Forbes.com

Chief Product Officer, Forbes.com

Lewis D'Vorkin serves as chief product officer, leading all editorial areas for Forbes and its related brands. Since joining the company in June 2010, D'Vorkin has initiated the redesign of Forbes magazine and launched a new digital publishing platform that seeks to put authoritative journalism at the center of a social media experience. Prior to joining Forbes, D'Vorkin founded and served as chief executive of True/Slant, an original Web-based content news network, which Forbes Media invested in and acquired in May 2010. He also served as executive editor of Forbes magazine from December 1996 to April 2000 and as senior vice president for programming at AOL, Page One editor of The Wall Street Journal, a senior editor at Newsweek and an editor at The New York Times.

How has the competitive landscape changed? Who do you view as competitors for the news media now versus 5 or 10 years ago?

LinkedIn, Twitter, Facebook and everything like it. I don't look at any traditional media competitors for anything.

We responded with a whole different mobile website, based on streams, not on the principles of article pages that have existed forever in news organizations. Everything was done based on the notion of how to integrate social into your product. We're moving to the world of streams – it's what we do. It's not a bunch of editors editing and editing again and then telling the reader this is what we think, now go away.

In the face of continual changes related to communication platforms and technologies, how does that affect your management strategies?

You either have to live the life or you have to eat the dog food. Most media managers do neither. When you live the life, you're online 24/7. When you eat the dog food, you're downloading 15 to 20 apps a day; you're out there looking for start-up companies; you're not having someone else do that. Most media managers are not eating the dog food, though there are plenty of people who say they do it.

It's a time-consuming, relentless job that doesn't stop. Most media managers still focus on the story, and that's OK, but that's being a chief content officer, not a chief product officer.

What is a chief product officer?

It's a whole different job. I'm a person who's focused on developing products that work for the consumer, the advertiser and the business. It's a whole different mentality than managing news. I create product experiences that work for audience, consumers and marketers.

Every journalist needs to understand business principles. That doesn't mean you're selling an ad, but you understand the economics; you think about the company and your own job. Twenty years ago, journalists thought, "There's not a problem in my business that selling another ad won't solve."

Are there management theories that you subscribe to, or are you essentially reinventing the approach as you go?

Get shit done; that's my management theory – end of story. New management theory? Get shit done faster, faster, faster.

Go back to [management guru Peter] Drucker; your mission comes before processes. Don't get wedded to your processes if they're not helping your mission. The essential mission is to inform, but 100 years of process has been developed and everyone's sticking to it.

Do you have any recommendations for media managers when it comes to content curation?

It will be very unusual that a traditional media journalist – reporter or editor – is able to make the transition into writing or being an editor in the world of social media. It's difficult because these people bring a certain set of skills and training and they close their minds about change, but there's an entire new generation of digital journalists that lives and breathes the way that people want to read, consume and share news today.

The first job interview I had in 1974 was at Dow Jones in Chicago. The bureau chief says, "We like to hire kids right out of college because we don't have to break them of bad habits." Today it's really difficult to break traditional journalists of the bad habits they've learned.

Is the Forbes strategy viable for other news organizations?

It's proven to be a viable strategy if you take the steps necessary to get rid of the politics or bureaucracy that would typically expel those kinds of things that make the strategy work. Forbes did this in unbelievable ways to make sure new ideas and new things were not blocked by people who were protecting certain ways.

Forbes has great strengths. I have not seen a big traditional media company that can make new ideas become integral to what they do. I'm not saying it can't happen, but it takes a lot of courage, a lot of answering questions from within.

User-Generated Content (UGC)

One of the best-known examples of an organization that has institutionalized UGC is CNN's iReport. The initiative was launched in 2006 as a way to allow people from all around the world to contribute pictures and video of breaking news stories.

According to the website, the unit's producers handle submissions from a reported 750,000 registered members, which translates into an average of 500 iReports a day. A fraction of those are vetted and approved for CNN's non–user-generated networks and platforms, which involves fact checking and

PHOTO 9-6 In October 2014, CNN's iReport asked for first-person stories from the front lines of the Ebola battle. In two weeks, they had 136 reports filed with seven of them used on CNN's broadcasts.[7]

Source: iReport.CNN.comRetrieved from http://ireport.cnn.com/topics/1179496 on Oct. 28, 2014.

verifying the details of a story. When a story is approved, the "Not Vetted for CNN" bar disappears and is replaced by a red "CNN iReport" bug that lets the community know a story has been verified.[8]

"CNN has built a strong relationship with our audience," says Katie Hawkins-Gaar. "We invite people to share their photos, videos and stories and select the best to be part of CNN's coverage. Building communities – people who connect around different topics and interests, for example – is especially important, as it helps us target the content we produce. I think audience participation will become even more important in the future; inviting people to share their thoughts on a topic or share content will be a key component of news coverage, not just a gimmick."

Hawkins-Gaar says news organizations moving more heavily into curation would do well to find topics or niche areas that aren't yet a part of the wider media conversation:

"There is no shortage of user-generated content online, and it's impossible to keep up with it all. I think developing strategies for curating content is essential; otherwise there's a big risk of burnout."

At the Associated Press, social media editor Andy Carvin says UGC is already central to that organization's newsgathering operation as well:

"And UGC is almost entirely about mobile, especially when it comes to photos and video. The reality is news organizations are going to have to find people who have some expertise to find this stuff."[9]

What Carvin and others recognize is that curation and verification are the value-added dimension that news organizations can bring to social media and UGC, but they often don't.

"The way user-generated content is used by the news industry is incredibly variable and inconsistent and in many cases problematic. We need to think about user-generated content the way we think about other sources – as unverified when we first see it," says Carvin. "We need to make sure that we know what we're looking at and that we're not essentially stealing content from people without their permission or proper credit."[10]

Hawkins-Gaar agrees.

"While this practice is relatively new in the news industry," she says, "I believe there are some basic rules that everyone should follow: Ask for permission before posting someone else's content on your site and always link back to original source. It's not always the speediest approach, but it's absolutely the right thing to do."

Theory in Practice – Disruptive Innovation

For new media managers, understanding the theory of disruptive innovation may be critical to success. A disruptive innovation is one that helps create an entirely new market; for example, the development of the iPad irrevocably changed a number of industries, including the communications and computing industries.

In the past, such innovations typically disrupted existing markets over a period of years or even decades, but social media consultant Steve Safran says those days are long gone.

"The evolution of media will never stop – or ever slow down," he says. "It accelerates. Newspapers have been around since the 18th century. Radio started in full in the 1920s. TV came along 30 years later. Now the change can happen in six months."

Safran, who was editor-in-chief of LostRemote.com, is a big fan of Clayton M. Christensen, who wrote "The Innovator's Dilemma." Christensen says established companies have such a hard time competing against start-ups because they have to sustain their existing businesses while they work to radically improve a product or service for a new set of consumers or create an entirely new product or service. With limited resources, that's a real challenge, but one Safran says media outlets and those who manage them have to meet.

"Companies need to innovate constantly," he says, "all while making their current business run smoothly. Managers and executives are no different – you have to keep evolving with the rest of the pack."

Strong media managers will strive to create processes within their companies that allow for disruptive innovation to occur while they continue to sustain the core business. This will almost certainly require reallocation of resources, a reworking of the company's value network and risk.

FOCUS ON THE FUTURE

The growth of audience participation in the newsgathering and agenda-setting processes seems to be a given for the future. For media managers who grew up in the top-down, "we decide what's news" generation, this new paradigm requires a radical shift in thinking.

For forward-thinking leaders, the willingness of news consumers to engage with and contribute to the news product is a business opportunity. When a community is passionate about a brand, they become more loyal and invested in that brand. At a more advanced level, there are also chances to capitalize on expertise outside your organization, as is the case with the Forbes "contributor" model and, in some instances, the CNN iReport approach.

Though some news managers continue to feel threatened by the change in media's traditional role, others are energized by what's ahead.

"I'm optimistic about the future of journalism; the news audience is more voracious than ever. Never before has it been easier for smart people to tell people what they need to know," D'Vorkin says.

Call it listening, engagement or an audience partnership, but the relationship between news producers and consumers is evolving and expanding.

EXECUTIVE SUMMARY

A new respect and appreciation of audience seems to be developing within successful news media organizations. News consumers are no longer content to accept that the media have all the answers or are even asking all the right questions. Social media and other digital technologies provide people with free or low-cost publishing platforms on which to express their views or to share important information on an infinite variety of topics. Smart news managers are leveraging this willingness to contribute and incorporating user-generated and other content contributions into their overall business strategies.

THINK AND DO

You've just been hired as a social media manager for a monthly magazine that serves "active seniors." Your social media presence has been described as anemic, with just a few thousand followers on Facebook and Twitter. Using the data on social media demographics from the Pew Research Center (http://www.journalism.org/2013/11/14/news-use-across-social-media-platforms/), determine which three social media tools you will use to build your social audience and outline how will you differentiate the content on each platform.

NOTES

1. Amy Mitchell, Jocelyn Kiley, Jeffrey Gottfried and Emily Guskin, "The Role of News on Facebook," Pew Research Center, Oct. 24, 2013, retrieved from http://www.journalism.org/2013/10/24/the-role-of-news-on-facebook/ on Feb. 27, 2015.

2. "Profile of the Social Media News Consumer," Pew Research Center, Nov. 13, 2013, retrieved from http://www.journalism.org/2013/11/14/news-use-across-social-media-platforms/5_profile-of-the-social-media-news-consumer/ on Nov. 18, 2014.

3. "Real Estate, Fashion, Graphics, Gadgets and More From The Wall Street Journal," Pinterest, retrieved from http://www.pinterest.com/wsj/ on Oct. 29, 2014.

4. Cory Janssen, "Digital Influence," Techopedia, retrieved from http://www.techo pedia.com/definition/28497/digital-influence on Feb. 27, 2015.

5. Brian Solis, "Report: The Rise of Digital Influence and How to Measure It," March 21, 2012, retrieved from http://www.briansolis.com/2012/03/report-the-rise-of-digital-influence/ on Feb. 27, 2015.

6. Ibid.

7. "Assignment: On the Front Lines of Ebola," CNN iReport, Nov. 30, 2014, retrieved from http://ireport.cnn.com/topics/1179496 on Oct. 28, 2014.

8. "How CNN iReport Works," CNN iReport, July 2, 2012, retrieved from http://ireport.cnn.com/blogs/ireport-blog/2012/07/02/how-cnn-ireport-works on Feb. 27, 2015.

9. Michael Depp, "AP's Carvin: News Battle Near for Twitter, FB," NetNewsCheck, Jan. 13, 2014, retrieved from http://www.netnewscheck.com/article/31368/aps-carvin-news-battle-near-for-twitter-fb/page/1 on Feb. 27, 2015.

10. Ibid.

chapter 10

Show Me the Money

"Our challenge with all these (new-media) ventures is to effectively monetize them so that we do not end up trading analog dollars for digital pennies."

—Jeff Zucker
Former Chairman, NBCUniversal[1]

BENEFITS

- In this chapter, we learn why some media organizations are economically successful and others fail.
- We look at the complex relationships between media companies that drive consumer media costs.
- We explore the struggle to monetize digital audiences and build future revenue streams.

STATE OF THE MEDIUM

As we have seen in previous chapters, audiences are in transition. Traditional media platforms are still important and many retain great value, but the shift in power to consumers has created a fragmented world in which new choices are not only vast, but growing, creating financial pressure on all media, large and small.

Because start-up costs for highly targeted new media, such as apps, are relatively low, large companies, with traditional staff and infrastructure costs, face the greatest threat from fragmentation.

Media companies, in general, are also at risk because of complex relationships between companies that constantly transfer revenue to one another. These factors include television programming agreements, retransmission fees, reverse network compensation and sharing agreements between newspapers, all of which we explain and explore in this chapter.

Government also plays a significant part in the complex business of media. Various forms of legislation, regulation and court rulings make government a wild card player that sometimes picks winners and losers.

How It Became This Way

Prior to the advent of the Internet, mobile, cable and satellite services, major media companies were protected from new competition by high start-up/operating costs and, in the case of radio and television, government regulations that limit the number of broadcast licenses in any area. The advent of cable TV channels in the 1980s and the launch of direct-to-home satellites in the 1990s began the audience fragmentation process.

At first, the competition grew slowly. Cable and satellite systems required substantial start-up and operating costs as well, so the initial effects of audience fragmentation were relatively small. Newspapers and television stations continued growing revenue, even as audiences shrank. As late as 2006, some newspapers and television stations were still reporting record profits.

Then came the real game changers: widespread broadband Internet access and smartphones. By the end of 2007, more than half of Americans were accessing online content via broadband connections.[2] The increased speed made viewing video and engaging in other online activities easier and more enjoyable for millions of Americans and resulted in further audience fragmentation.

Just a few years later, smartphone adoption took off. No longer was new media consumption limited by Internet access at home or at work. Smartphones changed the paradigm, offering untethered access to new media choices 24 hours a day.

Along with smartphones and tablets came the introduction of mobile apps. Apps lowered the cost of entry for new media start-ups. The introduction of iTunes and Google Play gave consumers the ability to become immediately aware of new apps and sort through all choices in a single place.

The competition between Android and iOS operating systems, along with competition among wireless carriers, accelerated the introduction of more smartphones and tablets, lowering the cost of entry to consumers. Reduction in entry costs dramatically accelerated fragmentation, creating new pressure on traditional media, especially newspapers and television.

More Challenges

To put fragmentation in full context, one must understand that consumption of news and information is only part of the story. Consumers are also faced with a continuing explosion of other media choices, from entertainment to shopping to games. Consumers must navigate a constantly changing landscape in what is still a fixed 1,440-minute day.

The recession of 2008 and 2009 fully exposed the economic peril of massive audience fragmentation. Newspapers and television stations that had continued to grow revenue and profit in spite of fragmentation suddenly found

PHOTO 10-1 By offering both immediate choice and connectivity, smartphones changed the media landscape by moving power to the consumer.

themselves facing dramatic losses in advertising.[3] Newspaper subscriptions, which ad rates are based upon, and which were already in decline because of media fragmentation, also dropped precipitously, further reducing print advertising revenue and profit.

Add to all of this the fact that before the recession, consolidation – the process of larger companies buying competitors – had caused many large newspaper and television companies to acquire massive debt. Even after dramatic employee layoffs and other cost reductions, many of these companies found themselves unable to make payments on their debt. For some, such as Tribune Co., bankruptcy was the only option.

Now, in the post-recession years, news media companies find themselves operating in a landscape with traditional media struggling to replace former profits. Most companies created new revenue by expanding traditional products onto new digital platforms, but new advertising on these platforms rarely has exceeded the cost of content production. New media, such as websites, apps and mobile advertising with no ties to legacy platforms, also struggled to find successful business plans.

In many cases, new websites and apps chose advertising as their revenue model, primarily because free, ad-supported models gain new users more quickly than paid models. This explosion of new ad-supported media choices reinforced a consumer perception that information, especially over the Internet and wireless, was "free."[4]

The 4 C's Strategy: Change

In 2008, when the economy collapsed and more uses for information technology burst onto the scene, most media companies were confused and lost and didn't know how to react to the double whammy. They had the choice of going with the beautiful seductive mistress called digital or fighting against the old man called economy. The majority selected digital, but unfortunately, very few entities have been able to develop a strategy for making money. In the sea of change, legacy media so far have tried to achieve some revenue from digital, but without much success.

So how can we learn from and use the big sea of change in our business model to depend more on the customer and make more money, whether the customer is a user, reader or advertiser? We have to end the "information welfare society." We have created a society that is accustomed to receiving content for free. In order for us to bring about the right kind of change, we need to create a start-up mentality in our news organizations, offering customers the kind of content for which they will pay.

The reality, of course, is that nothing is ever free. A media organization of any kind must create infrastructure, pay employees and cover myriad recurring hard costs. This is as true for a new app as it is for a traditional daily newspaper. Launching and maintaining a new digital business may be far less expensive than printing and distributing a newspaper, but nonetheless, at some point costs must be covered and a level of profit created.

MEDIA REVENUE MODELS

There are three major business models for monetizing media. The all-access model, in which content is free or one price for all content on all available platforms; the "bait and switch" model, in which companies offer limited free access and then charge for frequent use; and finally, the a la carte approach, in which every form of delivery is priced separately, sometimes called the iTunes model.

Advertising, subscription fees or one-time payments are at the heart of all revenue models, and it's not unusual for a single company to make money using multiple revenue models. For example, newspapers, cable systems and magazines are platforms that both sell advertising and charge a fee to the consumer. Television and radio, available over the air for free, have been historically supported by advertising but now also receive indirect payments from cable, satellite and phone company video distributors.

Understanding the true value of content is difficult because of factors such as exclusive newspaper distribution networks and the ability of television stations to receive copyright fees from cable systems. A newspaper that owns a large distribution system can sell content for a higher price than a paper with limited distribution. Some television stations receive copyright fees from cable and satellite providers called "retransmission fees," in return for allowing station programming to be distributed via the systems. Smartphone content must first go through a cell provider's exclusive wireless network, for which consumers typically pay.

The value of content also varies because of competition. Television advertising rates depend, in part, on what competing television stations charge. Cable subscription fees vary based on the availability of competing services from phone and satellite companies.

The value of media is further muddled by the practice of websites aggregating content that was originally produced by others. Aggregation of news is a complex issue that has resulted in lawsuits and mixed court rulings.

In the end, the cost of producing product is always passed on to the consumer, either by direct payments or indirectly through the cost of advertised goods and services.

Newspaper Revenue

Newspapers are the classic example of media organizations funded by dual revenue streams. More than 70 percent of a typical newspaper's revenue comes from advertising. The remainder comes from subscriptions and single-copy sales. Newspapers base advertising rates on the number of copies sold, known as "circulation." The circulation of major papers is measured by the Alliance for Audited Media, an independent agency.[5]

As the post-recession value of newspaper advertising declined, papers that had offered free access to their websites began to see those sites as potential sources of new revenue. Newspaper consultant Gary Randazzo says making newspaper websites profitable has been extremely difficult because of a serious structural mistake early on:

"When they created digital products, most newspapers in the United States bundled the Internet with the print. They were giving the Internet ads away free. It happened all across the industry. They put it together in a nice package, and they did that many times with other distribution products and ROP [run of paper] products. What that does is make it very difficult to determine the real value you have created. You don't know if you are making a profit or what that profit is related to."

Specialty newspapers with exclusive content, like The Wall Street Journal, charged subscription fees for the Web content, called "pay walls," early on, as did other unique printed products, including many magazines. Seeing those successes, newspapers realized they must eventually find ways to move the newspaper subscription model to the Web.

The first entry of a major metro newspaper into a pay wall was The New York Times in 2011. In 2012, Gannett, the nation's largest newspaper chain, announced all of its metro papers would eventually create pay walls. Randazzo says these efforts might eventually be successful, "but anytime you make a strategic misread and you go back to correct it, it is very expensive and sometimes not possible."

What is possible, according to Randazzo, is for papers to create "a symbiotic array of products that creates value across a number of metrics and allows you to see how the market is morphing so you can manage it better. As soon as one part becomes more valuable, you go to it."

Randazzo is talking about using the unique strengths of media platforms to support each other, then expanding the consumers' favorite choices. For instance, a static car ad in a newspaper might point the reader to the paper's website or a specialized app to view video of the car and access more details. Should the app be especially successful, it could serve as a model for other new, similar apps.

Newspapers have also worked to reduce the cost of payroll and infrastructure, cutting staff and introducing technological solutions wherever possible. Some newspapers have also exited the printing business – instead they outsource that task, creating an opportunity for other papers to make more efficient use of their presses.

But simply erecting pay walls and reducing costs in today's consumer-driven world is not enough. As the result of a 2014 internal study, former New York Times editor Jill Abramson said in a staff memo that "our competitors are often taking our stories and advantaging themselves with our content on their platforms, even developing paid apps from stories that were ours originally." She also said the newsroom needs to create "greater cooperation and harmonizing with our business side colleagues."[6]

PHOTO 10-2 As the audience for traditional print drops, newspapers struggle to convert to new platforms. Ironically, the majority of revenue still comes from the traditional printed product.

©iStockphoto.com/ 3Dmask

For many publications, "cooperating and harmonizing" between editorial and advertising departments means adding paid content to publications. Changing the relationship between advertising content and journalism content is controversial. Major news organizations are faced with the difficult task of finding new content-based advertising opportunities while still protecting news reporting from advertiser influence.

Though newspapers have somewhat stabilized in recent years through staff cuts, print outsourcing and improvements in technology, they continue to face a maze of challenges and an uncertain future. Not the least of these challenges is the trend of traditional media companies to spin off their newspaper assets into new companies. In 2014, Gannett, Scripps Howard, Tribune and Journal Communications all announced the separation of newspaper and television assets. As a result, newspapers owned by these new print-centric companies are no longer able to rely on profits from television to support the papers.[7]

Gordon Borrell, a media industry researcher, believes newspapers will survive, but not as mass media. "I don't think you can call newspapers mass media anymore," he says. "They are niche media. You don't find newspapers that are in more than 50 percent of homes."

Borrell's view is that newspapers will not go away, but they will dramatically change. "No media has died as a result of a new one coming along. It's just the new media has kind of peeled away the growth and affected the margins. I think that trend will continue. I think every medium, even paper, has its own benefits. It will be a struggle to morph into something and change, just like radio had to morph, but in the end the only medium I don't see viability for is Yellow Pages."

Leadership Report – Gary Randazzo

PHOTO 10-3

Courtesy of Gary Randazzo

Founder, GWR Research

A former senior executive with the San Francisco Chronicle and the Houston Chronicle, Gary Randazzo develops and implements marketing, financial and management programs for major media companies throughout the United States.

As you look at the newspaper landscape today, you certainly have been part of some great ones and consulted others. What do you see as the future?

I think there are some bright people really trying to figure out how to move forward, and I think over time they will. I will tell you that from my perspective, there were some misreads that are going to be very difficult to correct.

Clayton Christensen says that leading industries fall by the wayside because new companies come in and start by serving the leading industries' least profitable customers

(Continued)

(Continued)

with a product that is good enough. Once that happens, they can make a profit where the industry leader might not.

Those are called disruptive innovations. There is something called a sustaining innovation. If it comes along, it is something an industry leader can use to serve its most profitable customers better.

The misread that took place back in the late '90s was that the Internet was a disruptive innovation. It wasn't a disruptive innovation, going back to the definition. It takes away your least profitable customers and provides a good enough product. Monster.com and all those things that revitalized the classified section did not attract the least profitable customer. It attracted a very profitable segment, and they did not provide just a good enough product; it was a product that was better than the print in its ability to find the right products for the right things.

What if there had not been a misread? What if they had understood exactly what was going to happen? What would they have done differently?

Rather than creating a separate entity that had Internet classifieds like newspaper classifieds, they would have put the Internet for classifieds in the classified department. They would have created Craigslist. Some ad director somewhere would have said, "Hey, this stuff makes it a lot easier. We can do these kinds of things."

Today's newspaper managers are aware of the issues. They know what is going on. How does today's newspaper culture affect the future? Are they able to make changes?

Changing culture needs to be focused on a business outcome. The culture can change, but I'm not sure it lends itself to print. I'm not sure print will be the answer, but it will be part of the answer for a good while. I think what the industry has to do is have a plan for transition. The strategy has to be evolutionary, so changes are made as they go along.

Do you think that's happening at newspapers?

Yes, I do. The building of social networks is part of it. There are newspapers that are looking at their audiences and saying, "Here's a group of people who are really interested in our local football team, so we are going to create a social network around that. We're going to have interactions. We're going to have events. We're going to have stories in the paper." So they've created a symbiotic array of products to serve that group that covers all platforms. That allows them to monitor what is happening and to determine which of the platforms are going to get the most use and how the transition is progressing.

And, some of these are able to create value and make a profit while they do that.

Let me ask you about pay walls. The New York Times created the first buzz. Companies like Gannett have said all their papers are going to pay walls. Will they be successful? What will it mean for the economics of newspapers?

I think that if you create a pay wall, you can replicate that subscription model that has worked so well for so many years. You are able to say to advertisers, "I can deliver to you a group of people every day." The thing that created it in the beginning with print product was value. Content value.

I think The New York Times and The Wall Street Journal both have cache, and they create real value. They have content you can't find other places. People will subscribe because "I read it in The New York Times" or "I read it in The Wall Street Journal" and because they can't read it someplace else.

How do you create that value with a local metro paper?

That's where the editors really have to start thinking. How do we create real content of value for our readers? For a long time a lot of smaller and even metro newspapers picked up wire services as a huge part of their newspapers. In recent years they've changed that.

It's up to the editors to find good reporters who can create good content that is controlled and owned by the newspaper.

Television Revenue

Like newspapers, content is at the heart of television. Television also faces many of the same challenges, primarily massive audience fragmentation. Unlike newspapers, television has the advantage of new revenue streams that have, for the moment, bolstered television's economic viability.

Local television stations and national networks receive the majority of their revenue from the sale of commercials, known in the industry as "spot" advertising. "Spot" refers to individual commercials, as opposed to program sponsorships. Local stations also receive advertising revenue from their mobile and websites and their digital sub-channels, often referred to as "D2" channels.

Commercial advertising rates for stations are usually based on demographic ratings measured by Nielsen Television. The demographics are measured using a variety of means including "people meters" and traditional household meters. After more than a half-century using paper diaries, in some markets Nielsen is now moving to technology designed to impute demographic ratings.

Nielsen demographic ratings are broken down in a variety of ways, including age, sex and race. By far the most widely coveted demographic for advertisers is "adults aged 25 to 54," but depending on the product being promoted, advertisers may choose to target a more narrow audience, purchasing access to other categories such as "women aged 18 to 49."

As we have seen in other chapters, media audiences are far more complex than simple demographics. By those measures Nielsen ratings seem to be an antiquated standard.

Wayne Freedman, vice president of sales for Raycom Media, says, "If I am the head of marketing for a big brand and you are telling me the only metrics you can give me are what people are writing in the diary four times a year, I don't have a lot of confidence in that. So, that's leading to the growth of things like Rentrak and set-top measurement."

Rentrak is a media measurement and research company that tracks viewing behavior from millions of televisions across all TV markets. The company gathers its data from set-top boxes – devices used to deliver cable and satellite TV to homes.

PHOTO 10-4 As you can see in the company's brand statement, Rentrak portrays itself as able to fully measure movie and television consumption on all platforms. While a notable goal, Rentrak's primary measurement tool is satellite television boxes. The company does not yet measure over-the-air television viewing, a factor that has limited its ability to replace Nielsen as the primary provider of television audience measurement.

RENTRAK

PRECISELY MEASURING
MOVIES & TV EVERYWHERE

Freedman also points out that ratings alone do not determine a station's revenue. "At Raycom we control what we can control and don't control what we can't," he says. "Things we can control are making sure our sales resources and our people are focused on local and business development and the Internet and mobile. Those are the growth areas in our business."

Unlike newspapers, which continue to experience a decline in advertising, some television stations are experiencing revenue growth and have rebounded to historical levels of advertising and profit. As Freedman points out, this is due, in part, to new platform revenue (sub-channel, Web, mobile). It is also due to retransmission revenue and to the fact that some former newspaper advertisers are moving to television.

Television also benefits from a biennial influx of political advertising. The fact that politicians still spend most of their advertising dollars on local television validates the continuing value of the medium.

Leadership Report – Wayne Freedman

PHOTO 10-5

Courtesy of Wayne Freedman

Vice President, Sales, Raycom Media

A former vice president of business development with Gannett Broadcasting and executive vice president and chief marketing officer for Wolf Camera, Wayne Freedman's mission is to leverage the collective strength, experience and success of Raycom stations to generate greater revenue across all broadcast and digital platforms.

Stations like those owned by Raycom currently have many lines of revenue in addition to spot commercials: D2 sub-channels, retransmission consent and Web. How do you see the future?

I'm extremely optimistic. There is a lot at stake, but I believe there will continue to be a role for local broadcast and our related platforms. I'm speaking specifically from the advertising side, but I think when anything big happens, particularly when it is local breaking news or weather, I think the sheer power and the critical role this medium plays in the lives of our viewers becomes evident. And I don't see that changing. I certainly see fragmentation as a big issue. I see time shifting as an issue – but when all is said and done, I think it is a very strong business model.

If you are selling cars, or any kind of big-ticket item, there seems to be a sense you have to have broadcast television in order to have reach. Would you agree with that?

To me, it's the mindset of the advertiser or the business person, and if the business person wants to grow and wants to have the top share of voice and wants to have the highest market share in their particular business or profession, then yes, they probably need to be on broadcast TV because it's the biggest megaphone and biggest way to make people aware of and respond to your message.

What about the smaller TV stations, the WBs, the independents, those that don't have the big megaphone and consequently don't have Web revenue, much D2 sub-channel revenue or retransmission consent? What's their future?

I think that it's still very good. We do have some myTV affiliates. We also have a lot of D2. We are an investor in the Bounce network, which is an African-American network that's been very, very successful.

I believe their dependency on traditional advertising is sustainable, at least for the foreseeable future. One of the things that we are seeing is that by using all the different channels that we have available – Web, mobile and digital sub-channels – we are able to be a lot more creative and provide a lot more robust solutions for our clients.

Do you think D2 sub-channels will at some point become full-service television stations when the technology enables that?

Yes. There's a fascinating statistic right now. According to Nielsen, there are 60 million consumers in the United States who rely on over-the-air television every day. They watch television in some form, maybe at their office or home, maybe on their mobile device where it's over-the-air. There is no cord, no cable, no satellite. A D2 to a broadcast-only household is a whole different value proposition than, say, in satellite or cable households. With over-the-top television and with people now relying on old-fashioned TV antennas, that puts the value proposition of the D2 in a whole different light.

(Continued)

(Continued)

We are seeing more and more stations streaming on cell phones. What's the future of television on smartphones?

We think it's huge. It's still very rudimentary and the numbers are not huge, but as the technology improves and as the promotion and awareness improves, I think this is a big, big part of the future. A phone that used to be a phone is now many, many other things. It's your calendar and it's your email and it's your Internet connectivity. And people have just come to recognize that their phone is basically their life. And they are coming to recognize that they can watch a lot of television on it.

Is there an opportunity for over-the-air broadcasters at some point to get direct consumer payments?

I know newspaper sites have been experimenting with pay walls. I think if you read the stock reports, they are trying to put a positive spin on that. We would love to look at it, but I don't see that happening anytime in the near future. There have been some statistics that viewers are willing to accept advertising in exchange for free access to content. I think there is much less willingness for people to pay for that content. Certainly there are many pay sites out there, but on the TV side, I think our future is more ad supported than it is pay wall.

Once you get down to stations that are in markets 40 to 50, a very interesting thing is happening, and that is newspapers have cut way back. Not just dropping their subscribers down, but they are not producing seven days. They are producing maybe three or four days.

And the newspaper is physically a fraction of what it used to be. Now they are trying to put more robust assets on their digital sites, but what is happening is, in many cases, our stations have become the de facto local news resource in those markets. And so, if there ever was an opportunity to charge, maybe $2.99 a month, or whatever the model is – your first 20 stories free – it probably would work more in a middle to small market where there isn't as much competition. So, I do think it is definitely an option for us to consider, and we are looking at it, but to this point we haven't implemented it, and I don't think it's going to happen anytime real soon.

Where do you see measurement going? Will we get to the point everything is measured?

I think it almost has to be because that's what clients are demanding. Clients want to know what they are getting, and I think that one of the reasons the Internet has grown so much is because it does provide metrics. I think that's a big challenge for our business. The good news is we know it works. We have hundreds, if not thousands, of success stories that we try to use, but I think for us to get back to a point where the business is growing with national marketers we have to have better metrics – and everything does have to be measured.

Beyond Advertising

Though advertising money is by far the most important source of revenue for television stations, many also receive fees from other sources.

Up until the early 21st century, television networks shared a percentage of their advertising revenue with local affiliates. This process, called "network compensation," was especially important to smaller affiliates that had lower advertising revenue than large market stations.

Over time, networks gained more power over their relationship with affiliates and began to phase network compensation out. Led initially by Fox, networks then began charging affiliates a programming fee known as "reverse compensation."

Retransmission Consent

Stronger television stations, primarily those that carry local news, are also able to demand copyright fee payments from cable, telecoms and direct-to-home services such as Dish Network and DirecTV. These copyright fees are known as "retransmission consent" payments.

Prior to Congress changing the law in 1992, cable and satellite companies did not have to pay local television stations copyright fees. The 1992 Cable Act gave stations a choice of two options in dealing with cable companies. Weak stations and nonprofits, such as PBS, were able to choose "must carry" status. Under "must carry," cable companies were required to carry a station, but paid no fees. Stronger stations elected "retransmission consent," meaning cable companies had to negotiate carriage. This usually meant paying stations a monthly fee per subscriber.[8]

As retransmission consent fees grew, networks began to demand stations share a portion of the fees as a copyright license to the networks. Called "reverse compensation," as mentioned earlier in the chapter, as much as 50 percent of a station's retransmission fees now go to the station's network. These fees are likely to grow over time.

Retransmission consent is controversial because negotiations occasionally result in a temporary loss of station service for the audience on a cable or satellite system at the end of a contract.

Cable/Satellite/Telecom Revenue

Cable companies, also known as multiple system operators (MSOs), gain the majority of their revenue from monthly subscription payments. Large MSOs also sell local advertising during cable network programs. Many cable companies also own regional cable news networks that compete with local stations for news audience and advertising revenue.

Direct-to-home satellite services are direct competitors to cable systems. Like cable, satellite services carry both local stations and cable networks. Satellite services are most prominent in rural areas that would be expensive for cable services to wire.

Satellite differs from cable in two important ways: Spectrum limitations mean few local sub-channels (D2) are carried on satellite; broader coverage areas make it difficult to sell local television commercials.

Many telephone companies also offer cable television services. Verizon's FiOS and AT&T's U-verse are prominent examples. Like cable companies, telecoms also have the ability to sell local advertising.

Cable, satellite and telecoms are able to compete directly with each other because all carry the same major cable networks. They pay a "per subscriber" fee to the networks they carry. These fees are then passed on to consumers as part of their monthly bills. "Per subscriber" fees are also paid to some television stations as part of retransmission consent agreements.

Newspapers, television and cable/satellite/telecoms are known as traditional media, in part because they rely on established distribution systems. These systems are a strength because they are generally exclusive and therefore a barrier to entry. But when technology leapfrogs the barrier, the cost of maintaining those systems can become a competitive liability.

Digital Media Revenue

Digital media can be broadly defined as any media that is transmitted via the Internet or wireless systems. Also called "new media" because it is not distributed by traditional systems, digital media can be highly targeted and enjoys the advantage of consumer interactivity.

The relatively low cost of entry means digital media businesses do not have a single method of earning revenue. Common funding mechanisms include:

Advertising Revenue

The most common form of funding is advertising revenue. Web and mobile sites sell numerous types of text and video ads. Most general news sites are funded by advertising primarily because general news has become a commodity, making it difficult to charge subscriptions.

Subscription Revenue

The most common form of funding for sites with exclusive products is subscription revenue. Sites with original reporting, such as The Wall Street Journal and Consumer Reports, are examples. Because they also contain original material, many magazine sites are funded by subscriptions. Led by The New York Times, many newspapers are also erecting pay walls. So far, success has been mixed.

Agenda Funding

Product manufacturers, political organizations, government agencies and other organizations fund sites to advance their message or agenda. In some cases, sites are funded in lieu of spending money on advertising.

Public Service Sites

Public service sites are often privately funded, offering their services without advertising or charge. Craigslist is perhaps the best-known site that does not collect revenue.

Blogs/Personal Websites

Some major blogs are funded by advertising, but the majority are funded by the author.

Because most digital media companies do not have the advantage of exclusive distribution platforms, they have a clear understanding that content is the key to their success.

This understanding of the importance of content has made many advertisers look for ways to produce their own articles, videos, apps and other forms of media to deepen their relationships with consumers, sometimes publishing and distributing the content on their own as well. Using content, rather than traditional advertising, is controversial. Some journalists believe any advertiser foray into content is somehow illegitimate, especially if it's published on a traditional news outlet. Others counter that advertiser-produced content, when fully disclosed, plays an important new role that is not only legitimate, but welcomed by consumers.

CONTENT MARKETING

Sponsored or paid content goes under a number of names, including native advertising and advertorials. It is produced by companies, their ad agencies or publishers themselves in a variety of forms.

The most common form of content marketing is native advertising. Native advertising is sponsored content, often written by an advertiser or advertising agency, which appears within what has traditionally been the editorial section of a publication. Because it is in fact paid advertising, these sections are often identified by terms such as Special Advertiser Section, Produced by (name of advertiser) or Advertiser Spotlight.

Native advertising can also be produced by a publication's staff. This practice can be controversial. As we saw in Chapter 2, a media company's brand value is dependent on consumer trust. Therefore full disclosure is critical.

Companies participating in native advertising are a Who's Who of mainstream media names, including Time Inc., Forbes, The Wall Street Journal, The New York Times and many others. Native ads are also found in new Web and app media publications, ranging from BuzzFeed to Slate.

Tony Hallett, writing in The Guardian, which has aggressively moved into native advertising, believes "the quality and scalability of native advertising means it is filling the gap between brand publishing and banner adverts," seeing it "as a subset of the catch-all content marketing, meaning the practice of using content to build trust and engagement with would-be customers."[9]

The fundamental difference between native advertising and traditional ads is that native ads are actually within the flow of editorial content, usually as stand-alone articles. To be effective, native ads must be factually based and of high quality, offering the user important and helpful information. In other words, native ads must offer genuine user benefits.

PHOTO 10-6 Notice the Taco Bell logo and body reference in the BuzzFeed screenshot. As an advertising partner with BuzzFeed, Taco Bell is able to produce consumer material that many traditional media companies would reject.

Politics   Tech   Lifestyle   Food   Rewind   Celeb   Music   LGBT   Sp

10 Photos From 2012 That Should've Never Been Shared

Some things are just meant to be kept to yourself, just like the new Taco Bell Loaded Grillers, amazing appetizers you don't have to share.

posted about 6 days ago

Taco Bell
BuzzFeed Partner

  Not everything needs to be shared.   LET ME SHARE THIS!
99¢ Loaded Grillers from Taco Bell. Appetizers for one.

Source: http://www.bing.com/images/search?q=native+advertising&FORM=HDRSC2#view=detail&id=4500F7E5E9E9CB659736B1AD9D086938E36714B6&selectedIndex=56.

Hallett says, "Those publications that are pioneering native ads are usually good at making sure the quality of the content is high. They won't just commission content (for money, we should make clear), but work with individual writers or marketers so that it feeds an audience need."

"And it seems to be working. According to research from IPG media lab, native ads are viewed for the same amount of time as editorial content and [a native ad] is much more likely to be shared than a banner ad (32% versus 19% of respondents said they would do so)."[10]

Of course, as we stated earlier, publications offering native advertising must also protect their journalistic credibility by identifying the source of native advertising to the reader/user.

Native advertising, and other forms of content-based advertising, are controversial and may remain so. Nevertheless, advertisers, their agencies and media companies themselves will continue to develop nontraditional ways to deliver their messages to consumers. The key to success will be doing so without breaking trust with the user.

EVENT MARKETING

Event marketing is the process of creating a special event, promoted and/or produced by a media company around a particular subject that appeals to a target group of consumers. Events are often live, but can also be online. The goal of the event is to offer a rich in-person (or virtual in-person) experience that creates great value to the consumer about a particular subject. Done right, events not only generate revenue; they deepen the brand relationship.

From the consumer's point of view, an event is a personal experience offering the opportunity for immersion in a subject the consumer is strongly interested in. The two-way nature of the event also adds value because it allows the consumer to become an active participant. Interaction with other participants adds further value and uniqueness to the event.

To be successful, an event must do more than leverage the media company's core brand and offer interesting subjects. It must provide a satisfying experience based on content that has real value. The Wall Street Journal, for example, offers a wide range of financial and investment events year round, some of which are seen as so valuable they are by invitation only.[11]

The New York Times Travel Show is an example of a live event that leverages the value of a sub-brand. Held annually at the Jacob K. Javits Convention Center, the Travel Show imputes The New York Times' Travel Section reputation to the more than 500 exhibitors and sponsors who pay The Times to be part of show. According to the event's website, more than 20,000 travelers and industry professionals attend, paying from $17 to $45 per person.[12]

The Times does not report profits from its individual events, but the Travel Show is clearly a revenue stream not directly dependent on newspaper circulation.

Like other brand extensions, successful event marketing does more than create new revenue. It builds on the existing relationship with consumers, further strengthening value of the brand.

PHOTO 10-7 The New York Times Travel Show extends the paper's brand and creates new revenue streams beyond newspaper and digital advertising.

Michael Loccisano/Getty Images

AMAZON.COM: A DIGITAL EXCLUSIVE DISTRIBUTION SYSTEM

Amazon.com began as an online bookstore, selling books as a commodity. Consumers would select a title on Amazon's website, order and pay on the site, then have the book shipped to their homes. Because it did not have the cost of a traditional storefront chain, Amazon was able to sell books at a lower price, forcing storefronts to compete on price. When a product becomes a commodity, low price always wins.

Amazon's business model allowed it to grow and add other categories, eventually becoming the world's largest online retailer.

But Amazon's success also created vulnerability. Consumers who buy on a commodity basis are only loyal to price. News organizations that give away their content for free have created a similar vulnerability, so they need a way to deepen consumer relationships beyond price.

In the case of Amazon, the answer was to create an exclusive distribution system called Amazon Prime. For $99 a year, Amazon Prime offers two things: free two-day shipping on eligible items and exclusive access to Amazon's video content. Amazon also sells a range of video players, known as Kindle Fire. Kindle Fire devices perform many of the same functions as mainstream tablets, but are characterized by their integration into the Amazon infrastructure.

Consumers who buy a Kindle Fire and subscribe to Amazon Prime are part of an exclusive distribution system built on the same principles as traditional newspapers and television stations. In addition, Amazon Prime members have access to unique content, including a recently announced sitcom produced by Woody Allen, unavailable anywhere else.

Though still vulnerable to other commodity sellers, Amazon has leveraged its exclusive distribution system to create new products and services consumers are willing to pay for. Newspapers and television stations have a similar opportunity to leverage existing networks. The key is to produce unique content readers/viewers are willing to pay for.

IMPACT OF REGULATION ON FUTURE BUSINESS MODELS

The First Amendment to the United States Constitution guarantees the right of a free press, able to print whatever the editors see fit without prior restraint. Framers of the Constitution saw the press as a "Fourth Estate," holding government accountable to the people. This means newspapers have traditionally enjoyed an absolute right to free speech.

One of the foremost questions in media is "How does the First Amendment apply to media beyond the traditional printed press, especially media such as television and radio, and now wireless media, that operate on spectrum licensed by the federal government?" That question will continue to play out over time and will certainly have an impact on the business models for news media companies. What is clear is that government is very involved in regulating the business of electronic media.

Spectrum, the means of transmission for all wireless media, is deemed to be owned "by the people" in the same sense that national parks and government buildings are owned "by the people." Like parks and buildings, spectrum is regulated. But what of wired services such as cable television? What about the Internet? What role does "net neutrality," the ability of Internet providers to speed up or slow down the delivery of Web content, play? These factors create a complex playing field that varies the regulation of new media.

The picture is further clouded by the number of government agencies involved with media regulation. The Federal Communications Commission (FCC) issues and regulates spectrum licenses. The Federal Trade Commission actively investigates collusion among media company competitors. The Federal Aviation Administration regulates broadcast and cell towers. The Justice Department prosecutes illegal activities such as fraudulent billing for advertising. Court decisions sometimes radically change business practices. In short, the congressional, executive and judicial branches are all actively involved with regulating media in a complex tapestry of rules and regulations.

The vast array of agencies, policies and politics means the effect of government on media is not always predictable. What is clear is that government sometimes picks winners and losers as in the current debate over Internet paid prioritization, also known as net neutrality.

Leadership Report – Mark Prak

PHOTO 10-8

Courtesy of Mark Prak

Partner, Brooks Pierce

One of the nation's leading media attorneys, Mark Prak serves clients who span the full range of media industries from television, newspapers, magazines and cable to new media enterprises. He is a frequent speaker on media issues at national and state bar associations and industry trade associations.

You work with the FCC, other government agencies and the federal court system on media regulation issues. How has regulation changed over the years?

The regulatory system metamorphoses over time and is influenced by issues of the day. For instance, net neutrality is perceived to be about blocking content, but no one really blocks content. The core argument is whether or not over-the-top providers have to

(Continued)

(Continued)

pay anything to interconnect with the ISPs [Internet service providers], notwithstanding the amount of traffic or number of bits they want to push through the pipe.

Then you are saying complete net neutrality cannot exist because usage varies.

That's a huge issue because at some point everything can't be free. There is a cost of transport. Somebody transporting billions of bits of information. Netflix transmits more information than you or I, so why should you or I pay for Netflix's business model?

"Net neutrality" is a great catchphrase, but it can mean all things to all people. To some it means as fast as they want it to be without any additional cost to them. That's one thing if you are a user like you or me. It might be another thing if you are a commercial provider of material.

Highly regulated media, such as television, argue they are disadvantaged by the fact most new media is unregulated.

I would argue many of the regulations are no longer rational. The Internet, which has not been heavily regulated, has been hugely successful and a great forum for free speech.

Take the newspaper/television cross-ownership rule. We've got newspapers going out of business every day. There is simply no reason for the government to say that a radio or television station couldn't buy a newspaper and combine the two newsrooms into one.

My response to people concerned about media consolidation is they are banging a useless drum. Anyone with $60 can start a website. We've got more media diversity today than has ever existed in the history of the world.

Once you put regulatory structures and principles in place, it is hard to get rid of them even after they have outlived their usefulness.

Retransmission consent, the right of television stations to be paid for carriage of their signal, is another hot future issue.

At the end of the day, intellectual property is critical. If you are going to pay a million dollars an episode to produce a Hollywood program and have exclusive distribution rights to it, it is simply not tenable to allow someone else to steal your product and then resell it without securing a license or sublicense from you.

Right now the networks and local stations are all trying to find a way to get their signals onto the platforms. Every possible platform they can. Every digital iPad, iPhone and Android device. You name it. They want to make it accessible wherever people happen to be and on whatever device they are using. I think that is going to happen.

Is the consumer the ultimate decision maker?

Absolutely. One way or another. The question is "How much do you value these products and services?"

At the end of the day, we will all be negotiating for things we value, and the argument will be how they are priced.

Theory in Practice – Revenue Management

Using revenue management theory, companies rely on a collection of strategies and tactics to scientifically manage demand for their products and services.

In the early 1990s, revenue management began to influence television ad sales. Companies like ABC and NBC developed systems that automated the placement of ads based on total forecasted demand and forecasted ratings by program.

Now other media and telecom businesses are leveraging revenue management, especially those that have typically attracted customers with discounted plans and then retained them at higher price points – the cell phone service providers, for example. The process of revenue management, which Robert Cross describes in his book "Revenue Management," can help companies understand niche markets and forecast demand, so they can optimize advertising and price points.

Data collection – the process begins by gathering as much information as possible about prices, demand and customers that can reveal consumer behavioral patterns, the impact of competitors' actions, and other important market information.

Market segmentation – using the collected data, customers are segmented into groups based on how much they will pay for certain products under certain conditions. That information is then used to calculate the maximum amount of revenue possible for the product.

Forecasting – the revenue management process also requires forecasting audience demand and total market, among other factors. The company's overall success with revenue management often depends on the quality of these forecasts.

Optimization – based on the first three steps in this process, optimization involves determining how a company should respond. This is where you decide how and to whom you will sell or deliver your product.

Re-evaluation – to be effective over the long haul, companies must continually go through all the steps in the revenue management process.[13]

As news media companies introduce new products or come up with new pricing schemes for their existing services, revenue management practices can be a useful tool.

EXECUTIVE SUMMARY

Like all other products and services, journalism must have a working business model. In the case of media, the model is funded by the consumer, through either consumption of advertising or direct payment.

Today's fragmented landscape requires traditional media platforms such as newspapers and television stations to compete directly with new media platforms such as apps and websites. The goal is to gain a portion of the consumer's fixed 1,440-minute day. The continuing introduction of new technology, particularly wireless devices, means fragmentation will continue to grow exponentially and competition will continue to increase.

To remain relevant in this changing landscape, media companies must now compete on the basis of content and brand value. Media companies and advertisers are also looking for new ways to leverage their content and brands using ideas such as content marketing.

Government also plays a role in today's media landscape, serving as business regulator and occasional wild card dealer.

Today's consumer wields tremendous power in the success or failure of all media. The future of all media companies is dependent on their ability to satisfy the consumer.

THINK AND DO

You are the advertising manager of WXXX, a major television station in Tulsa, Oklahoma.

Research shows that Tulsa viewers have a very high interest in local weather, especially during tornado season.

Your station is the market leader in local news and weather. Part of WXXX's success is its emphasis on weather coverage, especially during tornado emergencies.

Because Tulsa is a competitive television market, the other major stations also place great emphasis on weather coverage. One has an arrangement with the local newspaper for its chief meteorologist to produce the paper's daily weather page. Another station has a website and app devoted exclusively to weather coverage. Weather.com is also a major player in Tulsa, as are at least two radio stations.

As the market leader, WXXX has a very successful news and weather website and a successful news and weather mobile app. The station now must decide if it should also launch a stand-alone weather app. You have been asked to lead a group that will make the decision. Should you put all emphasis on the current app or also add a new weather-only app?

Things to Consider

- Your current news and weather app is very successful. Will a weather-only app dilute the use of your current app?
- Another market station already has a weather app. Does it make sense to add another?
- Weather audiences in Tulsa are already fragmented. Won't this new app just add to the fragmentation?
- What about the effort it will take to make the app successful? Won't this take attention from other important projects? How do you decide?
- Will new advertising sales support the new app?

NOTES

1. Miguel Helft, "CNN's Jeff Zucker: Digital Is Our Future," *Fortune*, July 23, 2013, retrieved from http://fortune.com/2013/07/23/cnns-jeff-zucker-digital-is-our-future/ on March 3, 2015.

2. Lee Rainie, "Internet, Broadband, and Cell Phone Statistics," Pew Research Center, Jan. 5, 2010, retrieved from http://www.pewinternet.org/2010/01/05/internet-broadband-and-cell-phone-statistics/ on Feb. 27, 2015.

3. The Pew Research Center's Project for Excellence in Journalism, "The State of the News Media 2012," retrieved from http://www.stateofthemedia.org/2012/newspapers-building-digital-revenues-proves-painfully-slow/newspapers-by-the-numbers.

4. Mary Ellen Gordon, "The History of App Pricing and Why Most Apps Are Free," *Flurry*, July 18, 2013, retrieved from http://www.flurry.com/bid/99013/The-History-of-App-Pricing-And-Why-Most-Apps-Are-Free#.U4DDPybD-tU on Feb. 27, 2015.

5. "Newspaper Media Revenue 2013: Dollars Grow in Several Categories," Newspaper Association of America, retrieved from http://www.naa.org/Trends-and-Numbers/Newspaper-Revenue.aspx on Feb. 27, 2015.

6. Joe Pompeo, "New York Times Completes 'Innovation Report' Led by Sulzberger Scion," *Capital*, May 8, 2014, retrieved from http://www.capitalnewyork.com/article/media/2014/05/8545059/emnew-york-timesem-completes-innovation-report-led-sulzberger-scion on Feb. 27, 2015.

7. Roger Yu, "Gannett to Spin Off Publishing Business," *USA Today*, Aug. 6, 2014, retrieved from http://www.usatoday.com/story/money/business/2014/08/05/gannett-carscom-deal/13611915/ on Feb. 27, 2015.

8. Jeffrey A. Eisenach, "The Economics of Retransmission Content," Empiris LLC, March 2009, retrieved from http://www.nab.org/documents/resources/050809EconofRetransConsentEmpiris.pdf on Feb. 27, 2015.

9. Tony Hallett, "What Is Native Advertising Anyway?" *The Guardian*, retrieved from http://www.theguardian.com/media-network-outbrain-partner-zone/native-advertising-quality-scalability on Feb. 27, 2015.

10. Ibid.

11. "Executive Conferences From The Wall Street Journal," retrieved from http://wsj.com/conferences/ on Feb. 27, 2015.

12. "The New York Times Travel Show," retrieved from http://nyttravelshow.com/ on Feb. 27, 2015.

13. Robert G. Cross, "Revenue Management: Hard-Core Tactics for Market Domination," New York: Broadway Books, 1997.

11

Road Map for the Future

"If I was going to go into the world and inform people, and I could pick the day I walked in the door, it would be today. The opportunities to learn, to be curious, to help the world, to grow and engage a community. Just think of it. And we've barely scratched the surface."

—John Lavine
Founder of the Media Management Center, Former Dean at Medill

BENEFITS

- In this chapter, we look at the trends that will continue to change the shape of media.
- We study the ramifications of consumer-driven media.
- And we explore the important role journalists will play in the future of media.

STATE OF THE MEDIUM

As we have seen throughout this book, media is in transition. For most of the 20th century, the production and dissemination of news content was dominated by large institutions such as daily newspapers, magazines and television stations. High production and distribution costs limited the entry of new media businesses. Government licensing of television and radio stations also limited entry, further contributing to the dominance of mass media by major companies.

Two cultural tsunamis, consumer choice and consumer connectivity, changed the equation for all media, growing the power of consumers and lessening that of institutions. Choice and connectivity created a fragmented media world in which large institutions still mattered, but targeted media, such as apps, websites and social media, also played important parts. This transfer of control to the consumer continues and is accelerating.

Because the dominance of major media lasted for decades, many of today's journalism practices and business models still reflect an earlier time in which these institutions wielded enormous power.

As journalism and news media move toward the future, it is important to understand how and why power is shifting, what these shifts mean to the future of both journalism and journalism enterprises and what skills future journalists and news media managers will need to be successful.

THE POWER OF CHOICE

During most of the 20th century, consumer access to news was limited. Daily newspapers were published in either the morning or the afternoon. Television news aired at fixed times, with the most important stories reserved for early evening newscasts. Radio served as a headline service during the day, but the audio-only technology of radio limited details.

Consumer choice first appeared not with news, but with entertainment. The growth of cable television during the 1980s and 1990s gave consumers more viewing options than the three to five television stations that served most communities. The advent of satellite television in the 1990s also moved choice in entertainment programming to rural areas that did not have cable.

The advent of CNN in 1981 gave viewers, for the first time, a 24-hour source for news. Slow to grow at first, CNN came into its own during the 1991 Gulf War. The success of CNN eventually spawned competing cable news networks from NBC and Fox.

High-speed Internet, an early 21st-century phenomenon, changed the playing field once again, offering users direct access to news, information and entertainment from around the world. High-speed Internet also enabled video to be transmitted digitally, further changing the media playing field.

At first, high-speed Internet was limited to universities, businesses and the government. Consumers who enjoyed the improved online experience at work or school soon clamored for home access to high-speed service. As a result, both cable and phone companies quickly saw an opportunity to become service providers.

Handheld wireless devices, the forerunners of smartphones, were also initially introduced for business use. The first BlackBerry phone, incorporating both email and a cell phone, debuted in 2003 and was an instant success with business and government customers.

As was the case with high-speed Internet, so consumers also clamored for advanced mobile devices. This void began to be filled by Apple with release of its 2G iPhone in 2007, followed by a 3G version in 2008 and 4G in 2010. Google's announcement of an Open Handset Alliance in 2007 led to the introduction of Android phones in 2008.

The game changer for smartphones, and the consumer, came in 2010 with the introduction of 4G LTE service. 4G gave smartphones video and speed capability on par with high-speed Internet. This meant consumers no longer had to be tethered to a desktop to take full advantage of the Web.

The iPad, also introduced in 2010, gave consumers an additional unwired tool. iPads had the ability to connect to home and public wireless services as well as 4G networks. The iPad's immediate success caused both Android and Windows to enter the tablet field.

The availability of high-speed Internet, both cable and DSL, and the widespread availability of 4G LTE networks eventually made some form of high-speed connectivity accessible to most potential users. As technology continues to advance, so will speed and new forms of connectivity.

The upshot is that today's consumers find themselves with unprecedented media choices, much of it available on demand. That also means consumers can access news media when and where they choose. The advancement of app-based experiences, the development of integrated wearable technology and the lower cost of entry brought on by competition will continue to expand consumer choice well into the future.

When considering the rise of consumer power, one must also understand that choice, or competition, is not limited to media. Any activity that uses time, from coffee at Starbucks to working out at a health club, reduces the time consumers have left to spend with media. The less time a consumer has to invest in media, the more powerful consumer media decisions become.

As we look to the future, choice – both media and nonmedia choice – will continue to grow. That means future consumers will wield even greater power than they do today. As that power grows and technology improves, consumers will become more discerning and more demanding. News media companies that ignore the power of consumer choice will eventually find themselves marginalized.

THE POWER OF CONNECTIVITY

The social media phenomenon is also playing a role in the rising power of the audience. Social media can be defined as the ability for consumers to connect with each other through technology. From texts to websites to today's mobile devices, social media continues to grow because it is a natural expression of human interaction.

FIGURE 11-1   Increasing media choices means power continues to move from media companies to consumers.

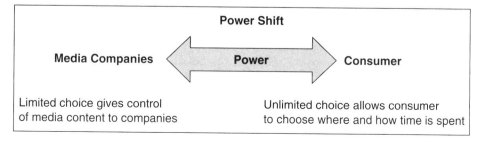

As consumers gain power through choice, and as technology enables social media, consumer expectations for media change. Institutional control of media had traditionally made the media experience passive. Mass media, by definition, was a top-down process that distributed one voice to many recipients. Choice changed that equation, empowering consumers to choose which institutions to believe and which to ignore. Connectivity further changed the equation, giving consumers a way to proactively exert their newfound power.

Consumer connectivity started with websites and the Internet, but the ultimate game changer was introduction of the smartphone. The ability of smartphones to take pictures, produce video, text, email and connect to social networks for the first time immersed consumers in the creation of media. The creation of media was a real-time experience. Real-time connectivity also changed expectations. The media experience was no longer passive. It was active, creative and two-way.

An active, creative, two-way media consumer directly conflicts with the traditional view of journalism as a process in which journalists serve as expert informers whose authority is unquestioned. Today's information consumer no longer accepts that as the only legitimate way for the journalism process to work. Emboldened by choice and connectivity, consumers demand a two-way conversation and a seat at the editorial decision-making table.

The continued movement of power from institutions to consumers through choice and connectivity is best understood not as a technological movement, but as a social one. Technology is only an enabler. Because technology will continue to advance the power of consumers, the role of the consumer in the journalism process and the relationship between the consumer and journalism organizations will continue to change. This will create both challenges and opportunities for future journalists.

To fully take advantage of these opportunities, journalists must have a clear, in-depth understanding of today's media consumer.

UNDERSTANDING THE MEDIA CONSUMER

Throughout this book, as we've considered new ways to understand consumers, we've made the case that it is critical to begin by recognizing that an

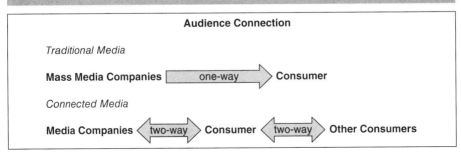

FIGURE 11-2 Although traditional one-way media still functions, connected media will continue to grow, making the future more and more a two-way conversation.

Audience Connection

Traditional Media

Mass Media Companies → one-way → **Consumer**

Connected Media

Media Companies ← two-way → **Consumer** ← two-way → **Other Consumers**

empowered consumer is in no less need of factual, important and fully reported information than a less empowered one. If anything, today's consumer, with independent access to raw information, is more in need of accurate and complete information.

In Chapter 2, we learned that different consumers have different expectations. Age, lifestyles and interests are but a few of the ways consumers align themselves. Thus, one way to understand consumers is to categorize them by mutual interests. Terms such as "tribes" and "psychographics" are ways of grouping consumers.

While grouping can be valuable, today's consumer is also an individual. Tools such as "persona" are designed to deepen the understanding of consumers and therefore aid in the creation of a deeper media experience.

Understanding today's media consumer is and will continue to be difficult. As consumers gain more power, they will exert themselves in new ways that are not always predictable. Serving tomorrow's consumer will require continued research and learning.

Meabh Quoirin, managing director of the Future Foundation, theorizes that consumers, especially 16- to 34-year-olds, "feel under pressure to always feel in control of their lives," that the pursuit of ever more control in their lives has become "aspirational" and that they will "look for new ways to emotionally express themselves." Quoirin believes that to survive brands must "relinquish control."[1]

John Lavine, founder of Northwestern University's Media Management Center and a former dean of the Medill School of Journalism, has spent his career understanding media consumers. Lavine was an early articulator of consumer power. He is an advocate of dealing with the reality of today's consumer's needs, interests and lifestyle.

Leadership Report – John Lavine

PHOTO 11-1

Courtesy of John Lavine

Founder of Northwestern University Media Management Center, Former Dean at Medill

John Lavine is a leading thinker on media futures. He was an early identifier of audience fragmentation, the rising power of media consumers, the Internet revolution and the importance of brand. He consults industry and educational organizations worldwide.

Tell us about the future.

First it was about journalism, and then it was about media and social and mobile, and now what? Back to the future. It's about being informed. Where, when and how users want it.

(Continued)

(Continued)

That sounds noncontroversial, but journalism, social, media – all of those words are silos, frameworks, and they have played an important role, they will play an important role, but they really are part of the larger picture.

What are Lavine's six laws?

The world is being constantly disrupted, and that won't ever stop, but there are six constants in this disruption.

First, there is an ever-rising content tsunami. This applies not just to journalism, but to media and every way we communicate. Every kind of communication. If you spent every day reading, you couldn't keep up with the rise.

Second, you and the people you reach only have 1,440 minutes every day. I've totaled up everything an average person does in a day. If you add that up, what you've really got is 40 minutes. No more time.

The third law is the audience, the users, are in control. Without their time and attention, it is as if your content doesn't exist. That's real. If you don't deliver it how, where and when they want it, it didn't happen. It just didn't happen.

Fourth, people's experiences drive engagement. I have an example of two coffee shops. Each shop offers a different experience. I ask people what's missing, and they say "coffee."

The fifth one is that brands are essential. With an ever-rising tidal wave of content, users start with the brand to decide if they are going to spend time with a particular set of content. When users see a brand, they instantly have a picture in their minds about what type of content it represents, who provided and created it, whether it is credible and can be trusted and much more. That's the good news.

The tough news is that to varying degrees providers'/creators' understanding of what their brand means to users may have little overlap with what the users think it is. Yet, if a brand is going to thrive, content providers must understand what the users value and are willing to invest their time in. A central driver of this is that those who create content too often think they know what the audience wants, and they don't. Or, even worse, they want to tell the audience what it "should care about," as they did in simpler, more one-way, monopolistic times. Today total control belongs to the users. If they don't allow a brand in, it's as if the content the brand presents did not happen. In addition, if users see the brand differently than the providers see it, that is an enormous barrier. If they have a shared view, that gives both sides a major advantage.

Finally, news and content. To last, content must be creditable, trustworthy, transparent, engaging and convenient.

John Lavine's Six Laws

- Ever-rising content
- Fixed 1,440 minutes per day
- Users are in control
- Experiences drive engagement
- Brands are essential
- Content must be creditable and trustworthy

What else do you see in the future?

In presenting the information, I dispel the idea that quality content can only come from traditional media. The Texas Tribune. OhmyNews. Citizens can create great content. The days of a monopoly are over.

You were the first person I ever heard say, "Quit thinking about platforms."

It's content. It's content. Content is what users find valuable.

Lavine believes that, despite the upheaval, many of journalism's foundational principles still apply to today's environment. "We'll recognize that what we really all got into this for was to help people be better informed," Lavine says. He also points to "experience" and "storytelling" as key ways journalists must communicate with consumers.

The key, according to Lavine, is "content you can trust." But how does today's consumer determine which content to trust and which not to? They make determinations based on brand.

MISSION CRITICAL: BRAND

Brands are important because they are a shortcut consumers use to help navigate today's complicated world. In its simplest form, brand is the first thought that enters a consumer's mind when seeing the image, name or logo of a product or service.

In Chapter 2 we studied the rise of brand and its definition as a core promise to consumers. Brands are not about advertising, nor are they easily created or changed. They are the result of the consumer's cumulative experience with a product or service. That means every interaction with the consumer, no matter how small, affects brand perception.

Brands are important in journalism because they help consumers identify trusted news organizations, avoid those they do not trust and frame the value of new information.

Brands Transcend Technology

No one can predict the future of technology, but our understanding of the consumer gives us some insight into the process that will shape the consumer's future relationship with technology.

There is now a clear link between consumer choice and technological development. The kinds of devices consumers choose, the particular features they access and the way devices are actually used are foundational to the development of future technology.

As Lavine points out, consumers are overwhelmed. They want their lives simplified. That means technology will become more integrated, easier to use and more normalized into daily life. Simplification also means seamlessness, not only making information easier to access, but prefiltering information that is of no interest.

Technological development will always create both risk and opportunity for journalists and media companies. This is why brand is critical to the future. Brand rises above platform.

Role of Media Brands

Much has been reported about the changing role of media. Some major newspapers have closed their doors while others are attempting to morph into digital information services. Individual television newscast ratings continue to decline even as television news mobile sites explode. New entrants, especially app-based news companies, are constantly being launched.

The future role of media companies will be determined by their ability to serve consumer needs, interests and lifestyles. As we have seen, the future is about brands that transcend platforms. Brands that serve consumer interests will be successful.

Writing in the Columbia Journalism Review, Bill Grueskin, Ava Seave and Lucas Graves theorize that although all digital news organizations "live in a brutally competitive environment" (driven by consumers), "some companies do much better than others because their managers respond more deftly to opportunities." They cite The Huffington Post as an example of a news media business that succeeded because it relinquished control and allowed the customer to be in charge.[2]

PHOTO 11-2 Because The Huffington Post has created a clear brand, seeing the site's logo tells users any content under the logo will be left of center. Seeing the Drudge Report logo likewise tells loyalists of that site that content will be right of center. Notice that neither of the logos contains any statement about content. Such is the power of a clear and unique brand.

©Stockphoto.com/GaryPhoto

iPhone/Alamy

It is also worth pointing out that The Huffington Post created a clear brand identity as politically left of center, just as Drudge Report earlier created a clear brand targeted to the right.

The transition to brand-driven media companies means coverage areas might also be redefined. Penelope Muse Abernathy, who has written extensively on the role of community newspapers, believes the traditional definition of community through geographic boundaries has evolved to include communities of shared interests. "Community is where you live, but it is also passions," she says. "That could be sports, parenting, hobbies, neighborhood gossip, politics, a whole range of things."[3]

Leadership Report – Gordon Borrell

PHOTO 11-3

Courtesy of Gordon Borrell

CEO, Borrell Associates

Gordon Borrell is one of the media industry's leading analysts. His industry papers and presentations provide insight to both consumer and advertiser trends. Gerson Lehrman Group ranks Borrell in the top 2 percent of 150,000 consultants worldwide.

You have been on the front edge of predicting media trends. How do you see the future?

There are many things people claim are tectonic or fundamental shifts in media that are not really true. People still need to get their message out so that people come in the door and buy stuff.

What has changed is that all advertisers now have their own medium at their disposal and can go direct to consumers. They have their own little newspaper, which is their website where they can advertise their hours of operation, their inventory. They can post jobs. You can like the page, and you can subscribe to it and get emails and specials.

They now have a direct communication with consumers that they've never had before. It used to be they only had the telephone. They can now punch a button and send out 1,000 emails.

They kinda, sorta don't need the media – yet they really do need traditional media because traditional media is mass, and what they do is advertise in niche.

One thing has changed in the past five to nine years. Local advertisers are spending 33 percent less annually on traditional, classic forms of advertising, which includes online. I'm talking about classic advertising where people aggregate an audience, then sell you access to it. Yet, they had spent 45 percent more last year on nonadvertising marketing.

(Continued)

(Continued)

If you are a media company and you are trying to be in the journalism business, what do you think the implications are of that revenue shift?

The implications are pretty big. If you are going to do business the way you have in the past, and you should, with your old business model of aggregating an audience, and you should if you are in television or radio or newspapers, and selling access to it, the future does not look great.

The way traditional media companies can grow again is to stop thinking of the Internet solely as something to support their existing medium.

When you look at how newspapers and TV stations and radio stations have utilized the Internet, they've basically used it as a technology to sustain the core product. The thing they miss, and the only opportunity for growth, is they need to create separate ventures. They need to create something that goes after a completely new audience and a completely new business model, not just enhance their current readership or viewership.

You have been talking about culture. Is it possible for traditional media companies to change culture?

I'm not really sure a change in culture is needed as much as everybody says it is. It is to some extent, because you need to do all these cool social media things, but do not take your eye off the ball of putting out a great product every single day. Don't divert your attention. While you are doing that, you need to also figure out what Pinterest is and Tumblr and everything else. You just diverted their attention from trying to win a Pulitzer.

What I'm saying is, it is a completely separate venture. Hire a whole bunch of people, and let them have nose rings and tattoos and flip-flops. Do cool things and make some money.

Do you think there will always be some form of mass media?

Yes, and I think television is it. I don't think you can call newspapers mass media anymore. They are niche media. You don't find newspapers that are in more than 50 percent of homes.

Broadcast TV is the only mass media, and that's OK. Everybody just got niched out. So there is room for the mass audience.

No media has died as a result of a new one coming along. It's just the new media has kind of peeled away the growth and affected the margins. I think that trend will continue. I think every medium, even paper, has its own benefits. It will be a struggle to morph into something and change, just like radio had to morph. In the end the only medium I don't see viability for is Yellow Pages.

I think newspapers will still exist and radio and TV, but it's going to be different and a lot smaller.

So, how does this affect the news business?

Ten years ago, it would have been inconceivable to think that you would pay for local TV news, yet the money the public is paying for content now is phenomenal. And it doesn't go, for the most part, to news organizations. Look at your cell phone bill, and you're going to think that's a utility expense, and it's not. You are getting huge amounts of content over your cell phone. Look at your cable bill. You are getting huge amounts of content.

ROLE OF THE CONSUMER JOURNALIST

Communities of interest have led to a significant boost in consumer production of news content. Every group that had to beg for media coverage in the past now has the capability to publish its own stories. As we discussed in Chapter 9 and elsewhere, news organizations able to harness this phenomenon will vastly increase their resources.

The most obvious consumer journalism tool has been the smartphone. The ubiquitous presence of smartphones means we expect coverage of any major event to include consumer-provided video and pictures, but this is only the beginning. Consumers now have the mobile tools, including wearable devices, to create a wide range of information, including fully produced stories.

There is, however, a cultural obstacle that must be overcome. Many organizations still see consumer-supplied content as something only to observe and report on. In other words, consumers are treated as sources to be interviewed rather than participants in a two-way conversation.

Journalistic organizations that learn how to understand and take advantage of the two-way conversation will gain unprecedented access to new consumer-produced information. This is not just a future prospect; it is a current opportunity.

ROLE OF THE JOURNALISM ENTREPRENEUR

As we learned in Chapter 10, though traditional media continues to lose audience, most ad dollars still go to traditional platforms, especially television.

We also learned that today's information user is willing to trade money for both time and information. This willingness by consumers to pay for unique or otherwise valuable information creates huge future opportunities for the journalism entrepreneur.

Thus, when choosing a business model, entrepreneurs have two potential sources of revenue: advertising and direct consumer payments. Those who choose consumer payments normally have three options: all-access, in which the consumer pays one price for access to all platforms; the "bait and switch" model, which gives limited free access before payment is required; and the a la carte approach, in which each piece of content is priced separately. Apple iTunes is an example of the a la carte model, as we stated in Chapter 10.

As time goes on, new revenue models will also be created. What seems certain is that the continued need for advertising gives the ad-based model long-term importance. That means ongoing audience fragmentation will cause ad dollars to continue their migration to new media. It also seems certain the consumer's willingness to pay for certain information and services will continue to grow.

The low cost of entry for new media, especially using the app-based model, means opportunity for innovative journalism services has never been greater. These services will continue to explode and serve media consumers in ever-growing ways over coming years.

MEDIA START-UPS

Media entrepreneurialism takes many forms but is usually thought of in the context of media start-ups.

Start-ups can be entirely new businesses, or they can be extensions of existing brands. For instance, in 2014, Hearst Magazines created a Dr. Oz magazine as a brand extension of the Dr. Oz syndicated television program. This example is important because it is an illustration of a "new" information enterprise launched on an "old" media platform.

It is fair to say that in today's media world one must not limit entrepreneurial thinking to only new platforms. The key is not new or old, but rather appropriate to the content and the way a consumer wants that content delivered. In the case of the Dr. Oz magazine, readers still have enough interest in a high-quality printed magazine to make the enterprise successful. Of course, the Dr. Oz magazine is also delivered digitally to tablets, but the launch was in traditional magazine form.

Because of lower start-up costs, most entirely new media businesses are Web-based. When Arianna Huffington launched The Huffington Post in 2005, the original site was a combination of blogging and news aggregation from a liberal point of view. That targeted point of view was so successful that in 2011 Huffington sold the site to AOL for more than $300 million. By 2012, The Huffington Post won a Pulitzer Prize for writer David Wood's reporting.

A less traditional media start-up is Gawker. Gawker is a combination of both serious and bizarre content written in an irreverent style. Gawker headlines and body copy often use words and phrases that would be considered obscene, even shocking, on traditional sites. In Gawker's case, what would seem irreverent and inappropriate other places is actually the foundation of the Gawker brand.

Neetzan Zimmerman, a former Gawker editor whose posts sometimes generated 30 million page views a month, describes what he calls "a deep connection to his audience's evolving, irreducibly human, primal sensibilities." Zimmerman says he chose stories based on this perception of Gawker users.[4]

A less well-known, but nonetheless successful, start-up is WebMD, a medical information site. WebMD's "symptom checker" allows users to self-diagnose some conditions. The site's business model is dependent on timely and accurate information, plus WebMD gains credibility by offering services to physicians, employers and health plans.

Not only is WebMD's content targeted; so it its advertiser base. WebMD advertisers are primarily pharmaceutical companies.

The opportunities for new media start-ups, especially using mobile and Web platforms, are unlimited. The key to success for new start-ups will continue to be consumer-targeted brands that fulfill consumer needs and interests.

Leadership Report – Terry Mackin

PHOTO 11-4

Courtesy of Terry Mackin

President, Remarkable Partners

Terry Mackin is a media entrepreneur. A former president of the Univision Television Group and executive vice president for digital development at Hearst Television, Mackin specializes in product development that creates sustainable growth.

As an entrepreneur, what does it mean for the audience to be in control?

I think the options are deeper now than they have ever been, both devices and services. The app has changed the way people think about media, and their device priorities have shifted. The smartphone is maybe the most important device for a lot of people. TV would still be No. 1, but the numbers have shifted.

The consumer wins again because all of these new opportunities are affordable.

The first choice of consumers would be to avoid all commercials. Giving them more contextual advertising is a big help.

Are you saying the consumer has control over everything, even advertising?

I think the consumer is doing what consumers have always done. It is just a little more overt. They really would like to avoid interruptions to what they are watching. They are there to watch favorite content, and they accept the commercials because there is no alternative. But, with the introduction of the DVR, pay channels, Netflix, this has changed dramatically.

What has not changed is that consumers still love their brands on TV. Because the consumer is now in control, the consumer says, "I can find a service that will let me watch episodes all day, all weekend, and I want to find a day when I can do that." So they are scheduling marathons, where in the past marathons have been scheduled for them.

It has been suggested the consumer is sitting as a judge. How do you take advantage of that?

I call it "finding the audience." Just like you produce a business model that says, "Can I afford to produce it?" I think there is now so much more information about audiences that there is more opportunity to build a good, solid foundation. Voids based on price or underserved markets. The market will still, more times than not, say, "I think I have a great idea," and the research follows.

The more sophisticated entrepreneurs are doing upfront analysis of the audience, from demographics to ethnography to psychographics, and then that leads you to testing a thesis, but that's not as expensive as saying, "Let's go build this and see if anybody wants it." Which is dangerous.

(Continued)

(Continued)

Do you think we will end up with one measurement system of how consumers use their time?

The Internet is still encumbered by multiple measuring systems. There is not a single standard of currency, which is better for the buyer of advertising than it is for the seller because the buyer can push down on price.

The research business is still a big opportunity for some entrepreneur to figure out.

How do you look at the future?

The consumer is in control. If you're not listening, and listening with enough quality data to make adjustments and measure objectively, then you are still just using what has worked in a less competitive environment. You must listen to the audience, and it must be bidirectional. Social media is really research. You can't please all the people all the time.

BIG DATA

According to Mackin, another exploding opportunity is big data: "Big data and algorithms help us understand what they [consumers] want and what they like. People are getting smarter and smarter about using data."

Big data is the analysis of massive amounts of information by advanced computing systems to reveal patterns and other information that would not otherwise be possible to understand.

Among other things, investigative journalists use big data to uncover government and institutional actions and trends. As big data becomes more mainstream, it will be a resource to further understand consumer trends and interests.

Big data is also important because it can automate certain information and present it much more quickly than would otherwise be possible. For instance, big data analysis of smartphone locations in moving traffic allows companies such as Total Traffic & Weather Network (www.ttwnetwork.com) to predict traffic flows and patterns of major cities in real time.

CONTENT COMPETITION

As the role of the consumer changes, non-news organizations are also developing content production and delivery strategies. By providing information and creating a two-way conversation, many different types of companies hope to deepen their relationship with consumers. The most effective content strategies are designed to "inform and engage" rather than "sell." One vehicle for engagement is native advertising.

The collaboration between Virgin Mobile and BuzzFeed is a good example of a native advertising partnership, a concept we first explored in Chapter 10.

Virgin and BuzzFeed collaborate to create content Virgin hopes will be picked up by social media. Virgin executive Ron Faris points out a Valentine's Day video "urging consumers to 'break up with their carrier'" was not only "liked"; it spiked Virgin's sales 95 percent that day.[5]

Native advertising is controversial and will remain so. Proponents point out that advertisers are in some cases the most knowledgeable sources of information. They emphasize that both the consumer and the advertiser benefit by the production of knowledgeable content that informs consumers and helps them make decisions.

Many magazines and even newspapers, most notably The New York Times, see native advertising as an important tool that will expand.

From a journalist's point of view, the key to native advertising is disclosure. The consumer must always know the source of information.

NEWS MEDIA MANAGER SKILL SET

The top-down nature of traditional mass media created internal cultures that were both clear and rigid. Newspaper reporters were promoted to editor; television producers were promoted to news director. This system created managers locked into specific cultures that functioned well in a time when media companies controlled the agenda.

Today's world of journalism requires a more flexible skill set and an outlook that is oriented toward the news consumer, not just the internal system. Managers must understand brand, research, targeting and the wide array of other skills that have been discussed in previous chapters.

Great managers must be great leaders, able to articulate a brand vision that helps journalists see and understand the enterprise's goals. The evolving relationship between media companies and advertisers means managers must also be able to make ethical decisions that achieve business goals while protecting the integrity of the organization.

As journalism continues to evolve and grow, so must the leadership of media companies.

JOURNALISM RULES

Because consumers now control the future, Tom Rosenstiel of Poynter theorizes that the next generation of journalists – and their leaders – are at a critical juncture. He believes journalism schools must continue teaching skills while also having a "larger responsibility and role to play in helping rethink and revive civic discourse and ensuring journalism has a sustainable and ethical role."[6]

In addition to writing and analytical skills, great journalists have always understood the value of content. Knowledge of history, sociology and government has also been among essential analytical tools.

In considering tomorrow's journalist, we must remember these skills remain requisite. Successful journalists forging the future must also have a broad tool kit of skills designed to help understand consumer needs and interests.

Additionally, journalists need new technical skills.

Journalists can no longer afford to limit their thinking and skill set to a single platform. They must be able to change and adjust in ways that make technology an opportunity, not a limiter.

Gordon Borrell sees today's new journalists as the key to the future. "I look at younger people as the savior of traditional media companies because they grew up with nothing but the technology of the Internet and are most adept at using it," he says. "They are in a great position to teach the graybeards how to use it to attract a new audience."

Those who lead news organizations must also have a fundamental grasp of traditional journalistic principles to know when and how to break the rules. It's clear that news organizations cannot conduct "business as usual" to remain both relevant and profitable, but they do play an important part in preserving a democratic society.

THE TRUSTED SOURCE

The fundamental role of journalism in society has not changed. It is to inform the consumer with accurate, reliable information that is contextually correct and, above all, truthful.

This means journalists must supply not only information the consumer wants, but also information the consumer needs.

In the past, the traditional one-way conversation between media and the consumer allowed media companies to control the journalism agenda, offering information on a hierarchical basis. A newspaper editor had the power to control information, offering the consumer whatever content the editor believed most important.

Today's empowered world means consumers now have the ability to control what information they receive. How, then, does a journalist fulfill the traditional role of journalism?

The answer is to remember that accurate news and information, even information the consumer would prefer to avoid, remains critical to every consumer's life. Consumers will accept important information they are not seeking provided it comes from a brand they have a relationship with and consider a *trusted source*.

At its most basic level, a trusted source is a trusted friend, which is why social media is such a powerful tool for journalists. Authentic interaction can help build trust at the personal level and then expand to organizational and institutional levels, but this will not be an easy task. Trust is based on fulfilling the consumer's self-identified needs in an accurate and truthful manner over time.

A friend who is not truthful will no longer be a friend. Trust of organizations and institutions is developed and maintained on the same basis.

In the past, media organizations and journalists were able to assume they had the public's trust. Today, that trust must be earned. Not every media organization or journalist will earn the *trusted source* brand, but for those who do, the exciting future of journalism is just beginning.

EXECUTIVE SUMMARY

Future opportunities for journalists and journalism companies have never been brighter.

To understand the future, one must think not of platforms, but rather of the power of technologically enabled consumers. The good news for journalists is that consumers not only want a role in the journalism process; they continue to want and need trusted sources to help them navigate the world.

As we look to the future, the business of journalism will continue to change. Fortunately, we are able to understand the forces driving change and thus begin to see the incredible and wide-ranging opportunities of the future.

The primary drivers of change, choice and connectivity, are the forces that have moved power from traditional media institutions to consumers. Consumers have actively embraced their new power, demanding a two-way conversation, a seat at the decision table and the opportunity to produce content. As technology continues to improve, consumers will continue to gain and exercise power.

In order to serve this powerful consumer, journalists must understand new tools such as research, market segmentation and the power of brand. Understanding these tools does not mean abandoning key activities such as ethics or truthfulness. In fact, if a journalist is to become the consumer's "trusted source," ethics and telling the truth are more important than ever.

One paradox is that even as new media choices explode and traditional media platforms lose users, traditional platforms continue to be efficient advertising vehicles and thus still generate cash flow while many new media ventures struggle. Over time, this will change. The consumer's new willingness to trade money for both time and information will create greater business opportunities.

No one can predict the future. But we do know this: The need for journalism will not change. Journalists willing to understand and take advantage of the things that are changing will have unlimited opportunities.

THINK AND DO

You are about to take on a new management role in your news media company.

In addition to your traditional journalism skills, you have a strong understanding of media fragmentation, new and old media, consumer research, funding models, the importance of brand and other factors that make up today's two-way conversation.

Consolidated Media, a major company that owns newspapers, television stations, radio and new media ventures, is impressed with your skill set and has invited you to submit a proposal for a new journalism venture of your choosing.

Things to Consider

- Will your venture be a new way to offer "general" news, or will it be a targeted product?
- Will the venture be part of an existing platform, independent or something else?
- How will you gauge consumer interest in the new product?
- Who will use the product, and why will they love it?
- How will you distinguish your product from others?
- What is your plan for funding?
- Why will the new venture be sustainable?

NOTES

1. Loulla-Mae Eleftheriou-Smith, "Brands Must 'Relinquish Control' and Let Consumers Feel in Charge," Marketing, April 6, 2014, retrieved from http://www.marketing magazine.co.uk/article/1297186/brands-relinquish-control-let-consumers-feel-charge on March 4, 2015.

2. Bill Grueskin, Ava Seave and Lucas Graves, "The Story So Far: What We Know About the Business of Digital Journalism," CJR, May 10, 2011, retrieved from http://www.cjr.org/the_business_of_digital_journalism/the_story_so_far_what_ we_know.php on March 4, 2015.

3. Meg Heckman, "Abernathy: Small Papers Must Seize Niche," NetNewsCheck, June 9, 2014, retrieved from http://www.netnewscheck.com/article/34306/abernathy-small-papers-must-seize-niche on March 2, 2015.

4. Farhad Manjoo, "Why Everyone Will Totally Read This Column," The Wall Street Journal, Dec. 1, 2013, retrieved from http://online.wsj.com/news/articles/SB100014 24052702304579404579231772007379090 on March 2, 2015.

5. "Does BuzzFeed Know the Secret?" retrieved from http://nymag.com/news/ features/buzzfeed-2013-4/index2.html on March 2, 2015.

6. Tom Rosenstiel, "Why We Need a Better Conversation About the Future of Journalism Education," Poynter, Apr. 15, 2013, updated Nov. 24, 2014, retrieved from http:// www.poynter.org/latest-news/the-next-journalism/210196/why-we-need-a-better-conversation-about-the-future-of-journalism-education/ on March 2, 2015.

Chapter 1

1. Jeff Jarvis, "A Degree in Social Journalism," BuzzMachine, April 26, 2014, retrieved from http://buzzmachine.com/2014/04/26/degree-social-journalism/ on Feb. 16, 2015.
2. Richard Perez-Pena, "Newspapers a Hot Commodity After Obama Win," The New York Times, Nov. 5, 2008, retrieved from http://www.nytimes.com/2008/11/06/business/media/06paper.html?_r=0 on Nov. 13, 2014.
3. "The Shirky Principle," The Technium, April 2, 2010, retrieved from http://kk.org/thetechnium/2010/04/the-shirky-prin/ on Feb. 16, 2015.
4. Thomas Baekdal, "What If Quality Journalism Isn't?" Baekdal Plus, June 12, 2014, retrieved from http://www.baekdal.com/insights/what-if-quality-journalism-isnt/10C3F189EE6048BBB4D5CB448CE6F069DAC6C08B6F9E7F72EF24FC33EAC1F946 on Feb. 16, 2015.

Chapter 2

1. "Newspapers Getting Started: The Development of the Modern Newspaper," Center for History and New Media, George Mason University, 2005, retrieved from http://chnm.gmu.edu/worldhistorysources/unpacking/newsmod.html on Jan. 20, 2014.
2. "The Early History of Newspaper Publishing in New York State," New York State Library, May 14, 2009, retrieved from http://www.nysl.nysed.gov/nysnp/history.htm on Jan. 20, 2014.
3. Mark R. Gould, "History of TV News – Part 1," American Library Association, 2012, retrieved from http://www.atyourlibrary.org/culture/history-tv-news-part-1 on Jan. 18, 2014.
4. Rick Edmonds, Emily Guskin, Amy Mitchell, and Mark Jurkowitz, "Newspapers: Stabilizing but Still Threatened," The State of the News Media 2013, retrieved from http://stateofthemedia.org/2013/newspapers-stabilizing-but-still-threatened/ on Jan. 18, 2014.
5. Barbara Boland, "Study: Network News Viewers at All-Time Low; Half Under Age 30 Never Watch News," CBS News, Jan. 10, 2014, retrieved from http://www.cnsnews.com/news/article/barbara-boland/study-network-news-viewers-all-time-low-half-under-age-30-never-watch on Jan. 18, 2014.
6. Susan Gunelius, "What Is a Brand? Part 1 – 5 Factors That Define a Brand," AYTM, 2015, retrieved from http://aytm.com/blog/research-junction/branding-factors/ on Jan. 18, 2014.
7. "A No Nonsense-Look at Newspaper Brand," Readership Institute, Northwestern University, 2012, retrieved from http://www.readership.org/brand/brandlook.asp on Jan. 18, 2014.
8. Ibid.
9. "Fox News Channel Marks Decade as the Number One Cable News Network," Press Release, January 2012, retrieved from http://press.foxnews.com/2012/01/fox-news-channel-marks-decade-as-the-number-one-cable-news-network/ on January 18, 2014.

10. Lisa de Moraes, "Rick Kaplan Out at No. 3 MSNBC," The TV Column, The Washington Post, June 8, 2006, retrieved from http://www.washingtonpost.com/wp-dyn/content/article/2006/06/07/AR2006060702355.html on Jan. 18, 2014.

11. "Rick Kaplan Exits: It's Time to 'Grow the Channel in a Way It Hasn't to Date,'" MSNBC, June 8, 2006, retrieved from http://www.mediabistro.com/tvnewser/rick-kaplan-exits-its-time-to-grow-the-channel-in-a-way-it-hasnt-to-date_b9996 on Jan. 18, 2014.

12. "MSNBC to 'Lean Forward' in Two-Year Brand Campaign," MSNBC News, Oct. 5, 2010, retrieved from http://www.nbcnews.com/id/39507182/ on Jan. 18, 2014.

13. Rick Kissell, "Fox News Remains Ratings Champ as 2013 Comes to Close: It and Rivals CNN, MSNBC Down From Last Year," Variety, Dec. 16, 2013, retrieved from http://variety.com/2013/tv/news/fox-news-remains-ratings-dynamo-as-2013-comes-to-close-1200964903/# on Jan. 18, 2014.

14. Dylan Byers, "In Crisis, CNN Aims to Rethink the Brand," Politico, June 26, 2012, retrieved from http://www.politico.com/blogs/media/2012/06/in-crisis-cnn-aims-to-rethink-itself-127385.html on Jan. 18, 2014.

15. Mike Allen and Alex Weprin, "Zucker Plans Massive Change at CNN," Capital, Dec. 3, 2013, retrieved from http://www.capitalnewyork.com/article/media/2013/12/8536789/zucker-plans-massive-change-cnn on Jan. 18, 2014.

Chapter 3

1. Todd Spangler, "Media and Entertainment Sector Profitability Forecast to Rise Again in 2014," Variety, Sept. 15, 2014, retrieved from http://variety.com/2014/biz/news/media-and-entertainment-sector-to-notch-highest-profitability-in-7-years-report-1201304744/ on Feb. 26, 2015.

2. Coursera, retrieved from https://class.coursera.org/contentstrategy-001/wiki/week on Feb. 20, 2015.

3. Steve Gray, "Part II – The End of the Mass Media Era," MediaReset, Apr. 31, 2012, retrieved from http://mediareset.com/2012/04/30/part-ii-the-end-of-the-mass-media-era/ on May 19, 2014.

4. Deborah Potter, Katerina-Eva Matsa, and Amy Mitchell, "Local TV: Audience Declines as Revenue Bounces Back," The State of the News Media 2013, retrieved from http://stateofthemedia.org/2013/local-tv-audience-declines-as-revenue-bounces-back/ on May 19, 2014.

5. Benji Cannon, "A Brief History of Disruptive Innovation, Part I," DisCo, Aug. 7, 2013, retrieved from http://www.project-disco.org/competition/080713-a-brief-history-of-disruptive-innovation-part-i/ on Feb. 26, 2015.

6. "Theories of Technology," Wikipedia, Jan. 22, 2015, retrieved from http://en.wikipedia.org/wiki/Theories_of_technology on May 19, 2014.

7. "Chicken or Egg: Consumer Driven or Technology Driven?" Innovation.net, Jan. 13, 2014, retrieved from http://venture2.typepad.com/innovationnet/2014/01/chicken-or-egg-consumer-driven-or-technology-driven.html on Feb. 23, 2015.

8. Vauhini Vara, "How BlackBerry Fell," The New Yorker, Aug. 12, 2013, retrieved from http://www.newyorker.com/online/blogs/elements/2013/08/blackberry-sale-announcement-iphone-smartphone-market.html on May 19, 2014.

9. Jesse Holcomb, "NBC Makes a Bet on Getting User-Generated Content From Citizen Videographers," Pew Research Center, Aug. 20, 2013, retrieved from http://www.pewresearch.org/fact-tank/2013/08/20/nbc-makes-a-bet-on-getting-user-generated-content-from-citizen-videographers/ on May 19, 2014.

10. Peter Marsh, "5 Things to Know About Content, Advertising and Trust," News-Cycle Solutions, Feb. 27, 2004, retrieved from http://www.newscyclesolutions.com/5-things-to-know-about-content-advertising-and-trust/ on Feb. 20, 2015.

11. "Broadcast TV Advertising Revenue in the United States from 2004 to 2013 (in Billion U.S. Dollars)," Statista, 2015, retrieved from http://www.statista.com/statistics/183366/ad-revenue-in-us-broadcast-television-since-2004/ on Feb. 20, 2015.

12. "'Magazine Media 360' Explained, The Mr. Magazine™ Interview With Mary Berner," Mr. Magazine, Oct. 13, 2014, retrieved from http://mrmagazine.wordpress.com/2014/10/13/magazine-media-360-explained-the-mr-magazine-interview-with-mary-berner-president-ceo-mpa-the-association-of-magazine-media/ on Feb. 20, 2015.

13. "Tribal Marketing," Marketing Tools, Jan. 28, 2009, retrieved from http://themarketingtools.wordpress.com/tag/tribal-marketing-definition/ on Feb. 20, 2015.

14. Larry Percy, "What Is a Behavioral Sequence Model?" retrieved from http://www.larrypercy.com/bsm.html on Feb. 20, 2015.

15. Allen Stafford, "Behavioral Sequence Model (BSM)," Marketing Binder, retrieved from http://www.marketingbinder.com/glossary/behavioral-sequence-model-bsm-marketing-definition/ on Feb. 20, 2015.

Chapter 4

1. Zacks.com, "Gannett to Expand Its Broadcasting Footprint – Analyst Blog," NASDAQ, May 15, 2014, retrieved from http://www.nasdaq.com/article/gannet-to-expand-its-broadcasting-footprint-analyst-blog-cm353557#ixzz32AN75sTY on Feb. 24, 2015.

2. "Across Platforms, 7 in 10 Adults Access Content From Newspaper Media Each Week," Newspaper Association of America, March 25, 2013, retrieved from http://www.naa.org/Trends-and-Numbers/Readership.aspx on Feb. 21, 2015.

3. Mark Jurkowitz and Amy Mitchell, "Newspapers Turning Ideas Into Dollars," Pew Research Center, Feb. 11, 2013, retrieved from http://www.journalism.org/2013/02/11/newspapers-turning-ideas-dollars/ on Feb. 21, 2015.

4. Ibid.

5. "Survey: Community Newspapers Still Tops for Local News," National Newspaper Association, Feb. 25, 2013, retrieved from http://nnaweb.org/article?articleTitle=survey-community-papers-still-tops-for-local-news--1361822263--502--1top-story on Nov. 16, 2014.

6. David Carr, "Times-Picayune Confirms Staff Cuts and 3-Day-a-Week Print Schedule," Media Decoder, The New York Times, May 24, 2012, retrieved from http://mediadecoder.blogs.nytimes.com/2012/05/24/new-orleans-times-picayune-to-cut-staff-and-cease-daily-newspape/?_r=0 on Feb. 26, 2015.

7. Andrew Beaujon, "USA Today's Circulation Up 67 Percent? Newspaper Industry Makes Comparisons Increasingly Difficult," Poynter, Oct. 31, 2013, retrieved from http://www.poynter.org/latest-news/mediawire/227958/usa-todays-circulation-up-67-percent-newspaper-industry-makes-comparisons-increasingly-difficult/ on Feb. 21, 2015.

Chapter 5

1. Neal Lulofs, "Top 25 U.S. Consumer Magazines for June 2014," Alliance for Audited Media, Aug. 7, 2014, retrieved from http://auditedmedia.com/news/blog/2014/august/top-25-us-consumer-magazines-for-june-2014.aspx on Feb. 26, 2015.

2. Emma Bazilian, "After Newsweek, Is Writing on Wall for Newsweeklies?" Adweek, Oct. 18, 2012, retrieved from http://www.adweek.com/news/press/after-news week-writing-wall-newsweeklies-144549 on Feb. 24, 2015.

3. "Key Indicators in Media and News," Pew Research Center, March 26, 2014, retrieved from http://www.journalism.org/2014/03/26/state-of-the-news-media-2014-key-indicators-in-media-and-news/ on May 19, 2013.

4. "'There's Always Going to Be Time for a Newsweekly,' Nancy Gibbs, TIME's New Editor, Tells Samir Husni. The Mr. Magazine™ Interview." Mr. Magazine, Sept. 25, 2013, retrieved from http://mrmagazine.wordpress.com/2013/09/ on Feb. 24, 2015.

5. "Newsstands and Retail: What's on the Mind of Top Magazine Executives? A Panel at the MPA/PBAA Retail Marketplace Provides the Answers," Mr. Magazine, June 13, 2013, retrieved from https://mrmagazine.wordpress.com/2013/06/13/news stands-and-retail-whats-on-the-mind-of-top-magazine-executives-a-panel-at-the-mpapbaa-retail-marketplace-provides-the-answers/ on Feb. 24, 2015.

6. Ibid.

7. Ibid.

8. Ibid.

9. Ibid.

10. Ibid.

11. "'There's Always Going to Be Time for a Newsweekly,' Nancy Gibbs, TIME's New Editor, Tells Samir Husni. The Mr. Magazine™ Interview." Mr. Magazine, Sept. 25, 2013, retrieved from http://mrmagazine.wordpress.com/2013/09/ on Feb. 24, 2015.

Chapter 6

1. "In Changing News Landscape, Even Television Is Vulnerable," Pew Research Center, Sept. 27, 2012, retrieved from http://www.people-press.org/2012/09/27/in-changing-news-landscape-even-television-is-vulnerable/ on Feb. 25, 2015.

2. "What Is Social TV?" The Digital Marketing Glossary, Aug. 1, 2013, retrieved from http://www.digitalmarketing-glossary.com/What-is-Social-TV-definition on March 2, 2015.

3. Deb Halpern Wenger, "Social TV May Mean Money, Viewer Loyalty, for News," RTNDA, Jan. 29, 2015, retrieved from http://www.rtdna.org/article/social_tv_may_mean_money_viewer_loyalty_for_news on Feb. 25, 2015.

4. Retrieved from https://www.facebook.com/WHSV.TV/timeline on Nov. 3, 2014.

5. Council for Research Excellence, "Following the Mobile Path of TV Content," TV Untethered, July 24, 2013, retrieved from http://www.researchexcellence.com/files/pdf/2015-02/id102_tv_untethered_presentation_7_24_13.pdf on March 2, 2015.

6. Patrick Goldstein and James Rainey, "Survey: Love of Mobile News Does Not = Pay for Mobile News," The Big Picture, Los Angeles Times, March 13, 2011, retrieved from http://latimesblogs.latimes.com/the_big_picture/2011/03/survey-love-of-mobile-news-does-not-pay-for-mobile-news.html?utm_source=feed burner&utm_medium=feed&utm_campaign=Feed%3A+PatrickGoldstein+%28 L.A.+Times+-+Patrick+Goldstein%29 on Feb. 25, 2015.

7. Deb Halpern Wenger, "Will the 'M' in Mobile Stand for Money?" Quill, July/August 2012, retrieved from http://digitaleditions.walsworthprintgroup.com/article/will_the_%27m%27_in_mobile_stand_for_money%3F/1132105/120451/article.html on March 2, 2015.

8. WCPO Cincinnati, retrieved from http://www.wcpo.com/subscribe on Nov. 3, 2014.

9. "Dual View: Newscast, Google Glass," WRAL.com, retrieved from http://www .wral.com/wral-tv/video/13379681/ on Nov. 4, 2014.

10. Patrick Kelly and Melvin Kranzburg, "Technological Innovation: A Critical Review of Current Knowledge," San Francisco: San Francisco Press, 1978.

11. Paul Trott, "Innovation Management and New Product Development," Essex, U.K.: Prentice Hall, 2005.

Chapter 7

1. "Statistics," ITU, 2015, retrieved from http://www.itu.int/en/ITU-D/Statistics/ Pages/stat/default.aspx on Feb. 26, 2015.

2. "eMarketer: Consumers Spending More Time With Mobile as Growth Slows for Time Online," Oct. 22, 2012, retrieved from http://www.emarketer.com/news room/index.php/consumers-spending-time-mobile-growth-time-online-slows/ on Feb. 26, 2015.

3. Jane Sasseen, "Digital: As Mobile Grows Rapidly, the Pressures on News Intensify," The State of the News Media 2013, retrieved from http://stateofthemedia.org/2013/ digital-as-mobile-grows-rapidly-the-pressures-on-news-intensify/20-top-sites-2012-comscore/ on Feb. 26, 2015.

4. "Digital to Account for One in Five Ad Dollars," eMarketer, Jan. 9, 2013, retrieved from http://www.emarketer.com/Article/Digital-Account-One-Five-Ad-Dollars/ 1009592 on March 2, 2015.

5. "Total US Ad Spending to See Largest Increase Since 2004," retrieved from http:// www.emarketer.com/Article/Total-US-Ad-Spending-See-Largest-Increase-Since-2004/1010982 on March 2, 2015.

6. "Google Takes Home Half of Worldwide Mobile Internet Ad Revenues," eMarketer, June 13, 2013, retrieved from http://www.emarketer.com/Article/ Google-Takes-Home-Half-of-Worldwide-Mobile-Internet-Ad-Revenues/1009966 on Feb. 26, 2015.

7. Rick Edmonds, "The Case for Paywalls: Gannett Gains While Digital First Experiments," Poynter, Feb. 5, 2013, updated Nov. 25, 2014, retrieved from http://www .poynter.org/latest-news/business-news/the-biz-blog/202897/the-case-for-paywalls-gannett-gains-while-digital-first-experiments/ on Feb. 26, 2015.

8. Ibid.

9. Dena Levitz, "10 Secrets of Successful Meters, Paywalls and Reader Revenue Strategies," American Press Institute, Sept. 24, 2013, retrieved from http://www .americanpressinstitute.org/en/Training/Transformation-Tour/10-Secrets-of-Successful.aspx on Feb. 26, 2015.

10. "Another Bloomberg First: Delivering Live Business News to Apple TV," Bloomberg, Dec. 11, 2013, retrieved from http://www.bloomberg.com/now/2013-12-11/another-bloomberg-first-delivering-live-business-news-to-apple-tv/ on Nov. 13, 2014.

11. Kenneth Olmstead, Amy Mitchell, Jesse Holcomb and Nancy Vogt, "News Video on the Web," Pew Research Center, March 26, 2014, retrieved from http://www .journalism.org/2014/03/26/news-video-on-the-web/ on Nov. 6, 2014.

12. Kelly Faircloth, "AOL's Patch Editor-in-Chief Leaves, Does Not Go Scorched Earth," Observer, April 12, 2012, retrieved from http://betabeat.com/2012/04/ patch-editor-in-chief-leaves-does-not-go-scorched-earth/ on Feb. 26, 2015.

13. Nicholas Carlson, "Exclusive: Now We Know AOL's Patch Revenue – and It's Tiny," *Business Insider*, Dec. 16, 2011, retrieved from http://www.businessinsider.com/weve-gotten-a-good-look-at-aols-local-ad-revenues-and-they-are-tiny-2011-12 on March 2, 2015.

14. Leslie Kaufman, "Patch Sites Turn Corner After Sale and Big Cuts," *The New York Times*, May 18, 2014, retrieved from http://www.nytimes.com/2014/05/19/business/media/patch-sites-turn-corner-after-sale-and-big-cuts.html?_r=0 on Feb. 26, 2015.

15. "Internet – Summary," How Much Information? 2000, retrieved from http://www2.sims.berkeley.edu/research/projects/how-much-info/internet.html on Feb. 26, 2015.

16. "World Wide Web," retrieved from http://www.w3.org/History/19921103-hypertext/hypertext/WWW/TheProject.html on Nov. 13, 2014.

17. "John Huey, Former Time Inc. Editor-in-Chief: Research Chat," *Journalist's Resource*, Shorenstein Center, May 16, 2013, retrieved from http://journalistsresource.org/skills/reporting/john-huey-former-time-inc-editor-in-chief-research-chat# on Feb. 26, 2015.

18. Ibid.

19. Excerpted from Dena Levitz, "6 Principles Clark Gilbert Used to Transform Deseret News," *American Press Institute*, Sept. 24, 2013, retrieved from http://www.americanpressinstitute.org/Training/Transformation-Tour/Six-Principles-Clark-Gilbert-Has-Used-To-Transform-The-Deseret-News.aspx on Feb. 26, 2015.

20. Seth Fiegerman, "Betaworks Vision for the Future of Online News," *Mashable*, May 7, 2013, retrieved from http://mashable.com/2013/05/07/betaworks-future/ on Feb. 26, 2015.

21. Google Analytics, retrieved from https://www.google.com/analytics/web/?hl=en#report/visitors-overview/a35535656w63365892p65008914/ on Nov. 13, 2014.

22. Excerpted from "The Journalists' Guide to Analytics," 10,000 Words, FishbowlNY, Aug. 3, 2010, retrieved from http://www.mediabistro.com/10000words/the-journalists-guide-to-analytics_b875 on Sept. 28, 2013.

23. Google Analytics, retrieved from https://www.google.com/analytics/web/?hl=en#report/trafficsources-referrals/a35535656w63365892p65008914/%3F_u.date00%3D20140101%26_u.date01%3D20141112/ on Nov. 13, 2014.

Chapter 8

1. Roger Fidler, "News Consumption on Mobile Media Surpassing Desktop Computers and Newspapers," *Reynolds Journalism Institute*, April 25, 2013, retrieved from http://www.rjionline.org/research/rji-dpa-mobile-media-project/2013-q1-research-report-1 on Feb. 26, 2015.

2. "News Consumption on Mobile Devices," *Pew Research Center*, Dec. 11, 2012, retrieved from http://www.journalism.org/analysis_report/news_consumption_mobile_devices on Feb. 26, 2015.

3. Jason Del Rey, "Mary Meeker's Internet Trends Report Is Back, at D11," *All Things*, May 29, 2013, retrieved from http://allthingsd.com/20130529/mary-meekers-internet-trends-report-is-back-at-d11-slides/?refcat=d11 on Feb. 26, 2015.

4. Fidler, 2013.

5. Alex Wilhelm, "Facebook's Desktop Ad Revenue Grew Only $69M in Q2, Mobile Rev to Outpace Desktop by EOY 2013," *TechCrunch*, July 25, 2013, retrieved from http://techcrunch.com/2013/07/25/facebooks-desktop-ad-revenue-grew-only-69m-in-q2-mobile-rev-to-outpace-desktop-by-eoy-2013/ on Feb. 26, 2015.

6. Dan Farber, "CNN's Jeff Zucker Trades Analog Dollars for Digital Quarters," CNET, July 23, 2013, retrieved from http://news.cnet.com/8301-1023_3-57595067-93/cnns-jeff-zucker-trades-analog-dollars-for-digital-quarters/ on Feb. 26, 2015.
7. "Local Mobile Ad Spend to Double in '13," NetNewsCheck, June 11, 2013, retrieved from http://www.netnewscheck.com/article/26729/local-mobile-ad-spend-to-double-in-13 on Feb. 26, 2015.
8. Amy Mitchell, Tom Rosenstiel, Laura Houston Santhanam and Leah Christian, "Revenue," Pew Research Center, Oct. 1, 2012, retrieved from http://www.journalism.org/analysis_report/revenue on Feb. 26, 2015.
9. "Paying for Digital News," Digital News Report 2013, Reuters Institute, retrieved from http://www.digitalnewsreport.org/survey/2013/paying-for-digital-news/ on Feb. 26, 2015.
10. Ibid.

Chapter 9

1. Amy Mitchell, Jocelyn Kiley, Jeffrey Gottfried and Emily Guskin, "The Role of News on Facebook," Pew Research Center, Oct. 24, 2013, retrieved from http://www.journalism.org/2013/10/24/the-role-of-news-on-facebook/ on Feb. 27, 2015.
2. "Profile of the Social Media News Consumer," Pew Research Center, Nov. 13, 2013, retrieved from http://www.journalism.org/2013/11/14/news-use-across-social-media-platforms/5_profile-of-the-social-media-news-consumer/ on Nov. 18, 2014.
3. "Real Estate, Fashion, Graphics, Gadgets and More From The Wall Street Journal," Pinterest, retrieved from http://www.pinterest.com/wsj/ on Oct. 29, 2014.
4. Cory Janssen, "Digital Influence," Techopedia, retrieved from http://www.techopedia.com/definition/28497/digital-influence on Feb. 27, 2015.
5. Brian Solis, "Report: The Rise of Digital Influence and How to Measure It," March 21, 2012, retrieved from http://www.briansolis.com/2012/03/report-the-rise-of-digital-influence/ on Feb. 27, 2015.
6. Ibid.
7. "Assignment: On the Front Lines of Ebola," CNN iReport, Nov. 30, 2014, retrieved from http://ireport.cnn.com/topics/1179496 on Oct. 28, 2014.
8. "How CNN iReport Works," CNN iReport, July 2, 2012, retrieved from http://ireport.cnn.com/blogs/ireport-blog/2012/07/02/how-cnn-ireport-works on Feb. 27, 2015.
9. Michael Depp, "AP's Carvin: News Battle Near for Twitter, FB," NetNewsCheck, Jan. 13, 2014, retrieved from http://www.netnewscheck.com/article/31368/aps-carvin-news-battle-near-for-twitter-fb/page/1 on Feb. 27, 2015.
10. Ibid.

Chapter 10

1. Miguel Helft, "CNN's Jeff Zucker: Digital Is Our Future," Fortune, July 23, 2013, retrieved from http://fortune.com/2013/07/23/cnns-jeff-zucker-digital-is-our-future/ on March 3, 2015.
2. Lee Rainie, "Internet, Broadband, and Cell Phone Statistics," Pew Research Center, Jan. 5, 2010, retrieved from http://www.pewinternet.org/2010/01/05/internet-broadband-and-cell-phone-statistics/ on Feb. 27, 2015.
3. The Pew Research Center's Project for Excellence in Journalism, "The State of the News Media 2012," retrieved from http://www.stateofthemedia.org/2012/newspapers-building-digital-revenues-proves-painfully-slow/newspapers-by-the-numbers.

4. Mary Ellen Gordon, "The History of App Pricing and Why Most Apps Are Free," Flurry, July 18, 2013, retrieved from http://www.flurry.com/bid/99013/The-History-of-App-Pricing-And-Why-Most-Apps-Are-Free#.U4DDPybD-tU on Feb. 27, 2015.

5. "Newspaper Media Revenue 2013: Dollars Grow in Several Categories," Newspaper Association of America, retrieved from http://www.naa.org/Trends-and-Numbers/Newspaper-Revenue.aspx on Feb. 27, 2015.

6. Joe Pompeo, "New York Times Completes 'Innovation Report' Led by Sulzberger Scion," Capital, May 8, 2014, retrieved from http://www.capitalnewyork.com/article/media/2014/05/8545059/emnew-york-timesem-completes-innovation-report-led-sulzberger-scion on Feb. 27, 2015.

7. Roger Yu, "Gannett to Spin Off Publishing Business," USA Today, Aug. 6, 2014, retrieved from http://www.usatoday.com/story/money/business/2014/08/05/gannett-carscom-deal/13611915/ on Feb. 27, 2015.

8. Jeffrey A. Eisenach, "The Economics of Retransmission Content," Empiris LLC, March 2009, retrieved from http://www.nab.org/documents/resources/050809EconofRetransConsentEmpiris.pdf on Feb. 27, 2015.

9. Tony Hallett, "What Is Native Advertising Anyway?" The Guardian, retrieved from http://www.theguardian.com/media-network-outbrain-partner-zone/native-advertising-quality-scalability on Feb. 27, 2015.

10. Ibid.

11. "Executive Conferences From The Wall Street Journal," retrieved from http://wsj.com/conferences/ on Feb. 27, 2015.

12. "The New York Times Travel Show," retrieved from http://nyttravelshow.com/ on Feb. 27, 2015.

13. Robert G. Cross, "Revenue Management: Hard-Core Tactics for Market Domination," New York: Broadway Books, 1997.

Chapter 11

1. Loulla-Mae Eleftheriou-Smith, "Brands Must 'Relinquish Control' and Let Consumers Feel in Charge," Marketing, April 6, 2014, retrieved from http://www.marketingmagazine.co.uk/article/1297186/brands-relinquish-control-let-consumers-feel-charge on March 4, 2015.

2. Bill Grueskin, Ava Seave and Lucas Graves, "The Story So Far: What We Know About the Business of Digital Journalism," CJR, May 10, 2011, retrieved from http://www.cjr.org/the_business_of_digital_journalism/the_story_so_far_what_we_know.php on March 4, 2015.

3. Meg Heckman, "Abernathy: Small Papers Must Seize Niche," NetNewsCheck, June 9, 2014, retrieved from http://www.netnewscheck.com/article/34306/abernathy-small-papers-must-seize-niche on March 2, 2015.

4. Farhad Manjoo, "Why Everyone Will Totally Read This Column," The Wall Street Journal, Dec. 1, 2013, retrieved from http://online.wsj.com/news/articles/SB10001424052702304579404579231772007379090 on March 2, 2015.

5. "Does BuzzFeed Know the Secret?" retrieved from http://nymag.com/news/features/buzzfeed-2013-4/index2.html on March 2, 2015.

6. Tom Rosenstiel, "Why We Need a Better Conversation About the Future of Journalism Education," Poynter, Apr. 15, 2013, updated Nov. 24, 2014, retrieved from http://www.poynter.org/latest-news/the-next-journalism/210196/why-we-need-a-better-conversation-about-the-future-of-journalism-education/ on March 2, 2015.

Samir "Mr. Magazine™" Husni, Ph.D., is the founder and director of the Magazine Innovation Center at the University of Mississippi's Meek School of Journalism and New Media. He is also professor and Hederman Lecturer at the School of Journalism. As **Mr. Magazine**™ he engages in media consulting and research for the magazine media and publishing industry.

Dr. Husni is the author of the annual "Samir Husni's Guide to New Magazines"; "Just Common Sense: Mr. Magazine's Ideas to Grow and Cultivate Magazine Media"; "Magazine Conversations"; "Magazine Publishing in the 21st Century"; "Launch Your Own Magazine: A Guide for Succeeding in Today's Marketplace"; and "Selling Content: The Step-by-Step Art of Packaging Your Own Magazine." Dr. Husni is also the co-author of "Design Your Own Magazine" and the editor of "The Future of Magazines."

He has presented seminars on trends in magazines and magazine media to the editorial, advertising and sales staff of Morris Communications Co., the Finnish media group Sanoma, the South African Media24 magazine group, iostudio, Highlights for Children Inc., Hearst Corp., Hachette Filipacchi Media U.S., Meredith Corp., Reader's Digest magazine, ESPN The Magazine, Sail magazine, American Airlines Publishing, the National Geographic Society, the Swedish magazine group Bonnier, Southern Progress Corp., New South Publishing Inc., the Society of Professional Journalists, the American Society of Magazine Editors, MPA: The Association of Magazine Media, Vance Publishing Corp., the Florida Magazine Association, the Magazine Association of the Southeast, the National Association of Black Journalists, the Japanese Magazine Publishers Association and the American Press Institute.

He is "the country's leading magazine expert," according to Forbes ASAP magazine; "the nation's leading authority on new magazines," according to media industry newsletter min; and "a world-renowned expert on print journalism," according to CBS News Sunday Morning. The Chicago Tribune dubbed him "the planet's leading expert on new magazines."

Dr. Husni has been interviewed by major U.S. and international media on subjects related to the magazine industry. He has been profiled and is regularly quoted in the New York Times, the Los Angeles Times, USA Today, the Chronicle of Higher Education, and many other newspapers worldwide, as well as the major newsweeklies and a host of trade publications.

He has appeared on CBS News Sunday Morning, Good Morning America, CNBC, CNN, CNNFN, PBS and numerous radio talk shows including NPR's Morning and Weekend Editions as well as On the Media.

Dr. Husni holds a doctorate in journalism from the University of Missouri–Columbia and a master's degree in journalism from the University of North Texas.

Debora Halpern Wenger, a 17-year broadcast news veteran, is associate professor and director of undergraduate journalism at the University of Mississippi. She is also a former associate professor at Virginia Commonwealth University. Prior to her academic appointment, she served as assistant news director at WFLA-TV in Tampa, Florida. She started her career as a reporter/anchor at KXJB in Fargo, North Dakota; moved on to producing at WBBH in Ft. Myers, Florida, and WMUR in Manchester, New Hampshire; then became executive producer at WSOC in Charlotte, North Carolina. Wenger conducts multimedia training in newsrooms across the country and is co-author of the broadcast, online and mobile journalism curricula for the Society of Professional Journalists' Journalism Training Program. She has been invited to work as visiting faculty for the Poynter Institute. She is co-author of "Advancing the Story: Journalism in a Multimedia World" and holds a bachelor's degree from what is now known as Minnesota State University and a master's degree from the University of North Carolina–Charlotte.

Hank Price is a veteran television executive who has led some of the nation's most prominent stations including WBBM-TV, the CBS-owned station in Chicago; KARE-TV, the Gannett-owned NBC affiliate in Minneapolis/St. Paul; WXII-TV in Winston-Salem, North Carolina; and WFMY-TV in Greensboro, North Carolina. He is currently the president and general manager of WVTM-TV, the Hearst-owned NBC affiliate in Birmingham, Alabama. Since 2000, Price has also been senior director of Northwestern University's Media Management Center where he concentrates on future journalism and business models. Earlier in his career, Price was a national television consultant with Frank N. Magid Associates. A frequent speaker at industry events, in 2000 Price was named a Fifth Estater by Broadcasting & Cable magazine for "innovation in television news." In 2010 he was given the North Carolina Association of Broadcasters' Distinguished Service Award for "outstanding contributions to broadcasting." That same year, he was named a member of University of Southern Mississippi's Journalism Hall of Fame.